LAND USE
A Spatial Approach

Editors

John F. Lounsbury
Arizona State University

Lawrence M. Sommers
Michigan State University

Edward A. Fernald
Florida State University

KENDALL/HUNT PUBLISHING COMPANY
Dubuque, Iowa, USA   •   Toronto, Ontario, Canada

SERIES: N.C.G.E.
Pacesetter Series

Clyde F. Kohn, Consulting Editor
The University of Iowa

Elizabeth Purdum, Manuscript Editor
The Florida State University

Cartography by The Florida
Resources and Environmental
Analysis Center, The Florida State University

Manson/Ridd: NEW PERSPECTIVES ON GEOGRAPHIC EDUCATION:
Putting Theory Into Practice

Richason: INTRODUCTION TO REMOTE SENSING OF THE
ENVIRONMENT

Richason: LABORATORY MANUAL FOR INTRODUCTION TO REMOTE
SENSING OF THE ENVIRONMENT

LAND USE: A SPATIAL APPROACH (Reviewers)

Professor Corey, Kenneth E.—University of Maryland

Mr. Rutherford H. Platt—Florence, MA

Professor John W. Frazier—SUNY, Binghamton

Professor Otto F. Jakubek—Central Washington University

Printed in the United States of America

C   402438   01

Contents

Section D

Implications for the Future

Preface

The mobility of the American people, the rapid changes in population in many areas of the country, and the ramifications of the technical revolution have resulted in changes, often drastic, in the ways that land is used in many sections of the nation. Some of the most pressing domestic problems, such as the decline of environmental quality, lack of sufficient recreational opportunities, improper use of hazardous areas and random economic development, are directly or indirectly related to land use changes. One approach to solving or alleviating these problems is to educate and train an adequate number of people to understand land use and the processes that affect land use change. As a result, many conventional academic courses and programs are being modified to keep pace, not only with recent advances in technology and subject matter, but also with rapid increases in land use problems and issues. This book is designed to support these curriculum changes.

The legal powers that influence land use have resided largely with local governments over much of this century. Today, many local governments are developing or revising land use plans. Further, it has been recognized recently that the states and the federal government are playing an increasing role in the development of land use policies. New forms of federal legislation will probably be enacted in the future requiring states and regions to play a more forceful role in guiding land use change and development. Such impending developments will create demands in the very near future for both an educated citizenry and specialists in land use analysis. It is hoped that this book will contribute significantly to meet these anticipated demands.

The book is designed to serve as the basic text for courses dealing with land use and as a supplementary text for courses concerned with applied research, land planning, and environmental studies both at the advanced undergraduate or beginning graduate levels. It is an outgrowth of a graduate program that was developed at Arizona State University, Florida State University, and Michigan State University. John F. Lounsbury, Edward A. Fernald, and Lawrence M. Sommers served as directors of the program at their respective universities, and program faculty developers are authors of many of the chapters of the book. The development of the program was supported by a grant from the National Science Foundation from 1975 to 1978. The Jessie Smith N Foundation provided fellowships for students enrolled in the program during the 1 period.

The editors wish to acknowledge major contributions to this book b manuscript editor and James Anderson, cartographer. Their patience to be invaluable to the editors.

Section A

Introductory Chapters

Chapter 1

The Spatial Character of Land Use

Lawrence M. Sommers
Michigan State University

Introduction

The relationship of people to the land has been a pervasive theme throughout human history and has shaped both the nature and quality of life on this planet. In the United States, land use[1] patterns have altered dramatically during the twentieth century. Technological advances and expanding population have put increasing pressure on lean resources and have created a variety of complex land use dilemmas which affect persons of all levels of society. Rural to urban migration, urban sprawl, energy-consumptive settlement patterns, private land ownership and control, and proliferation of federal, state, and local land use regulations continue to give rise to dynamic and often conflicting land use patterns and policies. Land use issues concern people's interaction with earth space, a topic particularly germane to the discipline of geography. Geographic literature has addressed the use, distribution, character and control of land since antiquity. Since the spatial approach of land use has long been a central theme of geography, it forms an apt focus for the discussion of land use characteristics, issues, and policies emphasized in this volume.

Evolving Land Use Patterns Since 1900

Many of the basic land use patterns in the United States were established by 1900. High value agricultural land had been identified, many forests had been cleared to provide agricultural land as well as building materials, the railroad network had been established, and the industrial revolution had continued to spur rapid urban growth.

Since 1900, the major changes in land usage have been urban related. As the population of the United States grew from 76 million people at the turn of the century to 227 million in 1980, the proportion as well as the total number of people residing in urban areas increased. Urban encroachment upon rural land became a major feature of land use change. Private entrepreneurs made decision after decision that consumed rural, mostly agricultural, land through construction of such facilities as factories, shopping centers, and housing developments. The amount of land in these specialized urban land use categories has increased substantially in the last eighty years while the amounts of land in other major classifications such as marsh, desert, and tundra; forestland; grassland, pasture, and range; and cropland have remained relatively constant (table 1.1). In addition to increased urban uses, other significant changes include decrease in hardwood forests, decrease in marsh areas or wetlands, increase in land devoted to recreational purposes, and increase in land for motorized vehicle transportation routes.

Table 1.1. Major Uses of Land in the United States

	(Millions of Acres/Percentage)		
	1920	1950	1974
Cropland	402/18%	409/18%	382/17%
Grassland, Pasture and Range	731/32%	701/31%	681/30%
Forest and Woodland	721/32%	721/32%	718/32%
Other Land			
Urban	10/0.40%	18/0.70%	35/1.50%
Highways	15/0.60%	19/0.80%	21/0.90%
Railroads	4/0.10%	3/0.10%	3/0.10%
Airports		1/0.04%	2/0.08%
Total Acreage	2,270	2,271	2,264

Adapted from Meyer, 1979.

Recent Population Change and Land Use Patterns

In many respects, changing land use patterns reflect the needs and values of an everexpanding population. The United States is growing at a rate of nearly two million persons per year, excluding several hundred thousand illegal aliens. Such population characteristics as birth and death rates, sex, age, race, education, migration and movement, income, occupation and household size all have an impact on the nature of land use and the rate of change.

One of the significant developments in the United States in the last twenty years has been an increase in population growth rates in non-metropolitan areas. Due to a recent reversal of the traditional rural to urban migration pattern, some of the fastest growing areas have been low density rural regions and towns and villages of less than twenty-five hundred inhabitants. The causes for rural repopulation include decentralization of manufacturing, increase in the number of people retiring in rural and small communities, lower living costs, desire for more recreational opportunities, government-sponsored stimulants such as interstate highways and sewer construction, and desire for an improved quality of life through rural amenities.

During the 1970s more and more people realized the American Dream of owning a single-family home, a trend which resulted in a rapid encroachment of urban functions and the diffusion of urban life styles into rural areas. Between 1970 and 1977, the central cities of metropolitan areas lost nearly 12 million people. During the same period the suburban ring areas gained 9 million, and the non-metropolitan areas gained 3 million.[2] Recent estimates suggest that urban sprawl consumes a million acres of prime farmland each year. Over half the acres removed from agriculture are subdivided for residential use and 10 to 20 percent for industrial and commercial use, the amount varying with the region. The problem is compounded because urbanization of rural residents has made the rural-urban classification increasingly blurred. Change of this magnitude is materially altering the patterns of land use in both urban and rural areas.

Land Use Problems—Current and Future

Prediction of the future in a dynamic society, in which social, political, and economic factors as well as values and attitudes are rapidly changing, is both difficult and dangerous. Unstable conditions have occurred in the United States during the last few decades as society has adjusted to unprecedented technological developments. There are a number of current land use problems, issues, and conflicts, however, that are most likely to become more acute in the 1980s. Some of these problems will have national impact either because they affect the country as a whole or because their pervasiveness at the local level fosters national awareness and concern. The most serious and demanding problems are and will probably continue to be the preservation of prime agricultural land in face of increasing urban encroachment, the conflict between future residential land use and the development of energy resources, the degradation of the environment, and the conflicts concerning the control of the land.

Conflicts Concerning the Control of the Land

At this time in history, there are no standardized land use controls and no national land use guidelines in the United States although decisions by local, state, and federal government have become increasingly important in determining the character and changes in land use. Federal laws, developed to control natural resources, pollution, and community development, have had a major impact on the nature of land management (table 1.2). These laws have all been enacted from 1938 to 1980. The rising impact of legislation is indicated by Congressman Morris Udall who counted nearly 140 federal programs that impacted on local and state land use decisions in 1977. Approximately 500 land use disputes were heard by state courts in 1976, and in that same year the American Society of Planning Officials reported nearly 200 new laws governing land use. These laws covered such topics as controlling mobile home locations, establishing criteria for waste disposal, managing geothermal resources, preserving open space, changing building codes and fencing off junkyards.[3]

The states have traditionally delegated land use control to the local governments via planning and zoning acts. There is great diversity regarding land use controls and land use planning from one local jurisdiction to another. The states are now beginning to assume a more direct role in land use planning, not only for the public lands, but also in the control of developments on non-state land. Several western states are challenging the federal government's right to administer land under the jurisdiction of the Bureau of Land Management.

Despite the growing trend of public control, decisions made in the private sector still determine the majority of land use patterns in the United States. As indicated both by recent urban to rural migrations and by the increase in the number of small households, the average United States citizen places a high value on independence and relative isolation, and this has been a major factor influencing land use patterns.

The increasing control of the use of land is related to the greater pressure upon the land by a growing population, a more complex style of living, and a desire of most individuals in the United States to own a plot of ground. Undoubtedly, not everyone will agree on how and by whom the land should be controlled. It may be anticipated that major conflicts over land use will characterize the coming decades. Conflicts may develop among local groups, between local and regional or state interests, and between state and national groups over mineral rights, power plant and mining sites, conversion of agricultural land to other uses, water rights and controls, development of energy resources, and so on. It is conceivable that these conflicts could become so severe and long lasting as to seriously threaten local, regional or national economic growth.

Table 1.2. Federal Laws Affecting Private Land Use Practices

Name (citation)	Administering Agency	Primary Purpose	Land Use Effect
National Resource Laws			
National Environmental Policy Act	Council on Environmental Quality	Reduce the degradation of the human environment and achieve a balance between development and resource use.	Requires federal agencies and licensees to analyze impacts of actions on land and water resources and to choose the environmentally preferable alternative or to explain why that alternative was not chosen.
Land and Water Conservation Fund	Heritage Conservation and Recreation Service	Provide financial incentives for state and local governments to provide recreation areas and opportunities.	Requires adoption of 5-year State Comprehensive Outdoor Recreation Plans to guide recreation land acquisition and development activities.
Coastal Zone Management Act	Office of Coastal Zone Management	Assist coastal and Great Lake states in preparing and implementing state coastal plans.	Requires states to adopt acceptable coastal plans as condition for continued federal assistance; plans generally designate permissible uses of coastal lands.
Floodplain Management Executive Order	Council on Environmental Quality, Water-Resources Council and Federal Emergency Management Administration	Reduce the risk of flood loss and restore or preserve natural floodplains.	Prohibits federal agencies and licensees from building in the 100-year floodplain unless there is no practicable alternative.
Protection of Wetlands Executive Order	Council on Environmental Quality	Minimize the destruction of wetlands.	Requires federal agencies to avoid construction in wetlands unless there is no practicable alternative.
Fish and Wildlife Coordination Act	Fish and Wildlife Service	Ensure wildlife conservation needs receive agency consideration when water-related impacts will result from federal projects.	Fish and Wildlife Service and state wildlife agencies can recommend modifications of projects to reduce impacts on wildlife habitat.
Water Resources Planning Act	Water Resources Council	Encourage the conservation, development and utilization of water on a coordinated basis.	Establishes River Basin commissions to coordinate water and related land development; statewide water resource planning must be consistent with these planning policies.
Agricultural Marketing Agreement Act of 1973; Agricultural Adjustment Act of 1938	Agricultural Stabilization and Conservation Service	Stabilizes prices, markets, and farm incomes and conserves resources.	Affects land use and crop management practices through set-aside programs, acreage allotments, and marketing limitations and subsidies.
Consolidated Farm and Rural Development Act of 1961	Farmers Home Administration	Finance real estate, operating, and emergency loans for soil and water conservation and rural industrialization.	Provides money for watershed and erosion protection, flood prevention, and soil and water projects.
Surface Mining Control and Reclamation Act of 1977	Office of Surface Mining	Protect society and environment from adverse effects of surface coal mining.	Regulates surface mining on both private and public lands and prohibits mining on critical lands.
Marine Protection, Research, and Sanctuaries Act of 1972	Office of Coastal Zone Management	Designate marine areas as sanctuaries for conservation, recreation, or ecological purposes.	Allows only activities compatible with marine sanctuaries protection to be conducted within sanctuary boundaries.

Reprinted from Council on Environmental Quality, 1979.

Table 1.2.—*Continued*

Name (citation)	Administering Agency	Primary Purpose	Land Use Effect
National Resource Laws			
Endangered Species Act of 1973	Fish and Wildlife Service	Conserve ecosystems for the use of endangered or threatened species.	Requires that federal agency actions anticipate threats to and be consistent with survival of endangered and threatened species and their critical habitats, whether or not the area is designated as critical habitat.
Watershed Protection and Flood Prevention	Soil Conservation Service	Prevent floods, conserve and utilize water and land resources.	Helps local organizations plan for community development and forecast demands for residential, commercial, industrial and recreational facilities in a comprehensive manner.
Community Development Laws			
Housing and Community Development Act of 1974	Department of Housing and Urban Development	Encourage comprehensive planning for the development of human and natural resources by state, region.	Provides grants for the planning and development of community facilities and services such as housing projects and recreation.
National Flood Insurance Act of 1968	Federal Emergency Management Administration	Reduce the risk of loss due to flooding.	Requires designated flood-prone communities to develop flood mitigation measures including land use, elevation and building requirements as a condition for flood insurance coverage.
Disaster Relief Act	Federal Emergency Management Administration	Mitigate losses from disasters and provide emergency assistance for major natural disasters.	Requires state and local governments to adopt measures which may discourage building on hazard-prone lands.
National Historic Preservation Act	Advisory Council on Historic Preservation	Protect districts, buildings, sites and objects significant to American history.	Requires that federal agency actions consider impacts of their actions on property registered in or eligible for the National Historic Register.
Federal-Aid Highway Act	Federal Highway Administration	Develop state and interstate highway system.	Provides grants to states for the construction of highway systems.
Urban Mass Transit Act of 1964	Urban Mass Transit Administration	Encourage the reconstruction and expansion of urban transit systems.	Provides grants to urban areas for public transportation.
Public Works and Economic Development	Economic Development Administration	Stimulate community development through a wide range of subsidized community projects.	Provides grants to communities to develop facilities such as public works and roads.
Water Resources Development Act of 1974	Army Corps of Engineers	Reduce the loss of life and property due to floods through dam and reservoir projects.	Provides for the construction of dams and reservoirs to reduce uncontrolled flooding and provide recreational benefits.

Table 1.2.—*Continued*

Name (citation)	Administering Agency	Primary Purpose	Land Use Effect
Pollution Control Laws			
Clean Water Act	Environmental Protection Agency; U.S. Army Corps of Engineers	Reduce water pollution and the discharge of toxic and waste materials into all waters.	Makes grants for sewage treatment plants, which may encourage or permit growth; requires state to regulate land use practices to control pollution from indirect (nonpoint) sources such as urban areas; requires wetland concerns to be considered in U.S. Army Corps of Engineers dredge and fill permits.
Safe Drinking Water Act	Environmental Protection Agency	Assure public is provided safe drinking water.	Permits Environmental Protection Agency to veto federal agency and licensee projects that could contaminate the watershed of a municipality's only source of drinking water.
Clean Air Act	Environmental Protection Agency	Reduce air pollution dangerous to public health, crops, livestock, and property.	Limits development in pristine areas, and affects siting of new industrial facilities in all areas.
Resource Conservation and Recovery Act of 1976	Environmental Protection Agency	Control of waste disposal and hazardous wastes.	Requires that all solid wastes, other than hazardous wastes be disposed of in sanitary landfill or utilized for resource recovery.
Rivers and Harbors Act of 1899	Army Corps of Engineers	Protect navigation, water quality, fish and wildlife, ecology, and aesthetics of navigable waters.	Requires that effects on wildlife habitat, wetlands, historic resources, and coastal zones be considered before granting a permit for activities in navigable waters.
Deepwater Port Act of 1974	United States Coast Guard	Regulate the construction and operation of deepwater ports on the seas to transfer oil from tankers to shore.	Requires land-based development effects to be considered in any port license and be consistent with state environmental laws or coastal zone programs.

Degradation of the Environment

The list of real and imagined threats to the national environment is long and diverse. Many are the result, directly or indirectly, of how the land is being used. The more visible examples include air and water pollution, destruction by mining industries, accelerated soil erosion, draining of wetlands, coastline erosion, forest depletion, and destruction of wildlife habitats. Many of these conditions result in irreversible changes in the physical or biological environment and many concern the interrelation of the atmosphere, hydrosphere, and lithosphere. Changes in one aspect of the environment will trigger changes in other features of the landscape. In a dynamic society, changes in land use are inevitable and will alter the natural setting.

The problems of the near future are not the changes per se, but rather the conflicts that result between groups and individuals over whether changes are damaging or otherwise undesirable. Degradation of the environment is in the eyes of the beholder and is dependent upon the values of a given society at a given location and time. As economic growth continues and population increases, trade-offs are essential. Conflicts and debates, often emotional, regarding these trade-offs will characterize the 1980s.

Urban Sprawl and the Preservation of Prime Farmland

The increasing role of agricultural commodities in foreign trade has important economic, political, and land use ramifications. Agricultural exports have increased to the point where they offset, to a significant degree, the fiscal drain of acquiring energy and manufactured goods from abroad. They have become major economic and political influences in international affairs, making the loss of almost three million acres annually of cropland (over one-third prime land) to permanent non-farm uses alarming. The demand to retain prime agricultural land for farming only will grow stronger year by year.

Land use and its regulation have been traditionally within the control of the local government. Only recently have the states become involved in the preservation of agricultural land. Unfortunately, the prime agricultural land—well-watered, level, and accessible to transportation—is also the land that often provides the best sites for residential, industrial, commercial and transportational land uses. The development and success of land use controls designed to prevent conversion of agricultural land to urban uses vary greatly from state to state. Urban sprawl can be contained either by government regulations or by the individual or collective decisions of people. It is essential that this process be instituted at local, state, regional, and national policy levels so that land, energy, and other resources can be conserved for use by future generations.

Conflicts Between Future Land Use Change and the Development of Energy Resources

A major problem confronting governments, individuals, groups, and enterprises is to find ways to change prevailing attitudes toward conserving finite resources and thus promote more rational land use policies. People, accustomed to the advantages provided by cheap energy, are unwilling or are slow to accept that the current wasteful and inefficient uses of land and resources must change.

During the cheap energy era of this century (1900–1973) the large sprawling industrial city became commonplace and will remain even though there are major movements of people into non-metropolitan areas. The automobile age provided the impetus and flexibility for the sprawl of urban functions and populations in a loose, unorganized pattern over the landscape, first into suburbs surrounding cities and then into rural, forested, agricultural, or vacant space.

This human settlement trend has been severely challenged as increasing demands and decreasing supplies of conventional energy cause prices to soar. The only way energy needs can be met is to preserve currently available fossil fuels through conservation while developing renewable forms of energy for future use.

There is an urgent need to restrain the sprawl of new housing and other urban structures into open land surrounding cities. The density of new and existing developed areas must be increased to foster conservation measures such as district heating, public transportation, and the recycling of urban wastes for energy.

Large amounts of land will be necessary to increase the available amounts of both conventional and renewable forms of energy. Fortunately, abundant amounts of coal are still available in the United States. In order to increase production, especially of low sulfur coal, large areas of the Great Plains and the West will have to be strip mined. Coal processing, which requires large amounts of water as does gasification of coal, will place heavy demands on this limited resource, particularly in the West. Increased exploitation of oil shale, tar sands and geothermal power will involve changing land use in many areas as large portions of the land surface will be affected in the development, processing, distribution and utilization of these energy sources.

The increased use of all types of renewable power—wind, biomass, solar thermal, and small scale hydroelectric—will greatly affect the land use in the areas where this type of energy is available. Much land will be required for solar collectors, windmills, and conversion of biomass to energy. Renewable energy sources will be important in rural and scattered settlements particularly in forested, wilderness, and outdoor recreation areas (fig. 1.1).

Thus, changing the source and type of energy will have a major impact on the future character of land use—both rural and urban. As land areas become involved in the production of energy, the intensity of land use in existing urban areas will need to increase in order to save energy through the use of such innovations as district heating and public mass transportation.[4]

In the coming decades, increased real costs of conventional fossil fuels and growing dependence on alternative sources of renewable and non-renewable energy will drastically affect the future patterns of human settlements. The spatial patterns of land use and the distribution of other resources in relation to needs of new households, businesses, industries, recreation and transportation facilities, and government and private services will be of crucial concern, especially at the community level. Adaptations in human settlement structures must begin with existing patterns and available energy resources. The tremendous spatial differences that exist from community to community, city to city, region to region, and state to state must play a crucial role in a flexible policy that will regulate the settlement evolution of farms, villages, and cities in the less energy-intensive future.

The result of such an energy future for human settlements could be increased community stability, improved economic and environmental conditions and reduced energy requirements. Individual energy efficient decision making, community energy systems, and rational land use planning are keys to making such settlement pattern change and associated land use change occur (fig. 1.2).

The Spatial Approach to Land Use

All of the above issues involve important spatial components. As United States and world population increases, the pressure on land and the importance of spatial analysis of land use are very likely to increase. Table 1.3 indicates some concepts, subjects and skills involved in the spatial analysis of land use developed by a national committee of land use scholars and practitioners in 1976. From Table 1.3, it is clear that the development of a useful land classification system, the application of the proper and most sophisticated techniques, the design of a model using the appropriate methodologies, and an analysis that leads to new insights, problem understanding and enlightened land use policy development are crucial for working towards solutions to the complex

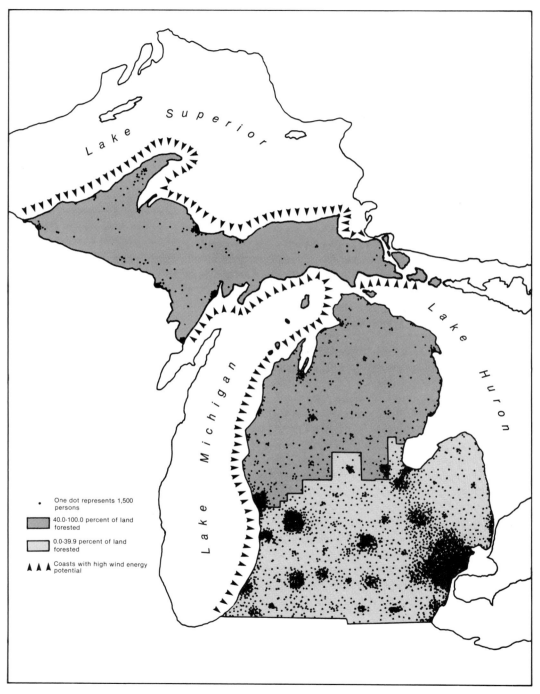

Figure 1.1. Forest biomass and wind energy potential in relation to Michigan population distribution. (From Frazier and Epstein, 1979.)

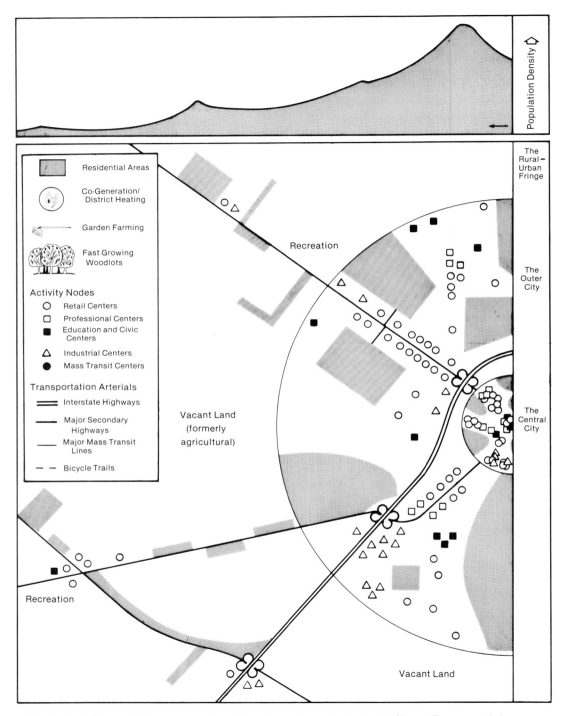

Figure 1.2. The contemporary metropolis and the future metropolis. (From *Energy and the Adaptation of Human Settlements: A Prototype Process in Genesee County, Michigan*, edited by Herman E. Koenig and Lawrence M. Sommers, Michigan State University, 1980.)

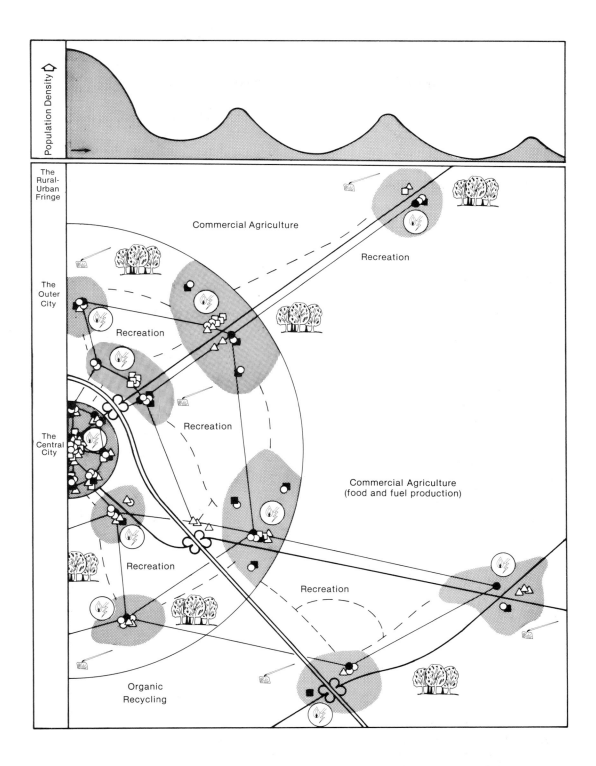

Population Density

The Rural-Urban Fringe

Commercial Agriculture

Recreation

The Outer City

Recreation

Recreation

The Central City

Commercial Agriculture
(food and fuel production)

Recreation

Recreation

Organic Recycling

13

Table 1.3. Concepts, Subjects and Skills Involved in the Spatial Analysis of Land Use

I. Techniques Concerned with the Acquisition of Land Use and Related Data

1. Development of classification systems for existing land use, land tenure, and related land resource data and ability in combining such types of data effectively.
2. Use of remote sensing data as it applies to land use and the natural and cultural environment.
3. Application of field methodologies in acquiring primary and secondary land use, socio-economic, and environmental data.
4. Assessment and evaluation of existing land use, socio-economic and environmental data, along with pertinent supplementary materials and information.
5. Statistical evaluations of data accurately and within limitations of techniques.
6. Documentation of the process of acquiring land use data.
7. Development of new or specialized land use classifications, including capability, suitability, and limitation concepts as related to classification.
8. Utilization of different data collection approaches in combination in both urban and rural areas (field observation, field enumeration, collection of secondary data from agency files, remote sensing, etc.).
9. Assessment of costs associated with using different techniques in acquiring land use data.
10. Evaluation of differing levels of intensity (micro-macro) or grain needed in the collection of land use data, including scale, resolution, minimum areal units, etc. appropriate for map and data compilation.

II. Methods of Data Processing and Analysis and Communication of Information

1. The use of quantitative methodologies for analysis of land use data (models, simulation, statistical analysis, etc.).
2. Development of new or specialized quantitative methodologies applicable to specific needs.
3. Application of existing computer graphics and spatial analysis programs (data bank generations, digitizing and editing, point searches, corridor analysis, etc.).
4. Development of new or specialized computer graphics and spatial analysis techniques (including compositing).
5. Application of cartographic design in presenting land use data.
6. Optimization of the existing technology alternatives (analytical, synthesis techniques, and communication).
7. Application of nondigital data organization and storage.
8. Use of concise verbal communication.
9. Selection of appropriate visual displays for oral or written reports.

III. Institutional and Other Frameworks for Land Use Decision Making.

1. History of land use policy.
2. Economic perspectives of the private and public sectors toward land use.
3. Political and bureaucratic aspects of the public management process.
4. Legal issues pertinent to land use policy.
5. Psychological factors manifesting themselves in public opinions and attitudes about land use policy.

IV. Ingredients of Research Design for Spatial Analysis of Land Use.

1. Regional concepts and regional conceptualization.
2. Overview and definition of substantive issues—political, physical, economic, social, and planning—within the regional framework.
3. Assessment of land use programs and policies including both macro- and micro-analysis of the public and private sectors.
4. Selection or development of the proper methodological framework.
5. Assessment and evaluation of cost effectiveness of land use research projects.
6. Statement of problem and methods of data gathering and analysis.
7. Design and preparation of professional reports and documents.

Adapted from material developed by Advisory Committee and Faculty Developers, National Science Foundation Supported Project, "Spatial Analysis of Land Use," April 1976.

land and resource problems we face. Land use problems are pervasive at all levels of society and in all regions. Thus, greater understanding of these important issues is crucial and provides the basis for the organization and emphasis of this volume.

The chapters that follow present more detail on the spatial aspects of land use. Chapters 2 through 4 spell out land use issues, underlying factors, and objectives of land use planning in the United States. Chapters 5 through 7 cover the acquisition and analysis of data necessary for dealing with land use problems, including graphic and quantitative methods of analysis. Chapters 8 through 12 detail the impacts of the many laws, regulations, and policies on the spatial nature of land use including the implications of recent developments in energy and waste disposal. The book concludes with a chapter emphasizing the need for rational land use planning and decision making if the United States is to make optimum use of its available land resources now and in the future.

Notes

1. Land Use is defined for the purposes of this book as all aspects of human activity on and in relation to land.
2. Council on Environmental Quality, *Environmental Quality*, 10th Annual Report (Washington, D.C.: U.S. Government Printing Office, 1979), p. 478.
3. P. Meyer, "Land Rush, A Survey of America's Land," *Harper's* 258 (1979), p. 54.
4. L. M. Sommers, and H. E. Koenig, "The Energy Future of Human Settlements," paper presented at American Association for the Advancement of Science Annual Meetings, San Francisco, California, January 1980.

Selected References

Albaum, R. et al. *Human Geography in a Shrinking World*. North Scituate, Mass.: Duxbury Press, 1975.

Barlowe, R. *Land Resource Economics*. 3d ed. Englewood Cliffs, New Jersey: Prentice Hall, 1978.

Council on Environmental Quality. *Environmental Quality*, 10th Annual Report. Washington, D.C.: U.S. Government Printing Office, 1979.

Frazier, J. W., and Epstein, B. J., eds. *Applied Geography Conference*. vols. 1 and 2. Binghamton, New York: SUNY-Binghamton, 1978, 1979.

Freeman, T. W. *Geography and Planning*. London: Hutchinson University Library, 1958.

Frey, H. T. *Major Uses of Land in the United States: 1974*. U.S. Department of Agriculture, Agricultural Economic Report No. 440. Washington, D.C.: U.S. Government Printing Office, 1979.

Isard, W. *Location and Space Economy*. New York: Wiley, 1956.

James, P. E. and Martin, G. S. *All Possible Worlds*. Indianapolis: Odyssey Press, 2nd ed. 1981.

Meyer, P. "Land Rush, A Survey of America's Food." *Harpers'* 258 (1979): pp. 45–60.

Mikesell, M., and Manners, I. A. *Perspectives on Environment*. Washington, D.C.: Association of American Geographers, 1974.

Morrill, R. L., and Dormitzer J. M. *The Spatial Order*. North Scituate, Massachusetts: Duxbury Press, 1979.

Perloff, H. et al. *Regions, Resources and Economic Growth*. Baltimore, Md.: Johns Hopkins Press, 1960.

Saarinen, T. *Environmental Planning: Perception and Behavior*. Boston: Houghton Mifflin, 1976.

Soja, E. "The Political Organization of Space." Resource Paper 8, Washington, D.C.: Association of American Geographers, 1971.

Stamp, L. D. *Applied Geography*. Baltimore, Md.: Penquin Books Ltd., 1960.

Zelinsky, W. *The Cultural Geography of the United States*. Englewood Cliffs, New Jersey: Prentice Hall, 1973.

Chapter 2

Perception and Land Use

Donald J. Patton
Florida State University

Introduction

Among the sets of factors that shape the evolution of land uses in particular areas are the cluster of laws, regulations and judicial decisions, together with some degree of guiding policy, which social groups bring into existence in response to an array of social concerns and objectives. But the original drafting of laws, regulations and court decisions, as well as the elaboration of policy by legislative, executive and judicial entities, normally involve debate and can at times engender deep-seated social conflict. In turn, to understand the debate and the conflict which can surround land use decision making, including decisions involving proposed changes in land uses, we need to recognize the underlying role of environmental perception in the development of individual and group attitudes toward the environment and the ways in which particular segments of that environment should be used.

Perception is a very complex and, indeed, ultimately a very mysterious process which relates each individual with the environment. In our everyday lives we are usually quite unconscious of our own perception, however, and quite unaware of the highly selected and filtered images of our environment which it is giving us. Recent work by psychologists and others clearly points to relationships between an individual's perception of the environment, attitudes toward that environment he or she develops, and actions he or she subsequently may take or try to take with respect to that environment. It is the purpose of this chapter, therefore, to examine some of the characteristics of perception that appear to have implications for the generation of attitudes and behavior relating to land use.

The subject matter of this chapter is organized into several parts. The initial section presents two specific examples of actual land use disputes illustrative of the deep concern people have for matters relating to the use of land. These examples open up the whole issue of the importance of perception to land use study. Following this initial section is an explanation of the meaning and nature of perception. Although the central concern of the chapter is not perception itself, but the implications of perception for land use concerns, the role of perception in land use cannot be fully appreciated without some understanding of perceptual processes themselves. Therefore, the general attributes of perception, which apply to most people regardless of age, background, experience and personality, are sketched first, followed by a summary of further aspects of perception highlighting differences as well as similarities in the way individuals or groups may perceive a given environment. The remainder of the chapter discusses the role of perception in a number of actual land use situations in the United States.

Environmental Perception and Land Use: Two Examples

Peter Meyer, in an article entitled "Land Rush: A Survey of America's Land: Who Owns It—Who Controls It—How Much is Left," in *Harper's,* describes an evening meeting in a downtown government building in Salem, Oregon.[1] Attending the meeting was a diverse group of people with only one thing in common: each owned land in the open country beyond the southern city limit of Salem. The purpose of the meeting, which had been called by the planning commission, was to consider the vote on a proposal to permit a ten-acre wooded tract south of the city to be used for a housing development. The issue at hand, whether the land use of a ten-acre parcel of land was to be changed from woods to residences, engendered debate and intense emotional reactions on the part of individuals present, even though the tract of land in question did not belong to them. Although it is not specified what percentages of the audience supported and opposed the proposed land use change, it is clear that among those present were those who heatedly opposed the proposal. The planning commission did vote in favor of permitting the development. The important point is that this meeting, with the conflicts which surfaced in it, is a vignette of land use confrontations all across the United States which have proliferated in recent years. It is estimated that as much as one-fifth of the total land area of the nation at any one time is in land use conflict embroiling planning and county commissions, municipal governments, courts, state legislatures, federal agencies, Congress, and private corporations, institutions and individuals. The issues are varied, the debate is often protracted, and feelings at times are emotional and intense.

People often take a deep interest in the way land is used when that land is in their general vicinity, and sometimes even when the land in question is remote from them. Land that arouses their preoccupation need not border their own property although concern with contiguous land tends to be stronger. Indeed, land use on the lot next door, land uses in the neighborhood, and even land uses along the route one normally travels to and from work are all of interest to most people.

People's tendency to be vitally concerned with land uses around them arises for a number of reasons. Different types of land use in the more immediate environment, such as arterial highway transportation, agriculture, various types and qualities of housing, manufacturing of various types, warehousing, and shopping centers, can all affect one's personal well-being. Consequences to the individual can include an increase in the property taxes, an effect on the assessed valuation and the marketability of property, the possibilities of enhanced or reduced income, enhanced or reduced aesthetic pleasure, and even changes in personal safety and health risks. A number of these issues are explored in some detail in other chapters of this book. Suffice it here to note that people react both positively and negatively to particular land uses and proposed land use changes for many specific reasons, but underlying their reactions are often their perceptions of their environment. Their reactions also arise from different sorts of happenings in their personal lives, which go beyond their direct perception of present land uses and their imaginative images of future land uses. Other sources of their attitude formation and cognition with respect to particular land uses are varied, ranging from viewing artists' sketches simulating future land use to reading newspaper articles concerning likely effects of a land use change on future real estate tax rates.

In addition to people's very widespread interest in land uses in their own areas of work, and especially residence, an increasing fraction of the American population has become interested in land use issues in areas remote from their particular locale. These more distant land use issues are rarely of interest to a person because of immediate financial or other practical considerations, such as health and safety; rather, they become of interest because of other beliefs and values possessed by the person, such as a concern for the preservation or protection of sound ecosystems. These beliefs and values help us to understand why the New Yorker becomes involved with land use issues in Wyoming—a long distance interest which may puzzle the citizen in Wyoming.

The second example illustrating contrasting ways in which the same area may be perceived by different persons or groups of people is drawn from the Echo Park controversy of the early 1950s. In 1948 the four states of the upper Colorado River basin, New Mexico, Colorado, Wyoming, and Utah, signed a compact allocating among them the upper basin's aggregate share of the total basin's water supply. In the period following the signing of the compact, planning for and implementation of water resources development in the upper Colorado River basin proceeded apace and included dams and reservoirs such as Flaming Gorge on the Green River in southwestern Wyoming. One of the places under active consideration as a site for a storage reservoir and hydroelectric power generating facility was at the confluence of the Green River and a left-bank tributary, the Yampa, in extreme northwestern Colorado, within the boundaries of the previously established Dinosaur National Monument. An intense land use debate ensued, not sparked by any danger of flooding dinosaur bones in canyon walls—they would have been unaffected—but by the question of what was, in the long run, the best use for Echo Park, the name given earlier to the confluence area of the two rivers. The following passages, taken from the debate on the use of Echo Park, eloquently illustrate the point that the same place may be perceived differently by two individuals. The first quotation is from a person who perceived Echo Park to be desirable for a form of land use combining water resource management and recreation; the second quotation is from a person who perceived Echo Park to be a place where the most appropriate land use would be only for a special form of recreation, the contemplation of spectacular scenery.

"The water level in the wild canyon would be raised 520 feet when the reservoir is filled. A crystal-clear lake of 43,400 acres would be created, extending 63 miles up the Green River and 44 miles up the Yampa. It is true that the river beds in the area would be obscured and their dangerous rapids eliminated, but the new crystal-clear reservoir would present to the tourist a calmer beauty of its own. Above the surface of the lake, canyon walls would tower 1,000 feet and more with all the beauty and grandeur now to be found there.

"This key Echo Park structure would regulate the flow of these rivers more effectively than any other sites that can be suggested. Six and a half million acre-feet of water would be stored here in highwater season for the year-round benefit of men all the way down the Colorado River Valley, from source to mouth. One and one-tenth billion kilowatt-hours of electric energy would be generated. Together with others in the project, the reservoir would be not only revenue-producing but self-liquidating over a stretch of 41 years, and at the same time it would create much new wealth in farms, homes and industries."[2]

Based upon a different perception of the same area is the second description, one contrasting sharply with that set forth above.

"The Yampa River at first was silent, beautiful, intimate, as it flowed through its deep sandstone convolutions. It led us down from open parks to overhanging cliffs, from ice-cream domes and sunburned terraces to the arched and polished contours of the canyons. . . . There were bank beaver, Canada geese, deer and the prints of big cats whose presence was felt but never seen. . . . On the fourth day the Yampa carried us to its junction with the larger Green River in the famous Echo Park, two miles upstream from the proposed dam. In the center towered Steamboat Rock, rising sheer from its sea of river sand. On three sides, beyond the green meadows and box-elder groves, climbed the white walls of the park, layer upon layer.

"It was one of those perfect sanctuaries which inspire awe from the moment one enters, a temple which has been in building for a hundred times the life of man on earth. Buttressed by the arched mountains, tiled by the wide green grass, illuminated by the stained-glass windows of the sunset, Echo Park commands silence. As with all temples, its value is not in the sounds one may startle from its ledges, but rather in the echoes which it may awaken within oneself."[3]

These two passages illustrate the concept of environmental perception and its significance in matters relating to land use. The debate over the Echo Park issue ultimately involved many individuals from coast to coast who had never seen the Yampa-Green confluence area, but whose attitudes were shaped by whatever mental images and broader values they had. The final resolution in this case was that Echo Park would not be used as a reservoir. The upshot of the controversy did rest, however, on more than the Echo Park image displayed in the second quotation. Also critical in the final land use decision was the camel's-foot-in-the-door-of-the-tent implication of allowing any land use at variance with national park management objectives to intrude into an area administered by the National Park Service.

The Meaning of Perception

The Physics of Perception

Imagine a viewer contemplating a particular area of land use, say a city park. The person visually perceives a pleasant, slightly rolling landscape dominated by a carpet of green grass, by the light-green foliage of scattered stately oak trees and the darker green of a few pines. Blue sky is reflected from the park pond in the middle distance. Several footpaths covered with fine-grained yellow gravel curve gracefully through the park lawns. In our common sense view we readily agree that the feeling of pleasure in the open space and greenery of the park is purely internal, as is the feeling that the scene is restful and even bucolic. But we tend to forget that everything about that park which we have described has an existence only as part of an interaction between two separate parts of the world: the park and us. The matter and the energy within the park exist whether we are there or not, but the attributes of the park we may find so attractive, such as its greenery, have no existence apart from us and our perception of them.

Let us stay with our hypothetical example a bit longer, while continuing to restrict our comments to what we perceive through our eyes. As we survey the park landscape, electromagnetic energy of various wave lengths reflected from all the surfaces of objects within our field of vision activates our retinal photosensors. Via a very complex set of processes the incoming energy is transformed into nerve impulses which travel via the optic nerves to that part of the brain where the sensation of vision occurs. There the incoming nerve impulses are decoded into a detailed image of illuminated colored objects. Although this decoding results in an amazingly detailed sensation of light and color in the visual sector of the brain, much or most of the potential stimulus information, although transmitted to the brain, will not be perceived: we will not be aware of it.

That part of the visual field that does register perceptually will be affected by our stored memory images, by other nonvisual aspects of our memory of this or other parks, by the play of our imagination and the images associated therewith, and by a myriad of other subtle, subconscious linkages with our thinking. Information or statements about the park previously received from newspapers, radio or television, or the comments of friends, can all affect the qualities we perceive the park to have on that particular occasion. Likewise, the hopes and plans which brought us to the park, and our momentary mood, will affect our perception. Our resulting perception of the park could include such qualities as beauty, congestion, or high crime potential because of many clusters of shrubbery. All of this is what we imply by the words "perception of the environment," unconscious as we normally are of all these aspects.

Through our perceptions we become aware of the world outside ourselves. In essence, perception links us with our surroundings but the linkage is far from simple. Recent research by scholars in fields ranging from the psychology of perception to color optics reveals previously unsuspected complexities in perceptual processes. Three interrelated sets of processes are involved in perception: purely physical processes such as the transmission of light and two interrelated sets of processes within the body sometimes distinguished as physiological and psychological. Most is known about the physical set of processes, much less about the perception-related processes within the body. Nevertheless, tentative conclusions from the work of psychologists and other scientists suggest some of the general characteristics of the ways perception appears to function.

When we perceive, we receive energy from stimuli. For most people much of the time the most important form of incoming energy is electromagnetic radiation reflected from the surfaces of objects, or stimuli, and received by light-sensitive cells in the retina at the back of each eye. Other forms of energy transmission involved in perception include so-called sound waves and chemical energy, received by sensory receptors in the inner ear and the nose, respectively. The several different forms of incoming energy are converted or "transduced" by the specialized sensory equipment of the human body into electrochemical nerve impulses which then travel via the peripheral and central nervous system to the brain. These physiological transmissions in turn activate special-function areas of the brain, such as the area responsible for the sense of vision or the area responsible for the sensation of sound. The sensory receptors and their nervous system linkages to the brain thus create and transmit "coded messages." The ultimate decoding is apparently deeply affected by other states or conditions of the brain, including pictorial or image components as well as nonimage components of the stored memory of previous experiences with the same or similar objects or environments as those being perceived at the moment, and ongoing cognition. The nature of perception is of course far more intricate than that implied by the above brief summary. This point can be illustrated through reference to two further attributes of one type of perception, namely visual perception.

Although visual perception is ultimately initiated and sustained by electromagnetic energy reaching the human eye from the surfaces of objects in the environment, the world as perceived is quite clearly not a world with a one-to-one relationship to those energy patterns. Consider just two cases in point. We look at a tree and as we do so the radiant energy traveling from tree trunk, branches and leaves through the atmosphere and then through the several components of our eyes, including the lens, reaches the retinal area at the rear of each eye in an upside-down pattern, comparable to that which reaches the film in a camera. Nevertheless, the pattern of stimulation of the photosensitive cells in our retinas is perceptually reversed in our brain; we "see" the tree as rightside up. Our second case in point baffled persons for generations. With our binocular vision the energy patterns reaching our two eyes from a nearby object are quite distinct, reflecting the separate angles of vision of the two eyes, yet the two separate retinal stimulus patterns are perceptually fused into a single three-dimensional image; we are not afflicted by double vision or blurred vision.

Environmental Perception

Much of our perception, including the perception that is significant for land use, is commonly called "environmental perception." The term "environmental perception" refers to the host of physiological and psychological happenings that occur in us during the simultaneous receipt of energy in several forms, such as light waves and sound waves, coming from the total array of objects, including people, which surround us. In order to focus the discussion on aspects of environmental perception relating to land use, the meaning of the word "environment" will be arbitrarily limited to the out-of-doors environment.

Environments are usually replete with a great diversity of stimuli from which multimodal signals reach the individual. Thus, perception via sound waves may reinforce perception via light waves, but at other times it might contradict or distract visual perception. Moreover, the environment is usually an unbounded segment of surrounding earth-space filled with objects and people. The sheer number, variety, and complexity of details in the environment produce a stimulus overload, resulting in marked filtering, and the perception of only a minute fraction of the total array of stimuli reaching the person. Also because of the large array of signals, some attributes in the environment may be contradictory; others may be ambiguous. The surrounding quality of the environment also results in signals reaching the individual from many directions. In the case of visual perception, this means that many environmental stimuli are only perceived via peripheral vision; other stimuli are not perceived at all. The large and surrounding nature of environments also invites movement. Consequently, memory appears to play a crucial role in perception as we move in and acquire experience of an environment. Together, the surrounding quality of the environment, its multimodality, its vast array of stimuli and their peripheral as well as central position with respect to us have collectively been called the "stimulus properties" of the environment.[4] These properties are largely self-evident, but they have been mentioned because they contribute collectively to our perception of environmental content and spatial structure. In other words, as we perceive any environment, we gain information for the size, shape, texture, illumination, color, relative position, and nature and relative significance of objects in our field of vision. We must remember, however, that even in terms of visual perception alone, the complexity of environments is so great, and the stimulus information carried to the retinas of our eyes is so extensive, that most of the incoming energy, although activating the photoreceptors within the retinas, is filtered out in the process of perceiving. Our perception of the environment is highly selective.

Up to this point the attributes of environmental perception have been considered at the more immediate level—the perception of the physical characteristics of people, buildings, vegetation, and other entities existing in the space around us. Important as is this level of perception, however, we also perceive our environments in terms of a deeper level of characteristics.[5] We now turn to these attributes.

We perceive environments as symbols. Again and again, studies of the reactions of people to landscapes and to particular environments have concluded people perceive environments as symbols. J. B. Jackson, a student of American environments, suggests a historical example.[6] In the second half of the eighteenth century, areas inland from the Atlantic Seaboard, where settlement had recently taken place and where forests were being slashed or burned to make way for fields, were nevertheless perceived almost universally in favorable ways by most foreign visitors as well as by local inhabitants. The rutted roads, the charred stumps, and the dead trees still in the midst of newly cleared fields were not perceived as ugly; rather, the whole landscape was perceived favorably. It was a symbol of a new, emerging American social egalitarianism and personal independence.

In our own century, reactions to environments often seem to rest in part on the symbols the environment is perceived to represent. Particular environments are regarded favorably because they are perceived to be a symbol of a sound, little-disturbed ecology or of a particular phase of American history elsewhere largely obliterated. Often they are regarded unfavorably because they are perceived as a symbol of the lifestyle of a particular social group to which one does not belong or of an excessive commercialism to which one does not subscribe.

We often perceive particular environments in terms of their aesthethic qualities. Attributes of volume, mass, texture, color and shape of objects within our visual ken, together with our perception of the degree to which the objects are harmoniously arranged in the landscape and are undistracted by discordant elements, all contribute to our perception of the environment as being beautiful, or ugly, or having aesthetic qualities intermediate between these extremes. Our reactions to particular environments—and indeed, to particular land uses—may be deeply rooted in the ways we perceive such environments aesthetically.

Environments are often perceived in connection with social activity. The quality of these social relationships may influence the ways we then perceive such environments. Moreover our environmental perception often includes a social component; we perceptually search environments for evidence of the social groups and the social activities that prevail in particular environments. Hence, our attitudes toward particular social groups and activities can come to affect the ways we perceive areas in which we infer that these groups and activities exist.

Ultimately, one of the most important ways in which environments are perceived is as places in which action can occur or is likely to occur.[7] Perhaps no other characteristic of environmental perception so clearly refutes the notion of the passive nature of perception or so clearly suggests the subtle cerebral linkages of perception to cognition. Environments appear to be perceived in several respects as potential arenas for action. First, they may be perceived in terms of the possible opportunities for them to be controlled or modified through human action. Second, they appear to be perceived in terms of the particular types of action needed to deal with them. Third, they may be perceived in terms of the likelihood that certain types of action may occur in them—action stemming from natural causes, such as the likelihood that a flood will occur in a particular area, or action arising from other individuals, such as the likelihood that a particular forest tract will be visited by hunters or campers. The importance of this facet of perception becomes evident when we consider the role it probably has played in the evaluation of particular areas by settlers, developers, industrial entrepreneurs, and others across the United States. Moreover, although we now possess many other so-called "objective" means of assessing the potentialities of particular areas for particular types of land use, there is much evidence that environmental evaluation and associated land use decisions still rest in part, and at times principally, on assessments of action possibilities, which are in turn rooted in the individual decision maker's perception of the area in question.

Group Similarities and Differences in Environmental Perception

Much of what has been said concerning environmental perception to this point has underscored that no two persons perceive the environment in precisely the same ways. One's own individual genetic make-up as well as one's individual experiences in life all contribute to the ultimate uniqueness of perception. But the opposite extreme must also be argued; that is, owing to the ways in which the sensory receivers operate for all of humankind, and owing to the common features of decoding which may operate in the brain of all people, there appear to be some broad fundamental similarities in the perception of all people.[8]

Between these two polar views of environmental perception, the ultimate differences in perception from person to person and the ultimate similarities in perception for all people, exists an intermediate area where particular characteristics of the environment tend to be perceived alike by members of particular groups or subgroups and where differences in perceived attributes emerge between groups. Although it might be argued that the fundamental similarities in perception of all members of humanity are ultimately of greatest importance, it is the differences at the individual level or the group level that are much more likely to be of importance to persons involved with land use issues, particularly when proposed actions are to be presented to segments of the public. At times, such as when a land use proposal is presented to members of an audience for their reaction, it will be the individual differences in environmental perception and the interrelated environmental attitudes that will often be reflected in their statements. At other times, however, individuals concerned with land use matters may encounter or work with different socioeconomic or ethnic groups living in different sections of a city or metropolitan area. In this latter instance, there is likely to be a tendency for certain common denominators of group perception to emerge.

Some of the types of group-to-group differences in environmental perception are part and parcel of deep-seated cultural differences. If culture is defined as the traditional patterns for behavior, transmitted by symbolic means, primarily language, then contrasts in these patterns between groups could well be expected to contribute to differences in perception.[9] Either manmade or natural elements of the environment can have varying significance to different culture groups and so be perceived differently. Many cultural variables ranging from languages to value systems may contribute to differences in the way two cultural groups in contact with each other perceive the same environment.

Cultural differences in environmental perception also arise from contrasts between groups in their previous experience with natural or man-made attributes of the environment. Thus, extant diaries, reports, letters, and other writings of early travelers to the area of the upper middle Rio Grande valley in the present state of New Mexico reveal that Spanish and Spanish-American travelers coming from the south tended to perceive the region as having a distinctly cold winter climate but not as being particularly arid or semiarid. American travelers entering the same general area from the east commonly reacted to New Mexico as being dry and desolate because of lack of greenery.[10] The role of cultural familiarity with artifacts of a culture has been shown in a study of the perception of photographs of American and Mexican village scenes by American and Mexican respondents. Contrasts in perceptual selectivity with respect to village scenes clearly emerged between the two groups.[11]

Differences in environmental perception may also appear among subgroups of a culture. In a detailed study by sociologist Herbert Gans in the West End of inner-city Boston some years ago before that area was demolished to make way for an urban renewal project, the mainly Jewish and Italian residents were shown to have perceived their urban environment in ways which contrasted with the perceptions of outsiders who visited the area.[12] Outsiders appeared to perceive West End as a charming neighborhood with ethnic diversity and stability for its inhabitants, whereas West End residents perceived neither charm nor ethnic variety as attributes of their neighborhood. Considerable evidence has now accumulated that various socioeconomic groups dwelling in different districts or neighborhoods of American metropolitan areas may differ in their perception of and attitudes toward particular features of an urban environment.

Environmental Perception and Land Use Debate

The mounting level of land use debate in the United States stems in considerable measure from the personal reactions of many thousands of individuals to objective data concerning the environment—data that can be displayed on maps or set forth in tabular form, and with which much of our collective work in land use is involved—but it also arises from differences in the way any environment will be perceived, from what Peter Meyer of the Salem, Oregon case cited earlier has poetically encapsulated as "the clamoring of people with different visions of the landscape." The role in land use debate of differing perceptions is illustrated by several further examples, starting with the case of the California redwoods.

The California Redwoods Case

In the 1960s a land use debate erupted in connection with some of the California redwoods clothing the slopes and valley bottoms furrowing the Pacific-facing side of the Coast Ranges in the far northwestern part of that state. Somewhat as in the Echo Park confrontation, the redwoods case came down to a choice between using the land for an economic purpose, in this case timber production, or using the contested areas for a national park. As at Echo Park, some types of recreation would have been compatible with the primary proposed economic land use of the area.

The redwoods land use controversy focused on more than 50,000 acres of redwood forest, which were privately owned by several large timber companies. The original redwood forests had covered the coastal slopes from southwestern Oregon to San Francisco Bay and beyond, but by 1960 much of the largest and most accessible timber had been logged off. Nevertheless, some very substantial stands of large redwood trees remained in the Coast Ranges, particularly in the two northwesternmost counties in California, Del Norte and Humboldt, where the land use issue was to come to focus.[13]

The issue evoked strong partisanship. A number of conservation groups had long supported expansion of the redwood preservation acreage in the Coast Ranges. The Save-the-Redwoods League had been especially conspicuous in this effort. On the other side of the issue were arrayed not only the major timber companies, who were not opposed in principle to a Redwood National Park—but not in the area of their holdings—but also most of the citizens of California's Del Norte County, a small county where the labor force depends heavily on employment in redwood cutting and processing. In the hearings held in Crescent City, in Del Norte County, it was clear that many of the people residing close to the contested redwood tracts perceived the standing trees as guarantees of future jobs and income. The role of the forests in helping to meet American housing requirements was also emphasized in the hearings. Some individuals were quite incredulous that national park status could seriously be entertained for such high timber-yielding tracts still relatively accessible on the slopes of the coastal valleys. With increasing distance from the privately held stands that would be purchased by the federal government if a park were to be effected, support for a transfer of redwood stands from a forestry to a national park use increased. Although it is evident that as distance increased, jobs were no longer at stake, the shift in outlook also appears to have resulted in part from indirect perception of redwood grandeur by a small but politically active component of the population who subscribed to the *National Geographic*. Two separate issues of that journal, during a critical period of the debate, carried major articles on the redwoods. In both issues viewers across the country, many of whom had never seen a redwood, were able to perceive some of the redwood forest qualities indirectly via colored photographs.[14] The imaginative imagery so stimulated might well have contributed to the public pressure on members of Congress in support of a redwood national park which developed subsequent to the publication of the two articles. Activities of other conservation agencies had somewhat similar effects. The upshot was the creation in 1968 of a new Redwood National Park in two separate segments of the north coast redwoods.

The act of Congress creating Redwood National Park not only ended an extensively debated land use issue, but it also departed from usual patterns with respect to land acquisition by the government. The enactment provided for full federal ownership at the moment the act was signed into law, therefore avoiding a possibly long condemnation interval during which accelerated timber cutting might have felled some of the very trees the act sought to save.

The Everglades Jetport Issue

Exactly two weeks before Redwood National Park came into being, a groundbreaking ceremony was held at what was to be called the Everglades Jetport. These two events, close in time but relating to areas at opposite ends of the country, also reflected very clear differences in the ways land use issues can arise. The proposal by the Dade County Port Authority to construct a new airport in the interior of South Florida had arisen when Miami International Airport, under the jurisdiction of that authority, had grown in its traffic flow to the point where it had begun to exceed its design capacity.[15] Flight training was also handled at Miami International, and a shift of this training function to a new airport would in turn mean that all commercial traffic could continue to be handled for some years at the Miami airport. In the more distant future, when even commercial traffic would surpass the design capacity of the Miami airport, components of that traffic could also be shifted to the proposed new airport.

The Dade County Port Authority considered several potential sites for the new airport, but for a number of reasons each of the early possibilities were rebuffed. Finally a site was selected some forty-five miles west of Miami, about an equal distance from the west coast of South Florida, and six miles north of the northern boundary of Everglades National Park. About two-thirds of the proposed airport was not even in Dade County, but rather in Collier County. Although the name "Everglades Jetport" was employed, the tract to be occupied by the airport, when eventually completed, was actually located for the most part within the eastern margin of a separate area bordering the Everglades on the west: the Big Cypress Swamp. Thirty-nine square miles were to be enclosed within the airport's outer boundary. The jetport site was also viewed as being capable of serving a succeeding generation of international jet aircraft, for which two of the runways ultimately to be constructed would be almost six miles in length. It was recognized that the location of the airport at such a distance from Miami posed potential surface transportation problems, but conversely the inland location was deemed to be an advantage since the large future jets would not be landing and taking off over a highly urbanized area. In short, South Florida's air terminal needs into the twenty-first century seemed to have been satisfied. Airline agreements to furnish pilot training could continue; Miami's international jet transport terminal operations, already second only to New York's Kennedy International Airport in the United States, could be assured future expansion when needed; and a new generation of possibly larger craft could be handled by the anticipated expansion of facilities inland. No active opposition to the planned new land use on the thirty-nine-square-mile tract existed, although certain individuals in other organizations and agencies involved with the same part of Florida did have some reservations in this early period concerning the eventual impact of the facility.

Substantial opposition to the planned airport land use in the Big Cypress area began in the months following the groundbreaking. The onset of hardening opposition was almost accidental. An official of the Central and South Florida Food Control District learned that possible construction of an airport access road across Conservation Area No. 3 was under active consideration.[16] Conservation Area No. 3 is one of several large tracts of land within the Everglades bordered by an enclosing levee in order to permit temporary storage of surplus fresh water, which from time to time is discharged southward from the Lake Okeechobee area following periods of high rainfall. Following this discovery, a meeting was convened in which the Port Authority was called upon to describe the environmental impact study of the possible affected region it had carried out in connection with the airport project. When the meeting revealed that the potential impact of the airport on surrounding areas had not been methodically considered, concern for the implications of the land use transfer mounted rapidly, leading rather soon to attention from segments of the federal government in Washington.[17] Eventually, plans for the first phase of the full-scale airport were abrogated with a renewed search elsewhere to begin. The Big Cypress site was to be confined to a small training facility.

Although the land use debate concerning the Everglades Jetport evoked as much national attention as did the earlier Redwood National Park case, the play of environmental perception and environmental attitudes seems to have been quite different in the two situations. Opposition to the continuation of land use for timber production in certain of the redwood areas in northwestern California appears to have been strongly prompted by the perceived grandeur and beauty of the tall trees. No comparable perceptual prizing of the Big Cypress occurred. It should be made clear that although the Big Cypress region did have some linear "strands" or strips of very large, old cypress, most of the area has been logged out. Over much of the Big Cypress area, thousands of acres of small, very slow-growing cypress are interspersed with patches of marsh, with tracts of slightly higher land covered with pine or dense tangles of hardwood trees, and with scattered ponds, often surrounded by a dome-shaped stand of cypress. In other words, landscapes within the Big Cypress contain many subtleties which intrigue those who really become familiar with the area, but seem not to be perceived by most visitors as exceptional manifestations of nature. In the words of one of the individuals involved with the Dade County government, there was nothing out there which would be affected by the jetport development except "a few alligators." Moreover, the thirty-nine square miles of the proposed jetport comprised no more than about 4 percent of the Big Cypress and this fact, when considerd in isolation, may also have served to ward off criticism of the proposed land use transfer.

One final difference between the jetport case and the redwood controversy should be underscored. Eventual opposition to a shift in land use in and adjacent to the proposed airport crystallized around the impact on Everglades National Park that would likely occur, rather than around the changes that would occur in the eastern margins of the Big Cypress itself. Maintenance of ecological relationships within the park depends critically not only upon adequate releases of water southward from the conservation districts within the Everglades, but also upon inflow of water from the Big Cypress. Although the boundaries of the jetport would encompass only a small fraction of the total Big Cypress watershed draining into Everglades National Park, it was particularly the impact commercial development around the perimeter of the airport would have on the quality of water flowing toward the park that ultimately proved to be the critical deciding factor in the rejection of the jetport site. Scientific study of the ecology of the jetport area and its ecological relationships with Everglades National Park, prompted by the hearing in which it became clear that potential environmental impacts of the airport had not been seriously studied, revealed a critical spatial linkage between jetport environs and the park. This spatial linkage was a consequence of shallow, dispersed seepage of wet-season surplus water from the Big Cypress area south and southeastward through the tract that would undergo transportation and commercial development. It was also feared that weak land use controls around the future airport might have an ecological impact on the park. The issue therefore ultimately turned on the objective findings of hydrology and other branches of science. The eastern border of the Big Cypress was not perceived sufficiently favorably by a sufficient number of the public to form a basis upon which a special-interest group's efforts could focus, in contrast to a Save-the-Redwoods campaign. In any event the surplus wet-season outflow from the Big Cypress toward the Everglades National Park was not a readily perceptible phenomenon of the environment. Only the perceived qualities of the Everglades National Park itself indirectly suggest some relationshp of environmental perception to the jetport case. Perhaps the greatest significance of the jetport issue in the context of environmental perception and land use is its illustration of the belated consequences of a failure to perceive a tract of land in terms of its possible linkages, actual and potential, with other areas and to organize scientific investigation before actions irrevocably changing land uses are taken.

Wye Island Case

The potential role of environmental perception and attitudes on land use decision making can often be most clearly revealed when particular land use issues affecting an area are studied intensively while they are occurring. An excellent example of this type of opportunity is a study, supported by Resources For The Future, of a clearly defined land use issue which developed with respect to Wye Island, a small tract of land surrounded by tidal creeks on the Eastern Shore of Chesapeake Bay in Maryland.[18] The land use confrontation was carefully observed as it unfolded. The issue was precipitated by the plans of the Rouse Company, which was building the new city of Columbia, Maryland, along innovative landscape architecture lines. The company planned to develop Wye Island in a way that would contrast not only with its present land use but also with the pattern of development that had already occurred in many parts of the Eastern Shore and elsewhere in the country.

The highly indented Eastern Shore of Maryland is a domain of peninsulas and islands washed by the sluggish undulations of a low tidal range. Wye Island, one such piece of low-lying land on the Eastern Shore, is a scant twelve miles southeast of the highway bridge across Chesapeake Bay. The island, four and a half square miles in area and six miles in length, has a total shoreline of forty miles owing to its highly indented nature. The level surface of the island was first cleared in the 1600s for tobacco plantings; today the land is mainly in corn and soybeans. Patches of oak, beech and hickory woods do exist, however, and even the cleared farming areas display a semblance of woods owing to thick hedgerows between many of the fields. The island's general landscape features have not changed much in the past 300 years, except that most of the few farmhouses still standing are unoccupied. The island has come largely into the hands of a single owner.

The proposed development plans for Wye Island were presented by the Rouse Company to the planning commission of Queen Anne's County in 1974. The land use plan was based on a series of land planning and ecological studies stretching back over the previous year which the company had either conducted itself or commissioned. The proposed land use plan detailed at the planning commission meeting was also couched within a land use philosophy of avoiding the unplanned or poorly planned sprawl of housing and commercial activity which was already changing the face of much of the Eastern Shore. In general terms, the land use plan was designed to accommodate a substantial influx of population onto Wye Island, yet retain the rural character of much of the island.

The land use plan involved 2,500 of the 2,800 acres of Wye Island; the remaining 300 acres were not available for purchase by the Rouse Company. Over 2,000 acres or 80 percent of the purchased land were to be used only for "estate residences," some 184 tracts in all, varying in size from five to over twenty acres. This part of the plan faced no major opposition since the entire island was already included within that section of the county zoned R-1, which required a minimum property size of five acres. On about 12 percent of the island a village containing 706 dwelling units would be built centered about a dock in one of the coves. Housing units would be a mixture of apartments and duplexes. Offices and shops for doctors, lawyers, and tradesmen were also planned, as were a small hotel and conference center, an eighteen-hole golf course, and a dock with slips for 200 boats, no more than twenty of which would be permitted to be powered solely by engines. In order to maintain Wye Island's "unspoiled" character, tight controls on land use were planned. Property subdivision would be forbidden. Owners of estate residences would not be allowed to build closer than 200 feet from the shoreline in order to retard further erosion of the river banks. Private boat docks in the estate areas would not be allowed. An architectural panel would need to approve all estate residence design and construction. Septic tanks would be used on the estates, but the village would be provided with an advanced treatment plant from which the effluent would be sprayed onto the golf course and fields and into ponds, but not into the surrounding rivers. Some 800 acres of estate land would be maintained as agricultural land, although how this would be accomplished was not clear at the presentation. About 400 acres would be designated as a wildlife sanctuary. Virtually all of the 500 acres of wooded land, particularly those wooded patches adjacent to the shore, would remain untouched. Some ponding to create new wildlife marshes would occur. In sum, about half the island would remain essentially undeveloped, and the one village would be comparable in population but smaller in area than most of the other larger settlements on the Eastern Shore.

The proposed land use changes on Wye Island failed to elicit the support of the government and citizens of Queen Anne's County, and were subsequently retracted by the Rouse Company. Although the deepening economic recession of 1974 contributed to the rescission of the plan, of crucial importance was the deep, if subdued, hostility to the plan which surfaced. Opposition to Wye Island development was county-wide even though the island itself was almost uninhabited. The negativism that emerged was not because land use change was to occur on land upon which people were living; rather it was a case of land use change within the neighborhood, and in a relatively rural county the neighborhood is the whole county. Moreover, the Wye Island case is especially instructive as an example of how deep, widespread opposition can develop toward a land use plan which, as imagined and designed by a development group, has much to recommend it.

Two other aspects of land use conflict also are clearly visible in the Wye Island situation. First, if the public is not directly involved at the outset in the formulation of a plan, careful land use planning is no hedge against widespread popular opposition once the plan is made public. The Rouse Company undertook very intensive study of the island's natural characteristics, and a series of alternative land use models were rather exhaustively studied, but the advance preparation had little effect on dampening the eventual public opposition to the entire plan. By the time questions, comments, and suggestions were elicited from the public, the main features of the land use plan had taken shape. Secondly, the Resources For The Future study cited previously presents clear evidence that land use planners in the Rouse Company failed to appreciate in advance the reasons why so much opposition to their plan would develop. For all those who in future may be concerned with land use change, the lesson is sobering. The public may oppose land use change for reasons little appreciated by the land use planner.

The strongly negative attitudes toward the projected land use changes on Wye Island appear to have arisen in part from citizen memory of environmental change which had ensued during an earlier spate of development on Kent Island within the county. Citizen attitudes, which were ascertained in interviews, also seem to reflect their contemporaneous favorable perception of Wye Island and other "undeveloped" parts of the county. People's statements also suggest that their negative attitudes may have been accompanied by their mental images of what Wye Island would look like once it had a settlement of apartments and duplexes.

Kent Island had been the first part of the Eastern Shore to undergo rapid development. The initial stimulus for this had been the opening of the Chesapeake Bay bridge, allowing automobile traffic from Washington, Baltimore, and other Western Shore points to reach the Eastern Shore without a long ferry delay. Kent Island previously had been almost entirely in agriculture, but most of the farms had been purchased and subdivided into some 6,700 narrow 50-foot-wide lots. Although many of the lots, purchased on easy-credit terms and held for speculation, had never been built upon, the change in the character of Kent Island was marked. Tilled fields were replaced by weedy tracts of land. Wherever dwellings had been built in clustered fashion on the subdivisions, the shallow water table had precluded adequate septic tank drainage; the effluent visibly and odoriferously upwelled at the surface. The negative perception of Kent Island's changing character had been clearly multimodal!

Unhappiness with the plans for Wye Island rested on much more than environmental perception and memory images. Fear of higher taxes and concern for the pollution, which could damage clam and oyster beds in the vicinity of the island, were two important reasons. The most persistent attitude, which was repeatedly articulated during the debate over the fate of Wye Island, was that one's neighborhood ought to remain familiar and unchanging. Except for a few of the other Queen Anne's County developments, local people put high value on the county's landscapes. They wanted no major changes. They liked the surviving fields and woods of the county, the interfingering of points and "necks" with tidal creeks and broader embayments. But the very crux of their favorable perception of most of the county was its social characteristics. It was a land of farms and small villages where one could expect to walk into almost any restaurant or store and recognize most of the people inside; where one knew one's neighbor and one's neighbor's neighbor. In essence, it appears to have been the environment perceived as a locale for familiar, comfortable social interaction that was at the heart of the resistance to change. Natives of the Eastern Shore wanted no further influx of people, but they were joined by relative newcomers who had retired or otherwise escaped from Washington and Baltimore, and other places it had been perceived desirable to escape from, and who wanted to enjoy the rural quality and the relatively uncluttered shoreline of Queen Anne's County. Old and new county residents tended to dislike intensely even the short-term visitor for the day—especially a "chickennecker" crowding the public boat docks and bridges with ropes and nets and metal collapsible baskets and chicken necks, fishing for Chesapeake blue crab. Most visitors were suspect. Thus all newcomers who would settle in Wye Island village would be suspect. The ultimate lesson of Wye Island is that reactions to proposed land changes will rest heavily on their social consequences and implications.

Clearcutting of Timber Stands

One final example of the role of environmental perception in land use debate, namely, the clearcutting issue, will be sketched briefly to illustrate an instance of where the question is not one of alternative types of land use, but rather alternative types of land management within a given type of land use. The clearcutting controversy has originated in recent years, mainly but not exclusively in the northern Rockies and in the Pacific Northwest, as the United States Forest Service adopted clearcutting and reseeding management on selected National Forest tracts. Clearcutting is an alternative to selective cutting of individually marked trees within a forest. From the view of silvicultural management, clearcutting offers certain timber production advantages, including efficiency of regeneration in certain cases, as with Douglas fir.

Opposition to clearcutting has been focused primarily in the West. The perceived geometric disfigurement of easily visible mountain slopes is quite evident, but other wellsprings of the generally adverse reaction to clearcutting can also be suggested. Many people not only perceive trees as a very attractive manifestation of nature, they also tend to perceive trees and hence forests as being relatively permanent unless cut down by man. Some would also argue that people tend to underperceive the forests as sources of products incorporated in the home or used in our daily lives. They also fail to perceive that clearcutting, as a way of managing a forest land use for timber production, is quite different from the destructive nineteenth-century cutting of many of the country's forest lands.[19] Opposition to clearcutting in the West also appears to rest in part on either perceived or imagined unfavorable effects on wildlife, and also upon possible consequences for erosion of steep slopes.

Regional differences in the tendency of people to perceive clearcutting as an undesirable pattern of land use is seen when the South is compared with the Pacific Northwest. Clearcutting of timber is a common practice on the pinelands of the Gulf Coastal Plain, but no serious opposition to the practice has been voiced. Clearcut tracts are much less visible on the relatively flat lands of the Coastal Plain than in the mountain lands of the West; hence, the aesthetic component of environmental perception figures less significantly in the perception of clearcut land in the South, but other regional contrasts between the West and South undoubtedly also contribute to differences in perception. Many Coastal Plain even-age stands of pine are growing on abandoned farmland, some of which, even on the Coastal Plain, had been badly eroded during farming. Economic dependence on forest industries is high in many Southern communities. Evidence of intensive management by corporate ownerships, often with seedlings of stock superior to that cut, may contribute to the muting of unfavorable attitudes to clearcutting. Rapid rates of regrowth under conditions of high temperatures and soil moisture may further help to reduce unfavorable perception of clearcutting in the South. Finally, in a country where there is a widespread tendency to be critical of federal activities, the comparatively small acreage of national forest land in the South may also be a contributing factor in the seeming absence of an unfavorable perception of clearcutting in the South.[20]

Land Use, Perception, and Behavioral Consequences

The implication of perception for land use extends beyond the debate over land use changes, actual or proposed, examples of which have been discussed in the previous section of this chapter. Particular types of behavior may become associated with particular types of land use. Considerable recent research in the social sciences has pointed up contrasting behavior patterns that tend to arise in diverse residential areas. Contrasts between neighborhoods in such features as the size and spacing of dwellings, and the materials used in building construction, seem to become reflected in the social behavior of people living in the different neighborhoods. Moreover, these behaviors seem able to maintain themselves with considerable persistence even when individual members of neighborhoods leave and newcomers arrive. Not only does the formation of particular acquaintanceship groups appear to be related to the physical lay-out or structure of residential land use, but other patterns of behavior in particular neighborhoods likewise seem to persist.

The work of Oscar Newman in his elaboration of the concept of "defensible space" provides a cogent example of the significance for human behavior of land use decisions, particularly decisions as to how space is to be structured within a particular land use.[21] Newman set forth his concept of defensible space in connection with his study of spatial aspects of criminal behavior in the United States. In his study of crime in New York City and elsewhere in the United States he found that its incidence was significantly related to the patterning of urban space. Newman employed crime statistics derived from the New York City Housing Authority Police Records to compare two public housing projects in Brooklyn which were basically comparable to each other in building materials, in size and in socioeconomic characteristics of their population.[22] One project, Van Dyke, contains 14-story apartment buildings separated by substantial open spaces; the other, Brownsville, across a street from Van Dyke, consists of comparatively low 3-to-6-story buildings arranged in such a way that the open spaces are relatively small and generally visible from the apartment windows. The incidence of crime has been substantially higher in the Van Dyke project than in Brownsville. Newman relates the contrast to differences in spatial design between the two projects. Contributing to the higher incidence of crime in Van Dyke are substantial areas not visible from apartment windows and the comparative absence of Newman's "defensible space"—comparatively small spaces where surveillance from dwellings is feasible and where a relatively small group of neighbors tend to perceive such spaces as part of their territory which they have a special interest in protecting. At Brownsville, in contrast, the criminal is more likely to perceive external spaces as extensions of the private dwellings of the project and hence under the surveillance and control of people nearby.

Perception, Image Formation, and Land-Use Change

The apparent role of perception in helping to form people's attitudes toward land use changes, actual or proposed, and therefore as an important factor in the large number of land use controversies now occurring in the United States has been discussed. It should be remembered, however, that perception and the imagery that may be associated with it also underlie land use change. A vast amount of land use change is the realization of a new land use which, figuratively speaking, is seen first in the mind's eye of the beholder. Nineteenth-century land use changes behind the westward advancing frontier are cases in point. But the role of perception and associated imagery also contributes in another fundamental way to the genesis of land use change: that is, as a stimulus to migration. Much migration in the United States is short-distance, of course, as within a metropolitan area. Such migration both responds to new housing available in suburban areas and encourages further investment in housing on the part of builders, thus serving to extend the urbanized area still farther outward. But long-distance migration was important historically in the United States, and remains so today.[23]

A family who in the early nineteenth century sold its land in the Virginia Piedmont and pulled up stakes might have wound its way slowly and arduously westward through the valleys and watergaps of the Appalachians, finally to reach and settle in southwestern Ohio. Such a family would certainly have been responding to its images of the new Ohio country. Imagination involves mental construction, and in this example the images of the Ohio country and its possibilities for farming were constructed out of reports and stories that had filtered back east to the Virginia Piedmont. Such reports and stories in turn rested in substantial part on the perception of Ohio lands by earlier travelers and settlers. The essential point is that images derived from imagination, but based in part ultimately on the perception of others, helped prompt a vast westward movement in nineteenth-century America, as well as immigration into the United States from Europe. In the late twentieth century long-distance migration flows continue with implication for land use change.

In extreme southern Florida a strip of land generally somewhat over ten feet in elevation along much of its length extends southwestward from Miami to Homestead. This tract of land, which comprises a southwestward arc-like extension of a low coastal ridge from Palm Beach to Miami, constitutes virtually the only relatively high and hence dry land in the entire southerly reaches of Dade County within which Miami is located. To the west of this "ridge" are the Everglades marshes; to the southeast, a sea level coastal fringe of saltwater marsh and mangrove swamp. Present urban development and most highway construction has been confined to the elevated belt. A virtually solidly built-up zone extends southwestward from Miami to Homestead along U.S. Highway One, but a considerable acreage of agricultural land also occurs, particularly on the northwest side of the higher land tract between Highway One and the edge of the Everglades. If current long-distance migration into South Florida from elsewhere in the United States continues, the surviving agricultural land use in south Dade County will be lost by urban encroachment.

Historically, several major waves of migration into South Florida have occurred, and another such influx is currently under way, prompted in part by a series of relatively cold winters, which began in the Northeast and Middle West in 1976–77, and by steep increases in fuel oil prices occurring in the late 1970s. In the case of our twentieth-century migrants, whatever imagery may be involved in prompting their move southward most often incorporates personal memory images derived from their perception of South Florida during previous trips to the region, as well as indirect perception of the area via television and other sources of imagery. In brief, the opportunities for direct and indirect perception of the area to which migration is to occur figure far more importantly in the case of present migrants within the United States than those which operated in our nineteenth-century example. The net effect still remains population influx into an area, with subsequent pervasive effects on land use change. That part of the total migration stream to Florida moving into south Dade County raises land use issues not only because of the size of the in-migration flow but also because of the relatively intransigent spatial limits to high-intensity land use development which exist in south Dade County. Although in theory the salt marshes seaward of the dry-land zone and the Everglades marshes inland from it could be sliced with drainage ditches and drained for residential expansion, this would in turn result in an unacceptable lowering of ground water beneath the valuable dryland zone. Moreover, there would be no practical way to protect residences on such low-lying land from the storm surges likely during major hurricanes. A further consideration restricting residential expansion outward onto the lower area of the Everglades border is the importance of this marsh area for ground water recharge into the major aquifer upon which the population of the southeastern extremity of Florida depends.[24]

The implications of the physical geography of southern Dade County for residential land use, together with the current rate of population movement into what, except for the Keys, is the warmest part of Florida during the winter are such that major economic pressures on the remaining agricultural land of the country are likely to be exerted during the 1980s. This prospect, unless circumvented by land use policy as yet not enacted, will produce land use changes from agriculture to residential and other nonagricultural uses. And although farmland is being transferred to nonagricultural uses around most American metropolitan areas, a shift of the remaining south Dade agricultural lands out of agricultural production will mean the loss of areas possessing climatic advantages for special types of crops. The tomatoes and winter vegetables now produced in south Dade County could be replaced in other areas, to be sure, but the loss of land for the production of two tropical fruits, the lime and the mango, could not be replaced by other areas in the continental United States.

Conclusions

The thesis of this chapter was that environmental perception and images need to be kept in mind whenever we are concerned with land use issues. The United States is veritably bristling with land use problems and land use controversy. All parts of the country are affected. The range of issues is wide. Outcomes determine land uses which we subsequently encounter repeatedly in our daily lives. Preservation of open land, the route selection of high-voltage electricity transmission lines, urban renewal attempts or urban homesteading in the inner city, the siting of both fossil fuel and nuclear power generating plants, strip mining of coal and its land use aftermath, the use of land for waste dumping, and other problems in the arena of land use debate seem almost limitless. The most important concluding point is that perception may be involved, often crucially involved, in these problems. Those directly involved with land use matters should be aware that at times it may be expedient to sample land use attitudes among those who will be most concerned or involved in particular land use issues.

Notes

1. P. Meyer, "Land Rush: A Survey of America's Land: Who Owns It—Who Controls It—How Much Is Left," *Harper's* 258 (1979): 45–60.
2. R. Nash, ed., *The American Environment: Readings in the History of Conservation* (Reading, Mass.: Addison-Wesley, 1968), p. 185.
3. Ibid., pp. 190–191.
4. W H. Ittelson, "Environment Perception and Contemporary Perceptual Theory," in *Environment and Cognition*, ed. W. H. Ittelson (New York: Seminar Press, 1973).
5. Ibid.
6. J. B. Jackson, "Several American Landscapes," in *Landscapes: Selected Writings of J. B. Jackson,* ed. E. H. Zube (Amherst: University of Massachusetts Press, 1970).
7. Ittelson, "Environmental Perception and Contemporary Perceptual Theory."
8. Yi-Fu Tuan, "Structuralism, Existentialism and Environmental Perception," *Environment and Behavior* 4 (1974): 319–331.
9. The relationship between language and thought has long been of concern to anthropologists. The Sapir-Whorf hypothesis, which states that the very structure of a language molds the way in which its speakers conceive of the nature of the world, is the classic articulation of this relationship. See, for example, B. L. Whorf, *Language, Thought, and Reality* (Cambridge, Mass.: Wiley, 1956); E. Sapir, (New York: Harcourt, Brace & World, 1921).
10. Yi-Fu Tuan, *Topophilia* (Englewood Cliffs, N.J.: Prentice-Hall, 1974) pp. 66–67.
11. J. W. Bagby, "A Cross-cultural Study of Perceptual Predominance in Binocular Rivalry," *Journal of Abnormal and Social Psychology* 54 (1957): 331–334.
12. Tuan, *Topophilia*, p. 65.
13. It should be noted that although the U.S. Forest Service administers a very large area of national forests in California, as elsewhere in the Far West, most of the remaining stands of large redwood trees had come under private corporate ownership before the reservation of what were to become the national forests began in the final decade of the nineteenth century. By 1960, however, some 58,000 acres of redwoods were already protected in twenty-eight state parks in California, and a small but magnificent stand was preserved in the Muir Woods National Monument north of San Francisco.
14. E. C. Crafts, "Men and Events Behind the Redwood National Park," *American Forests* 77 (1971): 20–28; 58.
15. L. J. Carter, *The Florida Experience: Land and Water Policy in a Growth State.* (Baltimore and London: Johns Hopkins University Press, 1974), pp. 187–210.

16. Ibid.
17. Ibid.
18. B. Gibbons, *Wye Island* (Baltimore and London: Johns Hopkins University Press, 1977). Published for Resources For the Future, a nonprofit corporation chartered under the laws of the state of New York, with headquarters in Washington D.C. It was established in 1952 with the cooperation of the Ford Foundation, and most of its work since then has been supported by grants from that foundation.
19. K. P. Davis, *Land Use* (New York: McGraw-Hill, 1976), pp. 259–283.
20. Ibid.
21. O. Newman, *Defensible Space* (New York: MacMillan, 1972).
22. Ibid.
23. Yi-Fu Tuan, "Images and Mental Maps," *Annals,* Association of American Geographers, 65 (1975): 205–213.
24. Davis, *Land Use*, pp. 170–182.

Chapter 3

The Nature of Land Use Problems in the United States

John F. Lounsbury
Arizona State University

Introduction

Many areas in the United States are experiencing problems directly or indirectly related to the way in which land is used. Recommended solutions to these problems often give rise to conflicts between groups within an area, or between citizens of one jurisdiction and another. Conflicts of interest and strong differences of opinion are especially common to areas undergoing rapid land use changes. The more stable areas where land use patterns remain essentially the same over a number of years experience relatively few land use problems and conflicts.

Certain land uses may have negative economic or social effects on contiguous areas. The use of pesticides, for example, may be necessary for crop production but may prove hazardous to inhabitants of adjacent urban residential areas.

Land use problems result from a complex array of factors. Principal among these are:

1. Changes in the number and distribution of population within an area, particularly those resulting from rapid growth or migration
2. Differences in values, attitudes, and perceptions of the inhabitants of an area or adjacent areas
3. Land developments unsuited to the natural characteristics of the land
4. The nature and type of land use controls and planning

These factors are interrelated, and changes in one will result in changes in the others. Further, resulting land use problems vary greatly in scale and severity. Some of the problems affect only local areas; others may have state or regional significance. A few may have repercussions at the national and international level.

Land Use Problems Related to Population Changes

The population of the United States is increasing about 0.8 percent annually. This present rate of growth is approximately one-half that of two decades ago. However, the current rate of increase is significant in that it represents almost two million more births than deaths annually. This natural growth of population has long range implications for land use problems, but many current problems are the result of sudden and drastic changes in population in certain areas of the country during the last few decades. This movement of people from one region to another has resulted in population increases considerably greater in certain areas than the national average.

For several decades the percentages of the country's total population living in the northeast and northcentral regions has declined while the percentages living in our western and southern regions have increased. Further, outmigration has been characteristic of predominately rural areas whereas urban areas have experienced a large immigration. Since the first federal census in 1790, the urban population of the United States has continually increased, at a more rapid rate in some decades than in others, although the rural population has continuously decreased. As recently as 1940, less than 60 percent of the country's population resided in urban areas. Today almost 80 percent of the population is urban (table 3.1).

The urban population of the United States may be found in several different kinds of urban environments. The largest share lives in central cities of 50,000 people or more; another group, almost as large, lives in areas peripheral to these central cities. These fringe areas include incorporated and unincorporated places, many of which serve as suburbs of central cities. Fringe areas also include localities outside of urban places yet within the greater urbanized areas. Today, about 80 percent of the urban population lives within the central cities or the fringe areas. The remaining 20 percent of the urban population resides outside of highly urbanized areas, mostly in towns of 5,000 or more people. In recent years, the urban population has increased at the highest rate in the urban/rural fringe areas and in localities outside of urbanized areas. This phenomenon has increased the pressure on the land and is largely responsible for present-day urban sprawl, traffic congestion, and loss of agricultural land.

The change in the urban/rural population ratio is primarily a result of the industrial revolution. At the turn of the century, developments in sanitation and other health measures made cities as safe as rural areas, and technological developments greatly increased the number and sophistication of manufacturing plants. The demand for labor in industry and associated urban activities increased several fold. At the same time, the dramatic increase in agricultural production, particularly in yields per area unit due to fertilization and hybridization, and the widespread use of machinery, reduced greatly the demand for labor in agriculture.

Dramatic changes in occupations from predominately rural activities to urban activities have brought about major shifts in the distribution of population. Almost one-half of the approximately 3,000 counties in the country, especially those that are predominately rural, have lost population during the last three decades. Urban areas, on the other hand, have experienced rapid growth during the same period. The number of farms and amount of land used for agriculture have also decreased from 1950 to the present time (table 3.2). The percentage of the nation's total labor force represented by farmers, as a percentage of the gainfully employed, has decreased steadily and today is only about 4 percent.

The movement of people from central cities to their suburbs has also had a major impact on land use for over twenty years. Most central cities have suffered a decrease in population, whereas the population of suburbs has increased at an astounding rate. It is not uncommon for the overall greater city area or Standard Metropolitan Statistical Area to have experienced an increase in population of 4 to 6 percent annually while its central city proper has actually lost population.

These changes in population distribution have resulted in changes in land use in the United States. Areas of declining population, essentially agricultural and mining areas, once contained thriving towns and hamlets as well as other settlement features. These settlements have deteriorated and are often no longer a visible part of the landscape. Changes in land use are more

Table 3.1. Urban and Rural Composition, and Rates of Urban and Rural Growth in the United States

Year	Percent of Total Population		Percentage Urban Gain over Preceding Decade	Percentage Change over Preceding Census	
	Urban	Rural		Urban	Rural
1979 (estimate)	77.5	22.5			
1970	73.5	26.5	3.6	19.2	−0.3
1960	69.9	30.1	5.9	29.3	−0.8
1950	64.0	36.0	7.5	21.8	3.4
1940	56.5	43.5	0.3	7.9	6.4
1930	56.2	43.8	5.0	27.3	4.4
1920	51.2	48.8	5.5	29.0	3.2
1910	45.7	54.3	6.0	39.3	9.0
1900	39.7	60.3	4.6	36.4	12.2
1890	35.1	64.9	6.9	56.5	13.4
1880	28.2	71.8	0.7	42.7	25.7
1870	27.5	74.3	7.7	59.3	13.6
1860	19.8	80.2	4.5	75.4	28.4
1850	15.3	84.7	4.5	92.1	29.1
1840	10.8	89.2	2.0	63.7	29.7
1830	8.8	91.2	1.6	62.6	31.2
1820	7.2	92.8	−0.1	31.9	33.2
1810	7.3	92.7	1.2	63.0	34.7
1800	6.1	93.9	1.0	59.9	33.8
1790	5.1	94.9	—	—	—

Reprinted from Bureau of the Census, *Census of Population, United States Summary, 1970.*

Table 3.2. Number of Farms and Land in Farms in the United States 1950–1975

Year	Number of Farms	Land in Farms (1000 acres)
1975	2,766,750	1,081,448
1970	2,949,140	1,102,371
1965	3,356,170	1,139,597
1960	3,962,520	1,175,646
1955	4,653,800	1,201,900
1950	5,647,800	1,202,019

Reprinted from United States Department of Agriculture Statistical Bulletins No. 316, 507 and 594.

dramatic, however, in the urbanizing areas. Rural lands are rapidly giving way to residential subdivisions, shopping centers, and roads and highways, often without serious consideration of the effects on the overall area.

Values, Attitudes and Perceptions

The culture of a society will have a direct impact on how land resources are utilized. The values and attitudes of the American people that have influenced the patterns of land use in recent decades include (1) the importance placed on economic growth, (2) the ability and willingness to change places of work and places of residence, (3) the reluctance to develop and utilize mass transportation, and (4) the desire for open space living.

Economic growth has long been regarded as a measure of progress at the national, state, local, and individual level. Economic growth implies expansion and demand for more resources, including land resources. Land use changes are necessary to provide more energy as well as space for expanding industrial, residential and commercial areas, and transportational systems. In recent years, economic growth has been closely interrelated with energy growth. The demands for additional energy have necessitated taking land out of some productive activity in order to use it for strip mining, thermal and nuclear power plants, power storage facilities, transmission lines, and hydroelectric sites. These land use changes often generate conflicts of interest and emotional responses from nearby property owners.

American workers are prone to move from one section of the country to another in order to improve their economic situation. The American society and the business community do not discourage this mobility in any major respect. Promotions, transfers, and new positions requiring drastic changes in residence are characteristic of the American way of life. Further, changes of jobs or of residences are the rule rather than the exception.

A change in an individual's economic status frequently brings about a change in residence. As a result of the extreme mobility of the American people, major changes in land use patterns have resulted, particularly in dynamic urban areas. At the present time, mass transportation has been developed only in a few cities in the country. The widespread use of the automobile and the development of excellent networks of highways and roads are characteristic of modern America. Along with the value placed on open space living by the American people, the automobile has been a major cause of urban sprawl so common to the urban landscape.

These values collectively create a life style that has encouraged large-scale intermigration and intramigration. Only recently, and then only in some localities, has there been a reversal of these attitudes. The quest for ever increasing economic growth, mobility, and individualism has placed demands on the land. In turn, these demands create conflicts or differences of opinion about how land should be used and result in land use patterns that are not compatible with one another or the natural setting.

The way individuals or groups perceive land use problems is often a source of conflict. Whether a specific use of the land in reality causes any economic or social problems may not be as important as what people perceive the problem to be (see chapter 2). Perceptions vary from group to group and may well differ from reality. Perceptions regarding land use changes may be reflected in spatial zones (fig. 3.1). Land use changes that *directly* affect the natural, economic, or social environment of a given locality (X) will occur in that area only (Area 1). This area of direct impact may be a few blocks or several square miles in extent. Among other results, the direct impact may manifest itself in changes in the natural setting, in traffic noise, in population densities or composition, and in property values. Common examples include the development of industrial or commercial structures in or near a residential area or perhaps the development of multi-family dwellings in a single-family area. In all cases, for the individual or group, land use changes have a direct real or imagined effect on locality X and usually result in some kind of action or reaction.

Surrounding the area of direct impact (Area 1), an area of indefinite size may be found within which land use changes will not directly affect location X but may indirectly affect the

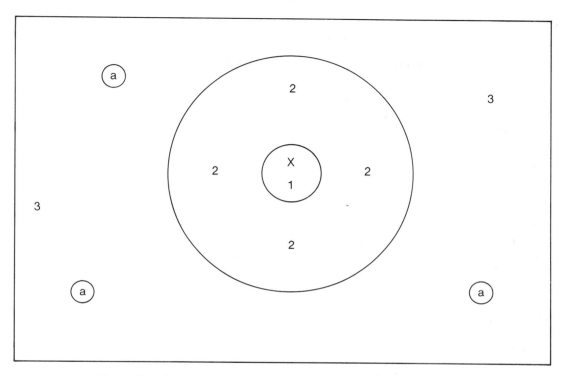

Figure 3.1. Spatial zone of impact (reactions to land use changes).

immediate environment (Area 2). Increased traffic or population density associated with the land use change in Area 2 will not directly affect location X but may cause the residents of locality X real or imagined inconveniences in traveling to other areas, or the change may lead to overcrowding of schools, stores, and so forth. Beyond the areas of direct and indirect impacts, land use changes per se will have no effect on location X (Area 3). However, land use changes in Area 3 may lead to reactions based on principles, values, or emotions. Wilderness areas, religious or historical sites, shrines, monuments, and the like may produce such reactions. This area (Area 3) may include the state, nation, continent, or much of the world depending upon the individual or group's interests and perspectives.

Land Uses Unsuited to the Land's Natural Characteristics

Land use problems may be the direct result of a specific use that proves to be poorly suited to a given natural environment. In some cases, errors in judgment or decisions made on the basis of insufficient data may not manifest themselves for many years. Factors that may be critical to the suitability of a given location for a specific land use include (1) slope of the land, (2) structure of the bedrock, (3) chemical composition of the soil and bedrock, (4) compaction characteristics of the soil, (5) porosity and permeability of the soil and underlying rock, (6) solubility of the bedrock, (7) depth of the water table, (8) depth of frost or permafrost, and (9) volcanic and tectonic stability.

The stability of the surface upon which structures are built greatly influences maintenance costs. High slope areas may be highly unstable, and, during periods of excessive rainfall, slips or slides may damage or completely destroy dwellings and other structures (fig. 3.2). Low slope areas are often subject to poor drainage, and flooding may result in crop and property damage. The underlying structure of the bedrock may cause surface motion, particularly if the rock is dipping and a porous layer is underlain by a nonporous layer such as shale. During periods of heavy rainfall, surface materials above the nonporous layer may move downward in the direction of the dip or tilt. Compaction qualities of soil vary greatly. It is not uncommon for heavy structures to subside, often unequally, resulting in irreparable damage.

Underlying materials also may have a major influence on how the land should be developed. To a large degree, the porosity and permeability of the surface materials determine how much precipitation will enter the ground water system and how much will become surface runoff. Some areas are excessively wet for long periods after light rains; other areas are always excessively drained, prohibiting vegetative growth and excluding various types of land use. Limestone and

Figure 3.2. Landslides in high slope areas are not uncommon. This particular slump flow was the result of building residential structures on a too-steep slope and was set off by a period of heavy rainfall. Seattle, Washington. (Courtesy, U.S. Geological Survey, U.S. Department of Interior.)

other soluble rocks are subject to the solution effects of ground and surface water. Constructing a dam or reservoir in such areas is risky because it is likely that solution channels will eventually develop, resulting in the loss of water. Depth of water tables and their seasonal and yearly fluctuations greatly influence the moisture content of surface materials. A given area may be swampy at times and adequately drained at other times. This condition, in turn, limits the types of land use that can be developed. The depth of the frost line is a factor that must be considered in construction of underground pipes and cables. Freezing water may cause heaving and disruption of underground structures. In areas of permafrost, structures will affect the energy exchange of solar radiation at the surface. Buildings, blacktop roads, and removal of the vegetative cover often cause changes in the permafrost line, resulting in unstable foundations and subsidence.

Perhaps the most spectacular examples of land use poorly suited to a given natural setting occur along active fault lines or near potentially eruptive volcanoes. The development of intensive residential and commercial land uses along the San Andreas and related faults in Southern California has resulted in periodic large-scale damage over the past several decades. Similarly, the volcanic belt in the Cascade Range from Lassen Peak in northcentral California to Mount Baker and northward into Canada is subject to eruptions at any time. The series of eruptions associated with Mount St. Helens in the spring of 1980 caused drastic changes in land use over large areas. The effects on the use of land hundreds of miles distant are yet to be determined.

Most land use problems of these types are the result of developing specific land uses without sufficient knowledge of the natural environment. To obtain such knowledge, however, may be costly in terms of both time and dollars. Unless forced by regulations, developers normally forego a study of the natural setting, which might have provided sufficient information so that preventive measures could have been taken or alternative sites developed.

Land Use Controls and Planning

Who devises and enforces land use controls and designs land use plans in the United States? The answer may be no one, or it may vary greatly depending upon the locality. As of the fall of 1980, a federal land use bill has not passed Congress nor is one likely to pass in the foreseeable future. This does not mean that there are no governmental controls or policies regarding the use of the land. About 40 percent of all the land in the country is owned or directly controlled by federal or state governments. Approximately 700 million acres or one-third of the nation's land is owned outright by the federal government through its various departments and agencies. Much of the remainder of the land, about 60 percent, is owned privately by individuals and corporations; but zoning laws, subdivision regulations, and tax structures may determine the type of land use that will develop. There are about 38,500 local governmental units, either municipal, county, or township governments, that regulate private land in the United States. Perhaps 15,000 of these jurisdictions exercise some form of land use control and planning; the rest do not.

Federal and State Controls

Federal policies regarding the use of federal lands vary depending upon the department or agency. Furthermore, federal policies have varied greatly over the past 200 years. Various acts have controlled the use of land within the public domain. More recent legislation has influenced the use of lands beyond the direct control of the federal government. Traditionally, states have delegated their land use control powers to the local governments via planning and zoning acts. Land controls, as a result, have been implemented at the local level.

Most public lands in the United States are located in the twelve western states, including Alaska. These lands are highly diverse in character encompassing a variety of climates and physiographic and vegetative environments. The public lands include the "public domain," lands ceded to the federal government by the original states, lands acquired from other countries, and lands obtained by the federal government for specific purposes. Most public lands are managed by the Bureau of Land Managment, Fish and Wildlife Service, Bureau of Reclamation, and National Park Service of the United States Department of Interior; and the Forest Service of the United States Department of Agriculture. In addition, large tracts of land are administered by various military departments and the Energy Research and Development Administration.

Policies regarding the use and management of federal lands vary tremendously depending upon the administrative department or agency and its policies. Although specific areas were taken out of the public domain in the late 1800s and early 1900s to create the national park and forest systems as well as for reclamation projects and a variety of other purposes, until recently the policy of the federal government was to transfer public lands to state and private ownership. Little regulation and management of public lands were undertaken and little public investments for improvement were made because it was assumed that the land would eventually pass out of federal ownership. In 1934, however, Congress passed the Taylor Grazing Act. This act, for the first time, called for the active management of unreserved public land, and its passage was the start of a trend to end the federal policy of unrestricted public land disposal.

In 1946 the Bureau of Land Management was created. Its major function was to manage federal land, pending eventual disposal to the states or private individuals or groups. However, the trend that began in 1934 to retain public lands resulted in the passage of the Federal Land Policy and Management Act (FLPMA) in 1976. This act changed the Bureau's operations drastically. The FLPMA replaced over 2,500 individual laws and contained 60 different sections covering all aspects of the Bureau's functions—some long established and some new. More important, the FLPMA established a basic national policy: the majority of the public lands should be kept in federal ownership and managed for their multiple uses. It served as a mandate to retain public lands for the benefit of the entire nation. The FLPMA changed the role of the Bureau of Land Management from range and livestock management to management of recreational activities, energy resources, wildlife habitats, and anthropological and cultural resources. Environmental concerns had to be fully studied and analyzed, and long-term land use planning became a basic part of all federal land administrative agencies' operations.

These new policies imposed strict regulations on many public land users. The resulting dissatisfaction reflected itself in organized efforts to assert states' rights over federal control.

Public lands are a valuable storehouse of resources. The majority of the nation's energy resources can be found within their confines. Including the outer continental shelf, they contain approximately 80 percent of the nation's known petroleum reserves, 80 percent of its natural gas, the largest known oil shale reserves in the free world, roughly 30 percent of the nation's coal reserves, and many geothermal deposits. Further, public lands include approximately 174 million acres of range, which grazes about 9 million head of cattle, sheep, goats, and horses. The value of merchantable timber on public lands is estimated in excess of $15 billion. Public lands serve as habitats for a great percentage of the nation's wildlife, and contribute considerable amounts of the nation's metallic and non-metallic minerals. Important archaeological and cultural resource sites are also found scattered throughout the public domain.

For the average citizen the recreational resources of public lands are perhaps the most meaningful. The tremendous increase in outdoor recreation during the last few decades has put great pressures on the federal parks, forests, and wilderness areas. Overuse is a serious problem and the use of vehicles, such as dune buggies, snowmobiles, trail bikes, and four-wheel drive vehicles, has disturbed the fragile ecosystems in many areas.

The magnitude and diversity of resources within public lands represent a very important aspect of the nation's present and future economy. The basic question focuses on the controls needed to ensure the sound development of these resources and at the same time provide for the rights and interests of private citizens and private enterprises. Further, who is to control and develop these resources? Is it to be the state within which the resources are located or the federal government? The potential conflict between regional or state and national interests over mining sites, water rights, power plant sites, and conversion of agricultural land could become so severe and widespread in the future that national economic growth could suffer.

Each state in the union has the power to enact legislation to protect the health, safety, morals, and general welfare of its citizens. Traditionally each state, to a varying extent, has delegated these powers to local governments. However, in the early 1970s, states began to assume a more direct role in influencing land use developments. First, many states began to assess and modify existing policies concerning administration of state lands. Problems of determining the optimum use of lands under direct state control were addressed, as well as those related to the need for increased revenues derived from the use of state land. Many states established new or modified existing policies regarding transferral of certain state lands to the private sector.

Second, some states began to pass new and innovative legislation to enable them to play a more direct role in the control of land developments on nonstate lands. The first critical areas to come under this new legislation were coastlines, wetlands, agricultural lands, and mountain areas. The role of the state in influencing land use developments varied greatly from one region to another. Such states as California, Delaware, Florida, Hawaii, Maine, New York, Oregon, and Vermont were among the first to develop innovative legislation. Others have left controls in the hands of local governments.

The case for state intervention in land use matters on non-state land may be justified in several ways. First, in certain cases, land use problems arise and there is no existing effective local control. In these situations, it may be argued that the state is responsible for providing plans and controls. The absence of land use controls is often the result of the lack of resources, and expertise, and the small size of local governments. Second, the effects of land use changes in one jurisdiction can spill over boundaries to affect conditions in neighboring jurisdictions. These spillovers may be highly visible as in the case of deterioration of air or water quality resulting from the development of industries or residential areas without adequate sewer facilities, or they may be as subtle as the flow of dollars from one jurisdiction to a new commercial area just across a jurisdictional boundary. A huge industrial complex may be located in one jurisdiction and bring in considerable revenue while the influx of new workers might settle in another jurisdiction placing a serious drain on its funds to provide additional schools and other services. The state's role in these cases should be to balance these inequities.

Third, it may be argued that states should take positive and aggressive action to preserve natural and historical areas of interest to the general public although such action may not be compatible with local opinion. Finally, the state's investments may be used as a mechanism to control land use. States may influence specific land use developments on private lands by determining the location and type of highway networks, water facilities, state hospitals, prisons, and educational institutions. These investments may have an important effect on local growth rates and subsequent land use changes. Police powers such as state tax, licensing, rights-less-than-fee-simple, and state environmental policies may be used as instruments to encourage or discourage specific types of land uses.

As a reflection of the states' new interest in assuming a more direct role in land use planning, several western states are developing strategies to challenge the federal government's right to administer millions of acres of land. The federal government controls about 87 percent of the land in Nevada, 43 percent in Arizona, 66 percent in Utah, and 96 percent in Alaska. The lands that are being challenged are under the jurisdiction of the Bureau of Land Management. The "Sagebrush Rebellion" began in Nevada in 1979 when the state enacted a law enabling the state to seize control of federal lands. Other western states have or are now preparing similar legislation. The legal rationale is based on "equal footing" and the "trustee doctrine." The "equal footing" argument asserts that certain restrictions were placed on the western states regarding federal lands as a condition to attaining statehood. These restrictions were not placed on the eastern states and, therefore, the states west of the Rockies were discriminated against in that they were denied the same treatment as their eastern sisters. The "trustee doctrine" maintains that the federal government holds the public lands in trust pending their disposal, a policy carried out in the past. It is argued, because the federal government has failed to divest itself of these lands in the western states, it is guilty of a breach of trust. It appears that the legal arguments will take years to resolve, since there is no sound precedent for the state challenge to federal ownership and management of public lands. This challenge, however, is highly significant in that it reflects the recent attitudes and interests many states have in becoming more directly involved in land use planning and management.

Local Control

In the past, virtually all land use controls and land planning regarding private lands were exercised at the local level of government. Today, even though the states are redefining their roles regarding land use and federal action is increasingly affecting land development, local governments still make the vast majority of land use decisions. Their active participation is essential to the success of any state or federal program. Local governments derive their power from the state. Each state, to some degree, has delegated the power to control land use to some level of local government. There is a great variation from state to state as to the types of power delegated at what level of government.

Local governments may utilize several types of mechanisms to control land use. These mechanisms include zoning codes, subdivision regulations, municipal planning, building codes, capital improvement programs, and local property taxes. Semigovernmental organizations, such as industrial development corporations and conservation commissions, can also exert influence on the type of land use that will develop.

Zoning codes enable localities to regulate the height and size of structures, the percentage of lot occupied, the size of yards and open spaces, the density of population, and the use of structures and land. Approximately 40 percent of the county governments and many hundreds of municipalities do not exercise zoning controls. In those localities that do have zoning laws, codes differ from one community to another. The manner in which variances, change of zone, special permits, and nonconforming uses are processed or enforced varies greatly.

Subdivision regulations provide standards to control the physical layout of streets, blocks, lots, and utilities. At least one-third of the county governments and many smaller municipalities do not have subdivision regulations. Municipal planning provides for development of a master or comprehensive plan, and building codes regulate the construction of structures. Capital improvement programs define a set of projects such as sewer or water line extension, acquisition of land for park developments, road construction, and the like. These have an important and direct bearing on future land use developments. The nature and structure of property taxes, as well as pressure applied by interest groups such as industrial development corporations, often encourage or restrict specific land uses.

The application and effectiveness of these mechanisms to control land use vary tremendously from one community to another. Further, it is not uncommon for areas to plan the development of land without a detailed inventory of the natural and economic potential of the land. Without this knowledge planning is neither sound nor orderly.

Within Standard Metropolitan Statistical Areas (SMSAs) is a great number of local governments, each with its own zoning code and master plan, which may not be compatible with that of neighboring jurisdictions. Several hundreds or even thousands of local governmental units exist in the larger SMSAs. Typically, it is difficult to attain any degree of successful regional planning. The lack of compatible codes and comprehensive plans as well as the lack of minimum standards create conflicts, problems, and issues in regard to the development and use of the land.

Frequently, taxation is used without due consideration given to its influence on land use. The inequalities of tax structures regarding major types of land use often encourage land use developments or land use changes incompatible with the natural or social environment. Similarly the influences of capital improvement programs, land speculation, highway, sewer and water extensions often are underrated in terms of subsequent land use developments.

In the final analysis, the type and degree of land use planning and land use controls vary greatly from one locality to another. Some areas have no zoning or planning whatsoever; in other areas, land use planning is so fragmented between different agencies or local areas as to be ineffective; in other localities, planning and controls appear to be effective. The important point, however, is that there is no standardization and that each locality proceeds at various levels of effectiveness. This usually results in land use problems particularly at the local scale. Because of these problems, the full potential of the area or region is not attained.

Existing and Future Land Use Problems

Although the underlying factors that cause land use problems are highly diverse, they are often interrelated. They may be natural, economic, social, or psychological factors, or almost any combination thereof. The resulting problems also vary greatly in type, severity, area of impact, and manner of possible resolution. The list of problems discussed below is not comprehensive, but represents land use conflicts and issues that are common in most areas of the country.

Urban Sprawl

The ramifications of metropolitanization and suburbanization have been a familiar part of the American rural/urban fringe for over two decades. The basic causes of urban sprawl are several. From the standpoint of residents, the widespread acceptance and use of automobiles, the development of roads and highways, the desire for open space or low density living, and the movement from urban to rural areas are among the significant factors contributing to sprawl. From the viewpoint of land developers, the economic advantages of going beyond the zone of high land values, high taxes and restrictive zoning and subdivision regulations are basic causes of urban sprawl. Urban sprawl does not always mean contiguous growth. It may develop in jumps, leaving rural land uses or undeveloped land between urban built-up areas. It may develop along major roads as a "ribbon" of predominately commercial or industrial land broken in places by tracts of vacant and undeveloped land, or it may radiate outward from a center leaving plots of rural land between subdivisions. This form of "leapfrog" sprawl at its most extreme becomes urban splatter.

Urban sprawl may be criticized on several counts: high costs necessary to extend water lines, sewers, and utilities; frequent lack of services in rural/fringe areas such as garbage pickup, and fire and police protection; disruptive effects on farming practices; and encouragement of visual blight in the form of poorly designed structures, billboards, amusement parks, and the like. The most serious effects of urban sprawl, at the regional or national scale, are the loss of highly desirable industrial or recreational sites and the loss of farmland. The loss of industrial and recreational sites is due primarily to the rapidity of urban sprawl and its characteristic random growth pattern. Potentially desirable sites for specific types of industries or for local or regional recreational developments are overrun by residential and commercial land uses before their values become known.

It is highly unlikely that urban sprawl can continue unabated as it has in the past twenty or more years. The skyrocketing costs of land, housing, construction, and financing as well as the shortage and costs of fuel and utilities will act as deterrents to some degree. However, a detailed inventory to determine the physical nature of the land and its economic potential along with the development of areawide or regional land use controls and planning, and revision of tax structures may prove to be long-range solutions to the problem. The determination and development of the optimum use of given segments of land, within the context of the regional perspective, should virtually eliminate random growth sprawl.

Preservation of Farmland

One of the most pressing contemporary problems facing local areas, states, and the nation as a whole is the preservation of agricultural land. A recent study by Soil Conservation Service, United States Department of Agriculture, reveals that between 1967 and 1975 about 48.7 million acres were put into new cropland and 79.2 million acres were taken out of crop production. Of the net loss of 30.5 million acres, 16.6 million acres were converted into urban uses and 6.7 million acres were covered by water. Thus, in recent years almost 3 million acres of cropland were converted to some type of essentially permanent non-farm use annually.[1] Approximately 60 percent of the land converted to urban uses and 40 percent of that put under water was among the most productive agricultural land in the country—Soil Conservation Service soil classes I, II, and III.

Figure 3.3. Urbanization of areas formerly used for agriculture is characteristic of dynamic areas. The rate of conversion may exceed several hundreds of acres annually in medium-sized and large metropolitan areas. Mesa, Arizona. (Courtesy, Water and Power Resources Service, U.S. Department of Interior.)

Unfortunately, prime agricultural land—level, well-watered, accessible to transportation, and adequately drained—is also the most economical for the construction of houses, roads, industries, and shopping areas. At the current rate of conversion, in about five decades 150 million acres of the current 400 million acres of cropland will be lost. Further, over one-half of this lost cropland will be in land classes I to III (fig. 3.3).

Is the urbanization of prime cropland a serious problem at the national level? Certainly not from the standpoint of the land's capacity to feed the American people in the foreseeable future. Only about 1.5 percent of the total land area of the country is presently in urban land use. Doubling or tripling this amount will still leave more than enough land, if properly utilized, to provide the necessary food and fibers for the American population. However, in recent years, the agricultural exports of the country, both in amount and in value, have increased enormously. Agriculture, today and in the future, must be viewed in a totally new perspective. United States agricultural exports have increased at a faster rate than even the most optimistic projection of ten years ago. The United States' share of world trade in agricultural commodities was 11.9 percent in 1951–1955 and 13.2 percent in 1968–1972. It has increased to over 17 percent for each year since 1972. In 1975, 52 percent of world grain exports originated in the United States compared to 31 percent in 1969. This increase in agricultural exports has had a major impact on the overall balance of trade by significantly lowering the United States' trade deficit.

At the local level, there are numerous examples of urban sprawl replacing productive cropland. Communities in the citrus producing sections in southern California and Arizona, or in the fruit belt along the southern shores of Lake Ontario in Canada, and in vegetable producing areas in the eastern seaboard provide a few examples. Local government units are attempting to preserve agriculture and open space by creating or enforcing zoning ordinances as well as by creating special tax structures such as assessing land at its use value rather than market value, providing tax deferral policies and transferable development rights thereby preventing individual windfalls or wipeouts. For the most part, these controls require state legislation. The current status of state programs regarding preservation of farmland varies greatly (table 3.3).

The preservation of prime farmland is not only a concern of the United States, but also of its neighbor to the south. Along the common boundary shared with Mexico, a dispute involving the loss of agricultural lands in Mexico developed as the result of water and land use practices carried on in the United States. This dispute has been the most serious single problem between the two countries since the early 1960s. Thousands of acres of highly productive agricultural land in the Mexicali Valley of Mexico had to be abandoned beginning in 1961 when the waters of the Colorado River entering Mexico became excessively saline. The increase in salinity was due to the changes in agricultural practices in the United States. These changes included building of dams to expand the irrigated lands and hydroelectric output in the United States. As recently as the fall of 1979, the government of Mexico refused to consider paying for the damage to the Texas coast from the runaway Ixtoc I oil well in the Gulf of Mexico on the grounds that the United States' government did not pay for damage done to the Mexicali Valley in the 1960s. Similar international issues have arisen between two or more countries sharing a common boundary when the effects of mining or agricultural practices in one country spill over to cause real or perceived damage to the other.

Development of Energy Resources

Although the population of the country is increasing at a slower rate than in the past, there is presently a net gain of almost two million people annually. Equally important, the resource consumption per capita is continuously increasing. This is particularly true in terms of energy resources. To meet these needs, the conventional sources—coal, gas, petroleum, water, and nuclear power—must be exploited at a faster rate, and the nonconventional sources of energy—oil shales, tar sands, geothermal sources, biomass, solar radiation, and wind power—must be developed. Large amounts of land must be converted from other uses to develop these energy resources. This conversion will necessitate major changes in land use patterns in various parts of the country.

Conflicts will arise between local groups or regional and national agencies for the control of critical mining areas, water sources, prime nuclear and thermal sites, power storage facilities and the like. If solutions to these conflicts are not found quickly, they will become more severe as the population increases. Another set of problems associated with the development of energy resources is concerned with the conversion of productive land into strip or open pit mines or locations for

Table 3.3. State programs for preservation of farmland by type of program.

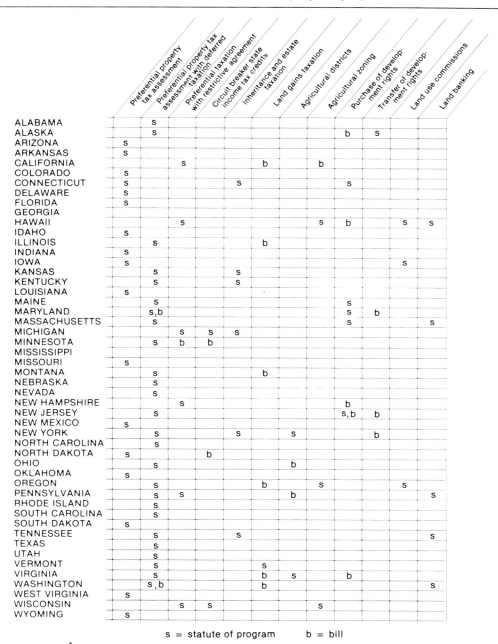

	Preferential property tax assessment	Preferential property tax assessment with deferred taxation	Preferential property tax assessment with restrictive agreement	Preferential taxation	Circuit breaker state income tax credits	Inheritance and estate taxation	Land gains taxation	Agricultural districts	Agricultural zoning	Purchase of development rights	Transfer of development rights	Land use commissions	Land banking
ALABAMA		s											
ALASKA		s							b	s			
ARIZONA	s												
ARKANSAS	s												
CALIFORNIA			s			b		b					
COLORADO	s												
CONNECTICUT	s				s				s				
DELAWARE	s												
FLORIDA	s												
GEORGIA													
HAWAII			s				s	b			s	s	
IDAHO	s												
ILLINOIS		s				b							
INDIANA	s												
IOWA	s										s		
KANSAS		s			s								
KENTUCKY		s			s								
LOUISIANA	s												
MAINE		s							s				
MARYLAND		s,b							s	b			
MASSACHUSETTS		s							s				s
MICHIGAN			s	s	s								
MINNESOTA		s	b	b									
MISSISSIPPI													
MISSOURI	s												
MONTANA		s				b							
NEBRASKA		s											
NEVADA		s											
NEW HAMPSHIRE		s							b				
NEW JERSEY		s							s,b	b			
NEW MEXICO	s												
NEW YORK		s			s		s			b			
NORTH CAROLINA		s											
NORTH DAKOTA	s			b									
OHIO		s					b						
OKLAHOMA	s												
OREGON		s				b		s				s	
PENNSYLVANIA		s	s				b						s
RHODE ISLAND		s											
SOUTH CAROLINA		s											
SOUTH DAKOTA	s												
TENNESSEE		s			s								s
TEXAS		s											
UTAH		s											
VERMONT		s				s							
VIRGINIA		s				b	s		b				
WASHINGTON		s,b				b							s
WEST VIRGINIA	s												
WISCONSIN			s	s				s					
WYOMING	s												

s = statute of program   b = bill

nuclear reactors, transmission lines, power storage sites, and reservoirs. The conversion process itself is costly when land must be acquired. Local organized resistance to these types of developments is not uncommon.

Lastly, the pollution produced when converting raw coal, petroleum, and uranium to energy affects more than just the local site. Although much of the pollution emissions can be controlled by utilizing current technology and at reasonable costs, regulatory laws are so recent that pollution is still a hazardous problem. It may be anticipated that in the near future demands for energy will increase significantly. These demands will result in additional conflicts regarding control of land and in land use changes affecting not only the area in which energy resources are being exploited but contiguous areas as well.

Environmental Hazards

The list of natural and artificial hazards that result in millions of dollars of property damage due to poor land use is a long and familiar one. The costs of damage resulting from urbanizing hillsides, floodplains, and fault lines have increased steadily in spite of large-scale federal, state, and local investments in protective measures. The costs of damage due to artificial hazards such as water and air pollution, solid waste disposal, radiation, and pesticides are even greater in terms of dollars and human health. Further, as technology progresses, the number of new potentially toxic or harmful substances increases. Protective measures frequently include buffer zones or greenbelts or other major changes in the local land use patterns.

In a like manner, the list of land uses that have caused damage to the environment, both locally and regionally, is long and well documented. Often the damage is obvious and takes place over a short period of time. The slow changes over a long period of time are more insidious in that they are difficult to detect and may become irreversible before preventive measures can be taken. To complicate matters, there is no universally accepted definition for an environmental problem nor is there agreement about whether a given change in land use or the environment is damaging or undesirable. Unless the health and well-being of people are impaired, a problem may or may not exist depending on the values of a given society at a given time. Organic waste may be a serious problem to some societies; in other societies it may be an excellent resource to be used as fertilizer. The familiar cases that are considered problems by most American people today include draining, tilling, and filling wetlands, open pit and strip mining, deforestation, eutrophication of inland bodies of water, soil erosion and depletion, destruction of wildlife habitats, and erosion of coastlines and beaches. In all the above cases the damage to the environment may be directly attributed to prior, often subtle, changes in the way land is used (figs. 3.4 and 3.5).

In this context, a new land use problem unique to our age has developed. The electronic smog of the communication's era may be a pollutant with possible harmful effects on the behavior and well-being of people. Recently, residents of a small community in Massachusetts went to court to force the closing of a giant radar antenna that was to be used to detect submarine-launched missiles. The legal rationale was based on the belief that radio waves could cause changes in behavior, increase anxiety, decrease the body's natural infection-fighting powers, and cause birth defects. The court case failed, but the wide publicity triggered similar concerns in other sections of the country. Since World War II, when the electronic age began, the lower atmosphere

Figure 3.4. The construction of residential structures caused the sand to form dunes and drifts rather than blow freely across the land as it did prior to the residential development. Thousand Palms, California. (Courtesy, Bureau of Land Management, U.S. Department of Interior.)

has been bombarded by radio emitters from low power garage door openers to high power sources associated with several industrial processes. Current research is not clear concerning behavioral or health effects resulting from radio waves. However, even if no actual impacts exist, the imagined effects could generate land use changes in many sections of the country.

Incompatible Land Use Patterns

Practically all dynamic areas have experienced, at some time, problems resulting from incompatible land uses located adjacent or near to one another. These problems are normally local rather than regional or national in scale, and are highly characteristic of areas undergoing rapid land use changes. The conflict between the urbanite and the farmer where agricultural and residential lands are located close together is typical in most rural/urban fringe areas. The farmer often objects strenuously to the development of subdivisions on the basis that they have distinct adverse effects on farming operations. Often their development raises taxes to excessive amounts, and the farmer objects to the urbanite's attitude towards certain necessary farming procedures. From the standpoint of the urbanite, certain farming operations are responsible for esthetic deterioration and, in some cases, pose a health hazard. Frequently, the customary services normally found in the city proper are lacking. Often local legislation is rural in outlook and not responsive to the needs of the urbanite.

Figure 3.5. Accelerated bank cutting due to land use changes along the drainage waterways. The increase of cultivated and overgrazed land has caused a significant increase in surface runoff which in turn accelerates the erosional processes. Longmont, Colorado. (Courtesy, Soil Conservation Service, U.S. Department of Agriculture.)

A problem that has developed to major proportions in recent years in many areas is the use of pesticides. The use of pesticides, insecticides, and fungicides may be necessary to prevent excessive crop, poultry, or livestock loss. In many cases, the effects spill over to adjacent residential land causing damage to vegetation, obnoxious odors, and real or imagined health hazards.

The litany of problems resulting from the proximity of industrial and residential land uses is a lengthy and familiar one. The nuisance factors, in terms of noise, smoke, smell, and excessive traffic, as well as the impact on the esthetic environment and property values are often causes for deep concern. The establishment of buffer zones, to separate industrial and residential land, is sometimes feasible, but necessitates taking sizable tracts of land out of some other type of productive use. Expanding transportational facilities often will trigger responses from the people occupying neighboring residential land. The real and perceived effects of airports on adjacent residential land in regard to noise, crash hazard, air pollution and property values are well known as are the effects of expressways and interchanges on adjacent lands.

Whether to allow multi-family dwellings to develop in predominately single-family areas has been a question that every zoning board in the country has had to face at one time or another.

The change in residential density must be accompanied by changes in traffic, parking areas, layout of parks, schools, and so on. These changes create new demands on existing land uses and necessitate land use changes. The threat or actual development of multi-family units in a single-family area has been the cause for legal action in many cities of the country. Institutional land uses, including governmental structures, religious structures, cemeteries, museums, and schools, usually require supporting types of land uses such as wide streets and large parking areas. These are of negative value to residential areas. Attempts to expand institutional land uses will normally evoke emotional responses and organized resistance from the owners of residential property. It may be anticipated that the development of mechanisms to conserve energy will also create serious conflicts with existing traditional zoning codes.

In many municipalities, the creation and enforcement of well thought out zoning codes prevent many of the above problems. However, in large urban areas where the political space is divided among many local governments, each jurisdiction may have its own zoning code which may be appreciably different from that of neighboring jurisdictions. As a result incompatible land uses exist side by side along a common boundary between two or more local jurisdictions.

Each major type of land use requires certain minimum services. In some cases special types of services are necessary. The costs to the local government to provide these services will vary greatly from one type of land use to another. Each type of land use will also provide revenue to the local community directly in the form of property and sales taxes and, perhaps, indirectly in the form of additional employment. In general, the revenue derived from residential land use does not meet the total costs of providing necessary services. This discrepancy is particularly noticeable in areas of low-cost housing and trailer parks. On the other hand, industrial land uses normally pay property taxes greatly in excess of the costs of services. Intensive commercial land uses also normally generate property and high sales taxes to more than offset the costs of services. Many institutional land uses, such as nonprofit charities, foundations, governmental, educational, and religious institutions, service and cultural organizations, and cemeteries, are exempt from property taxes. In most urban areas, the tax-exempt land represents about one-fourth of the total land. In some larger cities, it may be 50 percent or more. The fiscal aspects of land use create an intense competititon among local governments for tax revenues. Industry and shopping centers are highly desired for their tax revenues and source of employment, whereas low-cost housing and tax-exempt organizations are discouraged.

Visual blight resulting from uncontrolled growth of billboards, fast-food outlets, gas stations, shopping centers and the like are matters of concern to some people in many communities. A similar type of problem centers around the destruction of older, and often unique or historic, structures and the replacement of them with buildings of modern design. The concern is not with the quality or usefulness of the new developments, but rather the loss, in part or in whole, of the community's uniqueness or atmosphere.

The Future

It is difficult to predict land use problems of the future. In one respect, the nation, states, and local areas, as well as individuals, are more aware and concerned with the use of the land resource today than at any time in the past. This awareness should result in detailed inventories and analyses to determine the most optimum use of each segment of land. Further, it should spur the development of controls, policies and tax incentives, at all levels of government, to encourage the best and most efficient use of the land. In another respect, population increase and economic growth will continue to put demands and pressures on the finite land resource. If solutions to existing land use problems cannot be found quickly, the combined effects of land control conflicts, increasing demands for resources, and threats to the environment could cause these problems to become so acute and widespread as to impair the national economy.

The majority of the existing land use problems are the results of human activities. They are, therefore, subject to human solutions. To resolve a land use problem, it is necessary to define the problem clearly, determine the types of relevant information, carefully analyze the acquired information, and, finally, determine and put into operation the necessary corrective measures. Many of these issues will be treated in more detail in subsequent chapters.

Notes

1. I. Dideriksen et al., *Potential Cropland Study* (Washington, D.C.: U.S. Department of Agriculture, Soil Conservation Service, 1977).

Selected References

Davis, B., and Belden, J. *A Survey of State Programs to Preserve Farmland*. Washington, D.C.: Council on Environmental Quality, Executive Office of the President, 1979.

Frazier, J. W., and Epstein, B. J. *Applied Georgraphy Conference*. vol. 2, Binghamton, New York: SUNY-Binghamton, 1979.

Healy, R. G., and Rosenberg, J. S. *Land Use and the States*. 2d ed. Baltimore, Maryland: Johns Hopkins University Press, 1979.

Lewis, P. F.; Lowenthal, D.; and Tuan, Yi-Fu. *Visual Blight in America*. Resource Paper No. 23. Commission on College Geography. Washington, D.C.: Commission on College Geography, Association of American Geographers, 1973.

Lounsbury, J. F., and Taylor, P. W. "Land Use Policy: The Conflict of Federal vs. State Control of Public Lands." In *Applied Geography Conference*. vol. 3. pp. 114 to 124. Binghamton, New York: SUNY-Binghamton, 1980.

Marsh, W. M. *Environmental Analysis of Land Use and Site Planning*. New York: McGraw-Hill, 1978.

Moss, E., ed. *Land Use Controls in the United States*. New York: Dial, 1977.

Platt, R. H. *Land Use Control: Interface of Law and Geography*. Resource Paper No. 75–1. Washington, D.C.: Commission on College Geography, Association of American Geographers, 1976.

Procos, D. *Mixed Land Use*. Stroudsburg, Pennsylvania: Dowden, Hutchinson and Ross, 1976.

Zeimetz, K. A.; Dillion, E.; Hardy, E. E.; and Otte, R. C. *Dynamics of Land Use in Fast Growth Areas*. Agricultural Economic Report No. 325. Washington, D.C.: United States Department of Agriculture, 1976.

Chapter 4

Developing Land Use Objectives

Edward A. Fernald
Florida State University

Introduction

Land use planning is more than making a decision regarding the location of dwelling places, parks, or shopping centers. It is an activity that not only establishes the land use patterns of a community, but also the quality of life of its members. Land use questions are complex and far reaching, and the formation of a rational plan requires a great deal of effort and information. The first step in making a land use decision is to gather and evaluate land use objectives of different individuals and groups, including institutions.

Historically, land in the United States has been viewed as a commodity.[1] When legally settled, inherited or purchased, land became a possession to be used as the owner saw fit. Individual or corporate owners made land use decisions and set land use objectives based on the right of freeheld property. If, for whatever reason, the quality of the land was degraded, the pioneer, following the belief of Manifest Destiny, moved south or west because "there was more where that came from."

In time, limited restrictions were placed on use of lands by an owner, first by laws prohibiting immoral or anti-social behavior and later by local zoning and subdivision ordinances.[2] Today, zoning has become the legal tool by which communitywide land use objectives are enforced. As more and more people with higher and higher levels of technology occupy the same areas of land, more public policies and legal tools are needed to ensure land use patterns that benefit a majority of the citizens. On occasion, these actions infringe on the ability of individual citizens to use their land according to their private objectives. The question of public objectives versus private objectives is, and will remain, a viable topic for discussion and research.

Land ownership has always been part of the American Dream, but today land speculation has become a national obsession. In 1980 over two-thirds of American families owned their own homes, and many of them owned other property as well. As cities have become larger and competition for land has intensified, these property owners have sought to maintain or improve the quality of the landscape and the value of their land through planning and zoning. Similarly, property owners in rural areas have generally, although not universally, accepted the need for land planning and conservation to protect agricultural land from urban encroachment and to preserve environmentally fragile areas.[3]

Because of demographic, technological and speculative pressures on the land, people are beginning to perceive land as a resource rather than as a commodity. Some people feel that land is a societal resource or property like air or water. Consequently landowners are seen as having a public responsibility to use their ownership rights in a socially acceptable manner. Both the strict commodity position and the societal resource stance have been criticized.[4] Bosselman and

Calles have attempted to resolve this conflict by explaining that land should be viewed as both a commodity and as a resource.[5] This position fails to provide clear guidelines by which to set land use objectives, but it does provide a middle ground and emphasizes the importance of the development of rational land use objectives.

Elements of the Land Use Decision-Making Process

This chapter is based on the assumption that making land use decisions is a rational process which may be applied to either a single parcel of land or to the development of an entire state. It is assumed that the difference between planning at each level is a matter of generalization, rather than a matter of different decision-making processes. For example, land use control laws are different for the various levels of governmental jurisdiction, but the way the planner approaches the problems of control is the same. The elements in the decision-making model or process used in developing this chapter are listed below. The aim of this chapter is to examine the first two aspects or elements of that process: the formulation of land use objectives at the individual and at the institutional levels. The elements of the land use decision-making process are:

1. Formulation of land use objectives (individual)
2. Identification of institutional land use needs
3. Gathering and analysis of land use data; methodology and technology
4. Evaluation of current laws, policies, and regulations
5. Identification and evaluation of trends, influences and tools
6. Evaluation of land use change models
7. Implementation of land use decisions (single-purpose plans through master plans)

The elements listed above represent the major elements required in the land use planning process. They are not sacred and may be expanded, reordered, or modified to meet specific land planning needs although each suggests a series of questions which should be considered in any land planning activity.

In order to understand the formulation of objectives in the land use process it is necessary to develop a framework for identifying objectives, to discuss the factors that influence setting objectives, and to identify those responsible for setting them. This chapter will also discuss techniques for increasing participation in the formulation of land use objectives, the processes through which they are set, and the significance of establishing a method for changing objectives during the land use planning process.

The Formulation of Goals, Objectives and Policies

Land use objectives should be formulated using the widest possible variety of sources, ranging from individual citizens to large governmental agencies or industrial enterprises. Elements 1 and 2 distinguish between objectives of individual citizens and those of governmental, economic, and other social institutions. Although the same people may make up both groups, the researcher is advised to seek objectives under each category. Private citizens quickly identify certain land use objectives in order to satisfy residential, commercial, or recreational needs, but they tend to forget less obvious needs such as solid waste and power plant sites or even agricultural and transportation land. These less obvious needs are voiced by institutions. Also, individuals are frequently inconsistent when stating land use objectives. The land use specialist must be prepared for that phenomenon. For example, individuals may want single-family detached housing for their entire residential area and a picturesque two-lane road into town, but in their role as city officials they may wish to develop a mass transit system that requires medium to high density housing areas and multilane roads for support.

The results people want from their land use planning are usually stated in terms of goals, objectives, or policies, an approach used in the Tallahassee-Leon County, Florida Comprehensive Plan. Goals are more general than either objectives or policies. They are statements of purpose and are intended to define an ultimate or end state, a condition toward which the community is constantly striving. A land use goal taken from the plan of Tallahassee-Leon County states: "To achieve a distribution, rate and type of growth and land development which is consistent with the social and economic needs of the community and with the supportive capabilities of natural and man-made systems."[6]

Objectives are more specific than goals and they identify the steps necessary for the satisfactory pursuit of a goal. An objective that was written to be compatible with the above goal is: "To coordinate the location and design of shopping centers with the populations which they will serve."[7] The objective gives direction to the planner by setting a task to be achieved.

Policies are more detailed than objectives, and they provide guidelines for specific actions which will satisfy particular objectives. Sample policy guidelines listed below for shopping centers are an example of a policy consistent with the previously stated goal and objective.

"Regional shopping centers having an areawide function in the sale of general merchandise should be located and designed as to have a:

a. Minimum supporting population of 150,000 people
b. Gross land area of at least 40 acres
c. Gross floor area of at least 400,000 square feet
d. Location at the intersection of arterial streets or expressways
e. Service radius of 10 to 15 miles, or more."[8]

Orchestration is a primary problem in setting objectives and policies. As guiding statements become more specific, compatibility must be maintained. Statements must also be adopted with a clear understanding of the limitations placed on the implementing group such as time, money, technical equipment, and planners' ability. An additional limiting factor is the value system of the people of the community involved.

All plans do not follow the goals/objectives/policy format although most plans do differentiate levels of generality. Some identify goals and policies, whereas others identify objectives as general and specific. These differences represent the conflict between traditional planning, which its critics condemn as too inflexible, and policy planning, which is criticized as too fuzzy to give direction.[9] The Tallahassee-Leon County examples are from a policy planning approach. It is not the purpose of this author to advocate one system over another. Land use specialists must define and understand the format that is chosen and must be able to explain it to those with whom they will work, including fellow planners, elected officials and the general public. For the remainder of this chapter, goals or policies will be mentioned, but the term objectives will be used as a general term and is meant to include goals and policies.

Initial Collection of Land Use Objectives

Individual Objectives

Recognition of the diverse land use objectives held by individuals is the first step in the development of a land use plan. The perceptions and desires of citizens, individuals in governmental agencies, and representatives of business and industry should be identified as explicitly as possible (see chapter 2). This process, which gives everyone a common starting point, identifies needs and realistic goals. Sources of land use competition and potential critical conflict will also become clear as a result of this process.

Needs for residential and commercial development as well as objectives for environmental protection are commonly voiced by individuals. Some of these are achievable; some are not. For example, citizens may call for a park in a developed area for which no money is available to purchase expensive land. This type of objective may be shown to be impractical through discussion and explanation, or it may be noted for consideration and rejected only when data become available to support such a decision.

During the initial collection of individual land use objectives, competition and potentially critical conflicts should be identified. In the case of probable competition for parcels along a specific major connector street by residential or commercial interests, the planner should give special attention to the desired character and potential hazards of communitywide connector streets (broad objectives) before developing more specific objectives or policies. The same precaution holds true for conflicts involving any sharp break from lower to higher density use, location of necessary infrastructure sites such as power relays or pumping stations in an urban area, or construction of solid waste sites in a rural area.

Institutional Objectives

Institutional objectives are just as important as those of individuals. This statement is not made to diminish the value of private citizen input, but to point out that in matters concerning the health, safety or welfare of their citizens, governments are in a position to aid planners. These objectives may also come from private sector institutions such as the Chamber of Commerce, business or other economic groups, or special interest groups such as the Sierra Club and the Audubon Society. The planner is usually an institutional agent, either for the government or for a professional planning firm.[10] Because governmental, economic or social institutions have singular tasks, it is not uncommon for the objectives presented by these groups to contain most of the same contradictions and even extravagances contained in the list of individual statements. Nevertheless the valid land needs of government, business, industry and the social sector must be inventoried and evaluated.

Generally, institutional objectives can be categorized by the headings of any land use classification system (for example, see chapter 5). Both government and economic groups may have different objectives for the same type of land. For example, governmental agencies may identify forests for recreation or open space whereas paper products or chemical companies may state their need for forest land as a source of raw materials.

The land use researcher, as an agent of government, has a responsibility to be aware of the preservation needs of society as well as the protection needs of fragile ecosystems. To the same degree, however, the researcher should be aware of the economic needs of society, including the provisions of raw materials for industry and the relationship of land use to per capita income and employment.

If not written carefully, land use objectives may be one of the strongest ways, along with taxes, of establishing a "negative business climate." This has happened in several states, which have modified their positions as having been too strongly stated. In no way should this warning be construed as encouraging lax land use objectives as a tool for economic development. It does, however, call for a serious evaluation of how objectives should be written.

Conflicts in Land Use Objectives

Conflicts in objectives like the ones suggested above are normal, and the land use planner must deal with them as positions honestly held by reasonable people.[11] Even when he or she must take a stand, which is well supported by data, the planner must state the position objectively, not as a crusader. Usually, it is the specialist who must keep a calm climate in which to resolve land use conflicts. A time for study is needed to allow the supporters of opposing views to reassess their positions and to allow land use specialists time to gather all pertinent data. After using maps to present a situation clearly, alternative positions are evaluated, and if a single solution cannot be agreed upon, the decision becomes a political one for elected officials.

Specific conflict situations can be handled more easily if the broad or goal type objectives allow, if not encourage, the use of flexible planning tools such as the transfer of development rights as well as old standards such as buffers, extended easements or the backing up of one use to another. In some cases, the establishment of objectives that encourage the use of intermediate densities and functions such as office-residential or medical-commercial will help mitigate conflict situations.

Land planners are not always on the firing line to make decisions about conflicts in setting objectives. When planners do not make decisions, their responsibility is specific: land planners should help spot conflicts as soon as possible and provide the planning commission, citizens' groups and elected officials with the best possible data so they can develop a rational set of objectives, be they specific or general. Of course, land use specialists are usually asked for recommendations and are often asked to write objectives for acceptance or rejection by the decision makers.

The Role of Citizens and Land Specialists in Establishing Land Use Objectives

This section is concerned with the quantity and quality of citizen participation. It is desirable in our system of government to go to the people for as much guidance as possible. Almost every state and all federal land-assistance programs require citizen participation.

A generalization can be made that land use planning, and thereby the setting of objectives, is like the weather in that everyone complains about it but no one does anything about it. This may be true, but people do not necessarily have to be negative about planning. When people are in dispute with a land use program they are frequently reacting to something they have had no part in developing.

Smith believes "that no planning will be successful unless there is a planning attitude within the affected area on the part of citizens, political leaders, and the power structure. Where this is not so, what is called planning can be an illusory gimmick used to develop a false sense of security on the part of those of us who are prone to apathy concerning local government and our community. . . . I suggest also that community planning with meaningful citizen involvement is one of the last ways available to us in trying to preserve a true democratic society."[12]

Even if one feels that Smith overstates the case, it is important both to planning and to the democratic system to have as many people as possible directly participating in the formulation of planning objectives. This policy allows the opinions of more people to become widely known and often causes individuals to rethink their own positions. In the end, if a person has had a part in developing a land use plan, that citizen is more apt to support and even defend the plan against inevitable complainers.

Good public relations are important for the acceptance of land use plans. Just as a wide range of individuals should be invited to participate from the beginning, members of the media should also be invited to take an active part. They help advertise, they ask questions, and they often give constructive suggestions. At the end of the process they can help sell a land use plan. Some words of wisdom applicable to this process are, "No one likes surprises in land use management." Publicity broadens participation and works against the situation in which a small, but vocal and active special interest group, be it either a business, social or neighborhood group, imposes its will on the community as a whole.

Greater citizen participation immediately causes a number of problems which interfere with the smooth operation of the planning process. First, more people mean more ideas and more conflicting objectives. Many of these ideas are rational and valid; yet many opinions result because average citizens have not thought beyond their own life experiences and expectations. It is at this point that it becomes necessary to educate the participating public to broader community needs.

This educational need may be met by a public workshop where citizens from the whole community come to hear about the planning process. Such a workshop can become unwieldly if too many people with divergent views show up. Such a situation can set the stage for conflict. One solution is to ask representatives from various parts of the town or from special interest groups to attend. An acceptable way to educate citizens prior to having them participate in formulating land use objectives is to use neighborhood organizations, garden clubs, service clubs, the League of Women Voters or other interested groups.

The creation of neighborhood groups is a positive trend in the United States. Many of these groups were originally formed to meet a crisis involving crime, school or drainage problems. They can also be used as a forum for writing land use objectives. Planners, informed members of the planning commission and elected officials can meet with neighborhood groups to explain the tasks confronting the community.

The neighborhood might be introduced to the planning process by using a model such as the one presented in this chapter. In this way the neighborhood is instructed on the components of a comprehensive plan, if that is the goal, or on the various influences on the land use plan to be devised. These influences would include, but would not be limited to, transportation, growth trends, fiscal resources and restraints, and present and planned utilities. This exercise should be followed by a discussion of a neighborhood's perceived land use problems.

The next step is to get members of the neighborhood to express what they perceive to be the problems of other segments of the city or county. In the course of that discussion the researcher should inform neighborhood members of communitywide factors that need to be considered in a land use plan, such as low income and high-density housing, solid waste disposal, infrastructure siting and compatibility of land uses in contiguous neighborhoods.

A series of neighborhood meetings is not as easy as sitting back with the counsel of a few interested community leaders and devising a plan to present at a public hearing, but in the long run these meetings are undoubtedly the best procedure for the community.

This process was followed in Tallahassee-Leon County, Florida, where maps of present land use and zoning and multiple blank maps for experimentation were distributed. First, the neighborhood group or committee evaluated present zoning and land use. They then identified all existing conflicts and incompatible uses and, in cooperation with the planning department, suggested broad policies and specific spatial solutions to those problems. They also suggested objectives to guide future land use change. A workshop was then planned to allow the various neighborhood plans to be tested for compatibility and to work out problems. Out of these exercises, the land use specialists constructed what they felt was the best plan from suggestions by the neighborhood groups and from the departmental plan formulated for those areas that were not covered by citizens' committees. The Tallahassee-Leon County plan is a modified policy plan. It avoids the pitfalls of a rigid traditional plan by setting policies yet gives specific guidance, through a land use map, to both the land developers and to the planning, city and county commissioners who must vote on specific land use changes.

In the process of developing objectives through citizen participation, land use specialists are required to be many things but most of all they must be competent and self-assured. That is not to say that they must know everything about the final land use plan, but they must know about, and be comfortable with, the land use decision-making process they choose to follow. Their role includes administering the process and being able to communicate it to others. In addition, they must be able to provide all of the participants with the data they need to do their jobs well. Where there are alternatives, land use specialists must be able to inform the participants at the citizen level, take their suggested plans, combine them into a workable scheme, and present this scheme clearly at public hearings, to planning commissioners and then to elected officials for their vote. These activities refer to every step of the land use decision-making process, but in this chapter the reference is to the formulation of objectives. At each level, the researcher's tool, the map, is a suggested method of presenting and clarifying issues.

Role of Scientists and Elected Officials in Setting Land Use Objectives

Now that the roles of the citizen and the land specialist in writing objectives have been discussed, a few words on the roles of the scientist and the elected official are in order. Possibly it is more to the point to note what they should not do. The exercise of writing objectives will identify scientific research needed to complete the job. Usually the broader objectives are based on value judgments, but achievement of the more specific objectives depends upon data and their analysis. Research may be needed on the extent or function of a marsh or a drainage feature or on an existing tax or millage rate. After the needed task has been identified, it is the responsibility of the land use researcher to find the proper scientist to collect, analyze and present the data. The scientist's role is passive in the development of land use objectives. Scientists may make recommendations based on their professional judgment, but they should not play the role of decision maker.

As a citizen, and possibly a well-informed one, the scientist might be encouraged to take an active part in establishing objectives although it should be noted that a physical scientist might not consider the political or economic aspects of implementing a position he or she feels is adequately justified by science. On the other hand, a social scientist might not understand the physical/biological impacts of a decision. The researcher is responsible for understanding and communicating the symbiotic relationships among various land uses and the physical/cultural environment. The generalization here is that a scientist, who is an expert in one area of land use analysis, is not necessarily an expert in all areas of planning.

Elected public officials have the responsibility of providing the planning staff with the means to do the job of developing land use objectives and of implementing them. They should give the planning specialists the verbal support they need, and officials should prevent special interests from putting undue pressure on them. If the elected officials do their homework and are representative of the people, they should be able to make critical suggestions and to be a part of the development process. Their final responsibility is in the rational acceptance or rejection of the objectives and in the implementation thereof. This includes rejecting, on occasion, an objective generated by citizen participation that they know from their knowledge as a public officials is not in the best interest of the public at large.

Case Study: Tallahassee/Leon County, Florida

An example of how to set goals, objectives and policies is taken from the work of the Tallahassee/Leon County Planning Department and the Tallahassee/Leon County Planning Commission. The following information was developed to meet the problem of a lack of knowledge on behalf of citizens and some elected officials. In this example an overall goal was developed, several assumptions of the future were made and a problem was stated. To meet this problem an analysis was done of its severity, causes and results, and an objective was stated. Finally, alternative approaches to meeting the objectives and an analysis of the implications of each approach were noted. This process provides an understanding of the situation as it was, a choice of alternative solutions and the information on which to base rational decisions. The following is taken from development papers supporting the Land Use Element, a section in the Tallahassee/Leon County Comprehensive Plan.

Land Use Element[13]

OVERALL GOAL: To achieve a distribution, rate, and type of growth and land development in Tallahassee and Leon County which is responsive to the social and economic needs of the community and is consistent with the supportive capabilities of natural and manmade systems.

ASSUMPTIONS OF THE FUTURE:
- — Countywide population will increase to about 239,000 people by Year 2000.
- — Although the price of fuel oil will continue to increase, stability of the local economy, in conjunction with more fuel efficient modes of travel, will allow substantial portions of the population to continue living in relatively low-density residential patterns.
- — Economic inflation will make expansion of public facilities and services less cost effective than improvements to existing facilities and services.
- — Despite the many dissimilarities between residential and non-residential land use characteristics the concept of mixed use developments could be accomplished through the effective use of compatibility criteria.
- — Public attitudes and values towards land development are not always attuned to long-term social, economic, and physical necessity.

PROBLEM

Traditional low density residential development in Tallahassee and Leon County is becoming increasingly more costly to provide and to maintain.

Problem Severity

An estimated one-third of Leon County residents cannot presently afford to buy a new, median priced, conventional single-family home. As construction and land prices continue to outstrip family incomes, this situation will become even more apparent.

Conventional, low density, single family houses account for over half of the county housing stock; mobile homes add an additional 13% to the total stock of low density housing. Beyond the existing, low density inventory of housing, an additional 12,000–13,000 lots are already committed in the form of platted, but as yet unused subdivision lots. Over half of these lots are located in the northern part of Leon County.

Continuing increases in low density housing are creating strains on the ability of government to adequately provide community facilities. Utilities extensions and street improvements and maintenance are costly when spread over a wide geographic area. Within higher density development, "the largest cost savings are in construction of residential dwellings, although important savings are attributable to reduced costs for roads and utilities, which are about 55% lower in the high density than in the low density community."

Studies at both the community level and the neighborhood level indicate that better "planning" and higher density result in lower economic, environmental, natural resource, and, to some extent, personal and social costs.

Problem Causes

- — Large amounts of attractive, undeveloped land.
- — Utilities revenues form the financial basis for city government; tends to encourage the addition of new revenue producing accounts.
- — Availability of utilities services from other public utility companies in outlying areas beyond the City of Tallahassee utilities service area.
- — Competition between the City of Tallahassee and other public utility companies for non-electric utilities customers.
- — Relatively less expensive land costs in outlying areas of the County.
- — An extensive highway and street system (including an interstate highway and other U.S. highways) which provides quick access to Tallahassee from outlying county areas, as well as from surrounding counties.

- A multitude of natural features throughout the County (lakes, rivers, rolling hills, large trees, scenic vistas) which make "county" and suburban living desirable.
- Uncertainties about future fuel oil supplies and costs.
- The desire of many Tallahasee-Leon County residents to live in single family homes in suburban locations.

Problem Results

- City utilities services are being provided in developing areas far removed from the City. While expansion of water and electrical service offers the potential for increased City revenues, extensions of sewer facilities are costly.
- Continuing urban expansion into previously undeveloped areas has a strong potential for degrading sensitive natural resource areas and for reducing the amount of existing and potential agricultural properties.
- Increasing investments in streets and highways are required; these facilities are heavily dependent upon uncertain supplies and increasing costs of petroleum. Improved highways encourage increases in low density development, and increased development, in turn, requires improved highways.
- Most recent land development has been in suburban areas; much of the committed residential development (i.e. recorded but unused subdivision lots) and potential residential areas are also located on the periphery of the urban area. All of this development comes at a time when the future of petroleum becomes more tenuous, and when people are beginning to look for more ways to cut the cost and uncertainty of commuting between their homes and places of employment, shopping areas, and recreational and cultural facilities.
- Operation of low density residential units is relatively energy intensive in terms of heating and cooling requirements as well as for transportation.
- Low density development tends to encourage commercialization along major traffic arteries.
- Mass transit is unable to effectively serve a dispersed population.
- Suburban development provides little incentive for downtown development or redevelopment.
- Creates demand for additional drainage facilities; increases costs for construction and maintenance of these facilities.

OBJECTIVE

In an effort to make future development more affordable to more people, encourage a distribution and type of land development which will be in keeping with the cost effectiveness of providing public facilities and services.

ALTERNATIVE APPROACHES:

PROBLEM / OBJECTIVE

Approach 1	*Approach 2*	*Approach 3*
Anticipate and provide the type, location, and amount of utilities facilities needed to serve probable urban growth (based on continuation of present trends).	Attempt to concentrate future development within the existing Tallahassee urban area.	Encourage future growth in multiple "satellite" areas (independent communities) with concentrated residential areas in proximity to employment centers.

BY TAKING ACTION TO:

POLICIES

Approach 1	*Approach 2*	*Approach 3*
a. Identify and clarify specific jurisdictional responsibilities for the provision of the various facilities and services.	a. Encourage the development of urban lands that have, in the past, been by-passed ("in-fill" areas).	a. Identify activity centers or development centers, suitable for "satellite" development.
b. Develop a capital improvements program that is responsive to anticipated need rather than one designed to control future development.	b. Encourage the redevelopment of older, under-utilized, and vacant urban lands.	b. Preserve and enhance current urban development.
c. Allow the private market to be the controlling force in land use decisions.	c. Encourage the upgrading of *urban* utilities facilities, while discouraging extension of these facilities to outlying areas.	c. Maintain and upgrade the transportation network linking "satellite" developments to the central urban area, and linking the "satellite" developments to each other.
d. Maintain a current socio-economic and physical data base for use in projecting future land use.	d. Improve the urban transportation network— especially mass transit, pedestrianways, bikeways.	d. Avoid linear land development along arterial roadways linking the "satellite" developments (i.e., through zoning, subdivision regulations, scenic and environmental protection measures).
	e. Encourage higher density residential development.	
	f. Centralize housing, employment, cultural and recreational opportunities, and shopping.	
	g. Discourage the rezoning of agricultural properties to urban uses.	

IMPLICATIONS:

a. ORGANIZATIONAL FEASIBILITY

Existing organization is adequate, although the City/Other public utilities service boundary would probably need to be redefined. Staffing would probably need to be increased to accommodate service to a larger geographic area.	Existing organization is adequate. Emphasis would be upon upgrading of urban area services and facilities rather than upon expansion. Jurisdictional responsibilities would remain similar to present situation.	Would probably require reconsideration of City/county joint services agreement, reconsideration of the City/Other public utilities service area boundary, or other instruments of agreement, as this approach would encourage concentrations of urban development beyond the present City jurisdiction.

Approach 1	*Approach 2*	*Approach 3*
b. LEGALITY		
No apparent legal problems; continuation of present actions; the Local Government Comprehensive Planning Act (LGCPA) gives land use controls legal status.	No apparent legal problems if direction of growth is based upon valid data supportive of a comprehensive plan; LGCPA gives land use controls legal status.	Same as comments for Approach 2.
c. COST		
Support of low-density residential development, which predominates in Tallahassee/Leon County would be more costly than Approach 2; depending upon techniques used, may or may not be more costly than Approach 3.	Probably less costly than Approaches 1 or 3. "Inplace" services and facilities would be improved upon, rather than expanded or duplicated.	More costly than Approach 2 due to need for facilities and services in multiple development centers; depending upon techniques used, may or may not be less costly than Approach 1.
d. LENGTH OF TIME TO IMPLEMENT		
Can be programmed to coincide with need.	Implementation would need to precede urban growth demand in order to centralize that demand.	Implementation would need to precede growth demand in order to encourage "satellite" development.
e. ENVIRONMENTAL IMPACT		
Would encourage low density development over large areas and would create more environmental disruption than approaches 2 and 3.	Less destructive to the environment in terms of total developed acreage, although sources of environmental hazards would be more concentrated.	Less negative effects on the environment than Approach 1; concentrations of environmental hazards would not be as extensive as in Approach 2, but presently undeveloped acreage would be subject to development.
f. ENERGY IMPACT		
Requires more energy consumption than Approaches 2 and 3 in terms of utilities installation and operation. Low density development requires more energy for transportation and space conditioning of structures.	Most energy efficient of the three approaches; limits transportation energy requirements; higher residential densities encourage reduced per unit energy requirements.	More energy efficient than Approach 1, but probably not as energy efficient as Approach 2 due to need for duplicative facilities to serve multiple activity centers.
g. HEALTH AND SAFETY IMPACT		
No significant effects.	Higher urban densities could increase public health problems and crime rates. Even with Year 2000 projected population, the overall effects would be relatively limited.	No significant effects.

Approach 1	*Approach 2*	*Approach 3*
h. REGULATORY IMPACT		
Can be accomplished under present regulations.	Would require a higher level of development regulation than Approach 1; would probably be less difficult to regulate than Approach 3.	Probably the most difficult approach to regulate due to multiple "satellite" areas, possibly with different development characteristics and different regulatory needs.
i. CONFORMANCE WITH NATIONAL POLICY		
No explicit national land use policy. This approach conforms generally to federal assistance programs which have tranditionally supported urban expansion; national energy issues appear to be directed toward increased concentration of population.	No explicit national land use policy. While federal assistance programs have traditionally supported urban expansion, national energy issues appear to be directed toward increased concentration of population.	Would tend to concentrate population in conformance with emerging national energy issues.
j. CONFORMANCE WITH STATE POLICY		
Generally consistent but does not support the concept of population concentration/land conservation as well as do Approaches 2 and 3.	Consistent; supports concept of population concentration/land conservation.	Supports concept of population concentration/land conservation and yet provides flexibility to meet local desires for relatively low density living.

Following public discussion and recommendations on these alternatives and the parcel specific land use exercises described earlier, a final land use policy plan was written. Approach 1, which represents the past growth and development of Tallahassee/Leon County, was followed approximately 65 percent of the time. The major reason for this was a strong support of the status quo by the local realtors and the fact that the local city/county planning department had kept major land use problems to a minimum. Thirty percent of the other objectives came from Approach 2. These were basically the more idealistic objectives concerning subjects such as conserving energy, mass transportation, environmental protection and "in-filling" of vacant areas. Approach 3 was followed only in regard to the further planning of existing satellite centers.

Both the policy plan and the land use map were evaluated as the policies were tested against the parcel specific map and vice versa. A final use of the plan and the map can be made by local citizens: they can evaluate their elected officials on the basis of how those officials act in relation to the objectives adopted in the comprehensive plan.

Techniques for Gaining Input for Writing Land Use Objectives

Objectives from Individuals

Interviewing, polling, delphi techniques, workshops, public meetings, and public hearings are all ways of gaining information for writing land use objectives. Several problems must be recognized when using interviews or polling techniques. First, those gathering the information must be at least minimally trained so they can avoid asking leading questions, or ones that are too technical. A poorly conducted interview or a badly worded poll may be used against a well-meaning land use specialist. It is suggested that a person who is qualified in the use of these techniques be consulted before using them. A factor to be aware of after the data are gathered is that the average citizen is frequently unaware of the land use options available in the choice of objectives. Citizens do not usually know what their choices will cost in terms of fiscal, social and physical resources. This situation emphasizes the need for information/education sessions.

The Delphi method is a controversial forecasting tool based on the best guess or intuition of a group of people selected as knowledgeable or expert in land use planning.[14] This group is given information pertinent to the task and then asked a series of questions on the assumption that a consensus of their subjective judgments will be helpful in developing a land use plan. There are several variations in use of the Delphi method. In some cases the experts are unknown to one another. The questioning procedure may be held only once, or the group reaction from round one of questioning may be shown to the group, after which the group may be asked to react to a second round of questions. In some cases, group members may be asked to respond individually. This approach minimizes the influence of dominant group members and assures the participation of all group members. In other cases, the expert group may be gathered together for the benefit of group interactions.

The Delphi method as applied to land use objectives is not without its weaknesses. There is a problem with the selection of the "experts." It is the duty of the organizer to know the biases and commitments of members of that group. Another problem, shared with interviewing and polling, is the development of an appropriate questionnaire. It must be remembered that the Delphi method is, at best, an aggregate of opinions.[15] The method can be too sterile since participants do not have an opportunity to benefit from a discussion of why other members of the group feel as they do. At best, data resulting from this method for obtaining objectives should be used carefully and only as advisory.

Objectives from Public Situations

An innovative approach for assessing public reaction to planning alternatives employs an indirect method of input. The most widely applied version is called judgmental analysis, developed and applied at the University of Colorado.[16] Applied to land use plans, the procedure presents several (perhaps thirty or forty) hypothetical land use plans to people. The plans are described in terms of their effects on various aspects of the community such as open space amount and degree of isolation of heavy industry. People are asked to rate numerically the attractiveness of each plan.

Analysis of the data reveals the way in which individuals, groups, or subgroups combine and trade-off various effects to arrive at an overall evaluation of the plan. Among other things, the technique can reveal differences in evaluation of effects by different groups and can predict how people will react to any hypothetical land use plan that can be described in terms of the same aspects as the ones in the study.

The advantages of the method are: (1) it yields data that can be useful for prediction; (2) it tells why some plans are preferred over others; and (3) it is probably more valid than more direct approaches because it requires people to perform trade-offs among the various effects and because it uses methods demonstrated to predict actual behavior in market situations much better than other techniques.

It has been shown that one gets different results in assessing the relative importance of planning goals, depending on whether polling, Delphi or a technique similar to judgmental analysis is used.[17] The principal disadvantage of judgmental analysis is that it requires specialized statistical expertise to set up the hypothetical plans and to analyze and interpret the data. A computer is a must.

Public meetings and hearings are both used in the process of writing land use objectives. They are not the same although they do share common characteristics. The public meeting can be used by the land use researcher to educate the public about writing objectives or to gather citizen input for their formulation (fig. 4.1). In each instance the researcher should control the meeting from the chair. The subject of such meetings should be well advertised in advance and the interaction should be kept to that topic. Comprehensive notes or a recording should be kept of the proceedings for future reference. Care should be taken to inform the audience to address only the chair and not each other in order to lessen the chance of arguments.

In contrast to a public meeting, a public hearing is not a forum for general education of the public. It is a well-advertised official meeting held, for example, to allow the public to react to land use objectives developed by planning departments.

During public hearings appropriate maps should be prominently displayed. Participants should be instructed to address the chair. In turn, the chair should limit his or her reactions to questions, and keep explanations to a minimum. A point to remember is that the land use planner is usually a presentor and should not be placed in an adversary position by the chair. Following the meeting the planner may be asked to reexamine some objectives in light of information gained at the hearing. It is important to remember however that forty to fifty loud voices at a hearing do not necessarily represent what is right or what is best for the community.

In summary, the public meeting is more informal than the public hearing, provides for give and take, and is run by land use specialists or their representatives. The public hearing is formal,

Figure 4.1. Public meeting held in conjunction with development of the Tallahassee/Leon County Comprehensive Plan. (Courtesy of Tallahassee/Leon County Planning Development.)

usually mandatory, and allows members of the public to voice their opinions. It is usually run by a formal leader such as the chair of the planning, city or county commission.

Workshops are participatory meetings where a manageable number of concerned citizens are first informed about writing land use objectives and are then encouraged to write them. With the guidance of the land use specialist, they evaluate their work as to its applicability, compatibility and acceptance. Each of the above techniques may be used to obtain information necessary to the development and evaluation of land use objectives, but it is important that land specialists understand how to use each one correctly. Where possible, it would be desirable for the land use specialist to work in tandem with a group process/needs assessment specialist in the design and implementation of such techniques.

Impact of Objectives on the Land Use Decison-Making Process

The importance of the proper development objectives for a land use plan cannot be overestimated. In fact, they become the plan. The maps and text of a completed plan are an expression of the objectives. They are the means of getting the job done through communication and implementation, as are other elements of the decision-making process. The following discussion will relate the writing of land use objectives to each element of that process.

As a result of writing, or attempting to write, individual and institutional objectives in elements 1 and 2, need for further data and analysis becomes clear. For example, in order to write adequate residential objectives it is necessary to know the population characteristics of the community. Much of these data are available in the United States decennial census, but they may be incomplete or out of date. Information is also needed on soils, types of vegetation and drainage. Identification of environmentally fragile areas is critical for land use planning and no land use plan should be started without this information.

Objectives can tell the land use specialist what scientific studies are needed. They tell the geographer how many data sets are needed and in what form. When the research tasks for a land use study are identified in this manner, time and money are saved because only the data needed are collected. An understanding of objectives gives the planner better control over what the consulting firm, university research team or the planning department staff needs to do.

Objectives tell the land use geographer what the community wants to do with its land. The next step is to identify and evaluate all local, state and federal laws, policies and regulations which affect land use. Laws that help or hinder the achievement of the objectives must be identified. Laws that keep one from attaining a defensible or desired objective should be examined and the possibility of changing the law considered.

In any land use plan there will be those objectives which will be difficult or impossible to achieve without inventing, testing, or borrowing tools, or without studying trends that will affect their successful completion (element 5). Present data were considered in the third element, but future demographic or economic trends must also be considered. Tools such as impact taxes, transfer and purchase of development rights, land banking, phased development techniques or agricultural exemption taxes may be formalized in the community. All of these tools should be evaluated for use in any plan. Additional tools may need to be invented to help achieve land use objectives.

Growth Management Tools That Help Achieve Objectives[18]

Many tools exist to help planners achieve their objectives. Familiar examples are zoning, easements, subdivision regulations and moritoria on development. Given below are descriptions of several other planning tools which have evolved to help manage growth and reach land use objectives.

Land Banking

Under the land banking process land is purchased at the prevailing market price and put into a public or private non-profit "land-bank." This "banked" land can then be used in the future in accordance with a comprehensive plan. One problem with this technique is that it can require a substantial amount of money for the initial purchases. To offset this problem, however, is the fact that these funds can be recovered, in whole or in part, through leases or sales to private developers of lands allocated to homes, industries or commercial establishments. In many instances, however, land banking is used to acquire land for future school or park sites.

Phased Development Ordinance

This tool is coupled with planning provisions that establish the nature, location, and timing of future growth. Under this type of ordinance, land development can take place only in those areas of the community which, according to the plan, will be served by adequate community facilities such as sewerage, drainage, parks, roads and water. Such facilities are constructed on a time schedule over a period of years, and permits for housing are geared to that schedule. This technique was part of the Ramopo, New York program and was supported by court decisions.

Planned Unit Development (PUD)

This is a residential development in which prevailing density regulations apply to the project as a whole rather than to its individual lots. Densities are calculated on a project-wide basis, permitting, among other things, the clustering of houses and provision of common open space. Potential advantages include improved site designs free of standard lot pattern limitations, lower street and utility costs made possible by reduced frontages, more useful open spaces due to reduction or elimination of the unusable side and front yards required by traditional zoning, greater flexibility in the mixing of residential building types, and possibility of increasing overall densities without loss of essential amenities.

Pre-emptive Purchase

This is a technique whereby a government body can buy a few strategically located parcels instead of a whole area. Wetlands are particularly suited to this type of action. By owning a few sections, the government can prevent the filling of whole marshes.

Preferential Tax Assessment

Preferential tax assessment is a tool for retaining open space and agricultural lands. It permits assessment of land on the basis of its actual use rather than its development potential. Under this procedure, farm lands located on urban fringes and therefore subject to imminent development will, if retained in agricultural use, be taxed at lower rates applicable to farm land rather than higher rates applicable to other developable land. More than thirty states have adopted this method in various forms and with varying degrees of success. The more successful measures include a "roll-back" provision requiring that a seller of such "tax-reduced" lands pay the tax differential plus interest for previous years if the land is sold for subdivision or other development purposes.

Purchase of Development Rights

Another tool for preserving open space, agricultural land, or other areas of critical environmental concern is public purchase of the partial or less-than-free interest in private land that represents developmental potential. The strongest protection is provided when, once purchased by a government body, the rights become public capital assets and cannot be sold or transferred without voter approval in a referendum. The private owner retains title to the land and can use it for any purpose except development.

Purchase and Leaseback/Sellback

Although initially expensive, the purchase and leaseback/sellback tool is effective for guiding growth. Under the leaseback arrangement, strategic acquisitions by a public agency are leased back to their present owners or others, subject to appropriate restrictions on land use. Such arrangements do not put the lands back on the tax rolls. Under the sellback process, parcels are resold for private use, but with conditions written into the deed to achieve legitimate public ends and to preserve resource qualities. These lands are returned to the tax rolls. Saskatchewan, Canada's biggest grain-producing province, has used both methods extensively in a program to maintain agricultural use on more than a half-million acres which otherwise might have gone out of production.

Land Use Change Models and Implementation

Element Six, the use of land use change model, is also dependent on the plan objectives.[19] This step forces planners to evaluate the methods or models they might use to get from where they are (present land use) to where they want to go (future land use) without compromising, unwillingly, any objective. Land use change models are more applicable to specific projects than to the development of a land use plan. Logically, the master plan is a change model itself. But the change of land uses, from the filling in of wet areas to the building of huge highway projects or the flooding of reservoirs, must be evaluated on the basis of their effects on the whole set of land use objectives for the area.

The final step on the land use decision-making process is implementation. The plan, which is the embodiment of the objectives, is no more than a statement of the best thinking at the moment in terms of the constraints of the physical environment, time, fiscal resources, technology and the abilities of the people who have developed it.

The plan should be used for information, education and land use decision making that achieves or moves toward the stated land use objectives.[20] One last point is critical. The land use planning process is a dynamic one. Every day much of the data that goes into the formulation of the plan (e.g., the people, economic conditions, the level of technology, and even the physical environment) changes. Therefore, land use researchers must not sit back satisfied that the job is complete, with a feeling that they can bask in the sunshine of a job well done. Instead, researchers must constantly reevaluate their plans and thereby ensure that the use of the land is, in fact, helping to protect or enhance the well-being of the community's citizens.

Summary

In summary, land use analysts must not fail to realize the importance of setting rational, achievable, land use objectives. These objectives provide the participants in the land use exercise with a common starting place. They take into account individual and institutional land use needs and desires. This allows the geographer to identify conflicts, potential conflicts and suggest resolution tactics. Well-stated objectives help the planner make better decisions about methods of data gathering and analysis and about legal, technical and academic tools to use for plan implementation. Finally, land use objectives generated by the citizens help provide a measure for evaluating the programs of a community designed to provide high quality of life for all of its members.

Notes

1. F. Bosselman and D. Callies, *The Quiet Revolution in Land Use Control* (Washington, D.C.: Council on Environmental Quality, 1971).
2. B. Bruce-Briggs, "Land Use and the Environment," in *No Land Is An Island* (San Francisco, California: Institute for Contemporary Studies, 1975), p. 1.
3. Ibid. for dissenting view. This reference contains a chapter by Senator Morris K. Udall, which calls for federal land use legislation and a change in attitudes about "ownership."
4. Ibid.; Aldo Leopold, *A Sand County Almanac and Sketches Here and There* (New York: Oxford University Press, 1949).
5. Bosselman and Callies, *The Quiet Revolution in Land Use Control.*
6. *Tallahassee/Leon County Comprehensive Plan* (Tallahassee, Florida: Tallahassee/Leon County Planning Department, 1979).
7. Ibid.
8. Ibid.
9. See W. I. Goodman, ed., *Principles and Practice of Urban Planning* (Chicago: International City Managers' Association, 1968), pp. 327–348 for a complete discussion of policy planning.
10. At this juncture an additional word needs to be said about the land planners and their institutional role in the setting of objectives. Some say planners must be objective, their decisions "value free." Others question this by pointing out that planning is a political activity and therefore cannot be value free. Land use researchers must decide what their "ethical" positions are before they begin their work or their own contradictions will hinder them. Their credibility may well be injured if they are challenged on this point and cannot articulate their position. See R. E. Klosterman, "Foundation of Normative Planning," *Journal of the American Institute of Planners* 44 (1978): 38–46 and Goodman, ed., *Principles and Practice of Urban Planning* for interesting and informative discussions of this question.

11. See the American Association of Planning Officials, *Problems of Zoning and Land Use Regulations* (Washington, D.C.: Commission on Urban Problems, Research Report No. 2, 1968), pp. 2–23 for a more comprehensive discussion of goal conflicts in land use.
12. H. H. Smith, *The Citizen's Guide to Planning.* rev. ed. (Chicago: American Planning Association, 1979), p. 22.
13. Comprehensive Policy Plan Alternatives (Tallahassee-Leon County, Florida: Tallahassee/Leon County Planning Department, 1979), pp. 1–D to 7–D.
14. For an in-depth discussion of both the Delphi and Nominal Group Technique (NGT) processes, see A. L. Delbecq, A. H. van de Ven, and D. H. Gustafson, *Group Techniques for Program Planning* (Glenview, Ill.: Scott, Foresman, 1975).
15. J. Pill, "The Delphi Method: Substance, Context, A Critique and Annotated Bibliography," *Socio-Economic Planning Science* 5 (1971): 57–64.
16. T. R. Stewart and L. Gelkerd, "Analysis of Judgment Policy: A New Approach for Citizen Participation in Planning," *Journal of the American Institute of Planners* 43 (1976): 33–41.
17. E. J. Baker and J. Louviere, "Weighting Goals in Planning," paper presented at the 74th Annual . Meeting of the American Association of Geographers, New Orleans, 1978.
18. The descriptions of the growth management tools were taken from "How Will America Grow? A Citizen's Guide to Land Use Planning" (Washington, D.C.: Citizens' Advisory Committee on Environmental Quality, 1976), pp. 14–16.
19. For an in-depth discussion of planning for change see W. G. Bennis, K. D. Benne, R. Chin, and K. E. Corey, *The Planning of Change.* 3d ed. (New York: Holt, Rinehart and Winston, 1976).
20. See F. S. Chapin and E. J. Kaiser, *Urban Land Use Planning* (Urbana: University of Illinois Press, 1979). See especially chapter 16, "Evaluation, Adjustment, and Synthesis of Plans for Review, Choice, and Adoption."

Section B

Land Use Data—
Acquisition and Analysis

Chapter 5

Land Use Data and Their Acquisition

Frank T. Aldrich
Arizona State University

Land use data, in their simplest form, may be defined as including only information that directly relates to the past, present, or future ways parcels of land are utilized. Such a simplistic and strict interpretation is both inadequate and unrealistic. Land use problems and issues of our contemporary society are more complex than such a definition warrants. In practice, a bewildering array of data extending well beyond this simple definition is required. Such data include related information on natural conditions of the land as well as on social, economic, and legal topics. Frequently, data that turn out to be the most crucial to a particular land use question at first appear unrelated when examined in a traditional and casual manner.

A Land Use Information Systems Model

A land use information systems model (fig. 5.1) indicates the range and type of land uses and data required in order to analyze most land use problems. Any given site or parcel of land provides four subsets of information: the land itself, its capability, its present use, and the resulting land cover.

Land

The raw material of a particular site is the land. Land can be defined as the totality of the natural characteristics on both the surface and subsurface of a particular site. These characteristics include soil type, the site's slope, climate, geology, hydrology, and biology.

Land Capability

These raw materials are evaluated through cultural filters which include viewpoints, attitudes, values, interpretations, customs, morals, and ethics. Based on these culturally defined phenomena, certain perceptions of land capability are formed. These perceptions may be conscious and structured or unconscious and highly unstructured and biased.

There are certain land capability parameters that are not produced through perceptive evaluations. These constitute the inherent productivity of naturally occurring fauna and flora without being modified by the hand of man, and are based on genetic capabilities and the existing complement of natural characteristics of the land itself. Together these two types of capability make up the "land capability potential" that exists for a particular site.

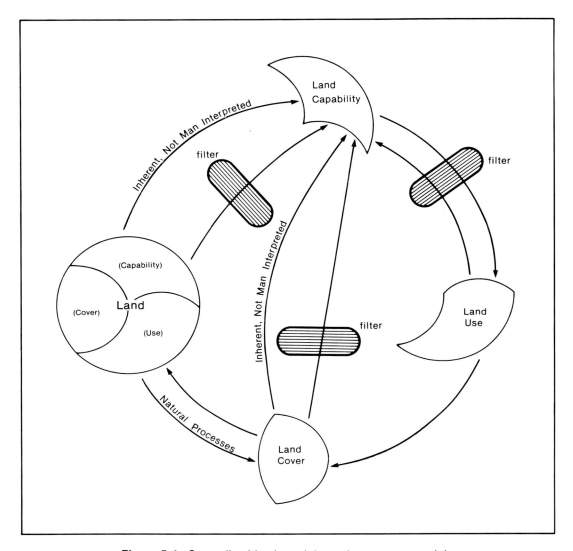

Figure 5.1. Generalized land use information systems model.

Data associated with land capability fall into six general categories:

1. *Adaptability of land,* as for example, for certain crops, agricultural activities, and related services.
2. *Productivity of the land,* including yields in dollars, volume, or amounts of crops or numbers and kinds of different activities.
3. *Hazards of the area,* including natural, economic, and social hazards of all types.
4. *Available technology,* which determines the range of possibilities for utilizing a given set of raw materials at a particular site.

5. *Feasibility of land use,* due to variations in technology, governmental policies, natural climatic cycles, and natural conditions of the site.
6. *Classified capability,* including the perceptive evaluation of soil, climatic, biotic or genetic, physiographic, and cultural characteristics.

Formal Capability Assessment

The assessment of land capability may be accomplished either by formal or informal processes. In the formal process, the potential or capability of a parcel of land is determined through standardized classification systems which rate the usefulness or value of a particular site for specific uses. A variety of land resource classification systems oriented toward agricultural land capability have been devised. Currently it is not popular to use these types of classifications in dealing with land use problems and issues. If used, however, more coherent planning and the highest and best use of land resource complexes are achieved.

The late Charles Kellogg addressed this particular problem and indicated that there should be a better distinction between the concepts of natural and cultural land, and that land should be classified and evaluated not only in terms of the cultural aspects of property, survey lines, and economic factors, but also in terms of its vegetation cover, relief, and other natural characteristics.[1]

In general, land classification in the United States has been carried out by public agencies and has been concentrated in three time periods. According to a National Resources Planning Board study in 1940,[2] the first period ran from the mid-1800s to about 1867 or 1869 when Powell, Hayden, King and Wheeler made their surveys of the mountainous West. These men were interested in the potential use of the land. They recorded their observations of natural resources as they discovered them.

A second period of classification occurred between 1933 and 1938, during the Great Depression. Approximately, nineteen different systems were devised during these five years.

The third major period was from about 1948 to 1951, but further attempts to classify land have continued from time to time during the past thirty years.

Land resource capability classifications seem to fall into five different types:

1. Classifications of land in terms of inherent characteristics,
2. Classifications in terms of present use,
3. Classifications in terms of use capabilities,
4. Classification in terms of recommended use, and
5. Classifications in terms of program implementation.

A Type 1 classification, in terms of inherent characteristics, uses natural aspects of the land as criteria for classification, including slope, soil type, climate, natural vegetation, water resources, and minerals. Over ninety percent of the projects identified by the Natural Resources Planning Board as being "land capability classification projects" fall within this category. They include topographic maps, soil survey maps, and forestry water resources inventories. This type of classification system only includes single features and not combinations of such items as soil, climate, and topography. Classifications systems combining these elements are found under Types 3 and 4.

Classification Type 2, land classification in terms of present use, is a grouping of the ways land is currently being utilized. This type of classification does not necessarily indicate the possible or potential uses of a parcel of land for agriculture or other uses.

Type 3, land classification in terms of use capabilities, is based upon appraisal value or usefulness of a particular site. This is done in two ways; first, the results of using the land in a certain way are evaluated, and secondly, the technology and management needed to produce a selected crop or item are determined. This type of land classification is more detailed than the others; however, it does not specify a best use. Historically, this type of land classification system has been used by farmers for centuries to determine the productivity of their fields. It comprises the largest number of land resource classification systems.

Land classification in terms of recommended use is the fourth type recognized by the National Resources Planning Board.[2] In this type the first three systems are integrated and the potential uses of the land are rated according to inherent characteristics, existing land use, and potentials for production for agriculture or forestry. Examples of this type are maps of recommended uses of forest land or maps of irrigation development sites. Type 4 criteria also include the cultural factors of land management and the types of resource converting or space adjusting techniques employed.

Type 5, land classification in terms of program implementations, is presented typically in map form and specifies how and when Type 4 recommendations are to be set up. The Land Resource Classification systems for the United States that emphasize agricultural resources can be grouped into data categories according to the criteria used in classification. There are systems with a soil emphasis, climatic emphasis, physiographic emphasis, genetic emphasis, and cultural emphasis. Most classifications, however, are based on more than one type of emphasis although they are commonly oriented to a particular set. For example, a system with a soil emphasis includes factors contributing to soil types, such as slope of land, texture, fertility, structure, depth, moisture content and erodability. Similarly, a classification system with a climatic emphasis may include data relating to temperature, precipitation, and wind, or variations of these.

A biotic emphasis may include facts of natural vegetation and native and domestic animal life. A physiographic emphasis may include factors of steepness of slope as well as land form configuration. The genetic emphasis may include criteria that are dependent on the genetic or physiological limits of domesticated plants as well as yields of the species. It may also include the adaptability of a specific crop type to a particular environmental situation.

As indicated, however, current practice is not to use a formalized land capability classification scheme. The land capability is more of an organizing construct in the land use conversion process. This process may be defined as the sequence of events that result in the change from one land use or lack of use to another.

Informal Assessment

Informal assessment of land capability is more frequent than formal assessment using established rating systems. If, for example, an individual wants to open a gas station, he or she first selects an appropriate site based on his or her perceptions of site factors that are important to the success of a gas station. This reflection might even occur at the subconscious level, and to the individual involved, a parcel might "feel" right or wrong for this new business. Nevertheless, an assessment of some kind is made at some level, the detail of which seems to vary widely.

Land Use

Marion Clawson defines land use as "man's activity directly related to the land."[3] It is a result of the information system modeled in figure 5.1. Land capability (whether determined formally in terms of a classification system or informally in terms of philosophical viewpoints and interpretations) is evaluated through filters representing the viewpoints, attitudes, interpretations, biases, morals, and ethics that ultimately result in a specific land use for a particular parcel. An abundant variety of data exists that relates to the conversion process and the end use.

All data pertaining to the description of a specific parcel of land such as area, dimension, location, and accessibility are desirable. In addition, legal and economic data such as value, taxes, land rent, transportation costs, capital costs, social costs, policies, goals, and attitudes are important before choosing particular land uses and changes from one land use type to another. Information is also needed on ownership, zoning, government policies, government objectives, perceptions of citizens, issues, demography, interest groups, energy constraints, attitudes, life styles, education, aesthetics, services, morals, and ethics. Finally, information concerning past land use in the dynamics of land use may be important. Rates of change, types of change, and reasons for land-use modification can contribute to a proper understanding of problems and issues confronting the land use analyst today.

Land Use Classification Systems

There are two approaches to the selection of a formal land use classification system. One technique is to ascertain the range of use that exists over the area of interest and then to subdivide this as required for the study at hand. A unique system such as this has an advantage in that it is tailor-made to a particular study. In the past, this has been the type of land use classification scheme employed on major projects. Examples include: the TVA classification, the rural land use survey of Puerto Rico, the land use survey of Great Britain, and other recurrent activities such as the inventory of major uses of land made every five years by the Economic Research Service of the Department of Agriculture, the National Inventory of Soil and Water Conservation, and the inventory of the Bureau of Public Roads and U.S. Urban Renewal Administration which resulted in the publication of the Standard Land Use Coding Manual in 1965. Each of these systems is different, with different purposes and scales, although they do have basic similarities.

Another classification which includes a crude land cover classification as well as land use, was developed by the U.S. Geological Survey in 1976. This was specially designed for small-scale LANDSAT (Earth Satellite) Imagery and was developed to be compatible with as many of the existing classifications as possible. The USGS classification has multiple level unit capability for both urban and non-urban land uses and land cover.

The alternative to making up a specific classification for a particular project is to select one of the standardized classifications referred to above. The Standard Land Use Coding Manual and the U.S. Geological System have the advantage of using terminology and definitions that are compatible with those employed by the U.S. Bureau of the Census. They have the advantage of being nested classifications having multiple levels suitable for computerized data storage and retrieval systems.

Land Cover

The fourth principal component of the land use information system model is land cover (fig. 5.1). This is the end product of land use. It may be positive or negative raw material for later changes, and may become part of the land itself (the land resource) even if it is produced by human activity. The land cover includes not just buildings and vegetation cover or modifications made directly by people, but also the results of natural processes that occur without human interaction. Thus, the flow lines in the systems model (figure 5.1) extending from land to land cover as well as the flow lines from land use to land cover are explained. The flowline directed from land cover to land represents those components of land cover which represent raw materials and which become a part of the land once again.

The USGS identifies land cover as the visible expression of human activities as well as the result of natural processes. Three general classes of data fall within land cover. One of these includes those structures built to serve human activities—their condition, persistence, modification, and description. A second data category is composed of biotic phenomena, and includes natural vegetation and animal life—their description, presence or absence of serial or climax conditions, changes, and rates of change. The biotic category might also include agricultural crops and animals, or any other cover modifications made as a result of land use decisions. The third type of data is more general and includes any type of development.

In the generalized land use information systems model, the three categories (land capability, land use, and land cover are diagrammed as shapes that fit together as a jigsaw puzzle (fig. 5.1). In a site-specific consideration all three actually fall within the entire circle of land or raw materials at a given site. The diagram also shows several feedback and intermediate loops. The feedback from land use to land capability is important when considering uses that heavily modify the landscape such as strip mining. Also, there is a dual feedback from land cover to land capability, both of which are important.

Figures 5.1 and 5.2 show the way that the land itself as well as its capability, use and cover are perceived and interpreted by the values, attitudes, and goals of the researcher. This is done by the insertion of filters. Four filters have been placed in figure 5.2 between the researcher and either the past, present, or future land use indicators, and between the researcher and the actual interpretation and resolution of particular land use problems and issues. These filters may be called the researcher's *reference frames*. They color the researcher's view of particular situations.

Differences in the filtering process may result in either a discrete or continuous view of phenomena. A discrete view is based on the assumption that all phenomena are clearly observable and have boundaries which may be mapped easily. Transitions, if they exist, are narrow and easily determined. A continuous view, on the other hand, is based on the assumption that within the study area, the units or categories identified, do not have boundaries which are observable. All aspects of a particular phenomenon being observed change with distance in a slow but not always regular manner. Most land use tends to be discrete, particularly when structures are involved or when the information is used at the parcel level. However, in a very small-scale view, such as that obtained from remotely-sensed satellite images, a continuous view becomes meaningful. Such differences, of course, are merely a result of the scale of the research. All continuous changes, if viewed at a small enough scale, will develop narrow boundaries and have the appearance of discreteness; whereas all discrete phenomena, if enlarged sufficiently will display boundaries that become wide and tend to be continuous.

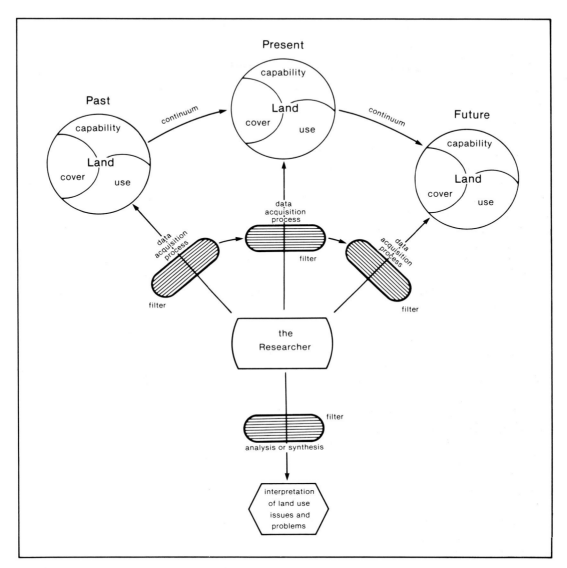

Figure 5.2. Conceptual structure of data acquisition for land use issues and problems as they change through time.

A Conceptual Structure of Land Use Data

At this point it becomes necessary to turn from the different types of data associated with land use problems and interpretation to a conceptual structure of the data acquisition process. figure 5.2 shows this structure and identifies its important components. In the center lies the researcher surrounded by his philosophical filters (perceptions) and the considerations that must be made in order to gather and interpret the data at hand. These filters, which change through time, have already been discussed. Across the upper portion of figure 5.2 are three circles, each of which represents the complex system model presented by land raw materials, land use, land capability, and land cover as they coexist over time at a specific site. Such relationships are present in the past (left circle), in the present (middle circle), and in the future (right circle). In a general way, facts in the past are secondary data having already been gathered and presently existing in the form of secondary source materials. Secondary data lie outside the experience of the present researcher in that another individual has studied the problem, possibly for a purpose different from the present interest. Secondary data are historical in nature. Even so, they comprise the most plentiful source for land use related information although they may become quickly outdated. This is particularly true in areas of rapid urban change where land use conversion processes are more active.[4]

Moving from the past through the present to the future, the three circles represent only discrete points in a temporal continuum showing spatial expressions of phenomena varying in area, linear extent, and intensity. At the present time (center circle) data must be gathered from personal experience or investigation in the field. The acquisition of these primary data is more costly than the acquisition of previously gathered, or secondary, data; however, it is frequently the only way to acquire the necessary and current information. On the other hand, primary data are gathered for specific projects. Such data may be more efficiently analyzed and synthesized. In some instance, it may be possible to gather historical data by active means. In this case, people involved in activities of interest in the past may be given questionnaires or they may be interviewed and their recollections documented. Such information, however, may not be entirely accurate since it may have become distorted in the interviewee's mind over time.

The top right circle of figure 5.2 in the land systems model represents the future. This may require simulated data which do not exist but which might be made available if specific scenarios were to be developed. Although in many instances a projected land use plan constitutes the end product of land use research, it might also constitute an intermediate product particularly if it forms the basis of more elaborate land use scenarios involving projected problems or activities.

A more complete understanding of the relationship of primary and secondary types of data may be gained from figure 5.3. Here, the process of collecting primary data is represented by the inner shaded circle and the acquisition of secondary data, the outer circle. Such a diagram may be superimposed over each of the circles in figure 5.2 to represent the temporal continuum of the data acquisition process.

Acquisition of Secondary Land Use Data

Secondary land use data may originate from either published or unpublished sources. Published sources range widely and include federal, state, and local government sources. The several hundred bureaus and divisions within the departments of the federal government publish many documents of value to land use analysis. Generally speaking, state and local government documents tend to be more regionally or locally oriented, although some federal publications are also regional in scope.

Many professional organizations publish periodicals or monographs that focus on specific topics and areas. These are likely to be of greatest help in conceptualizing a problem and in developing a methodology although occasionally a researcher may find detailed historical studies that can be used as base-line data for present land use problem.

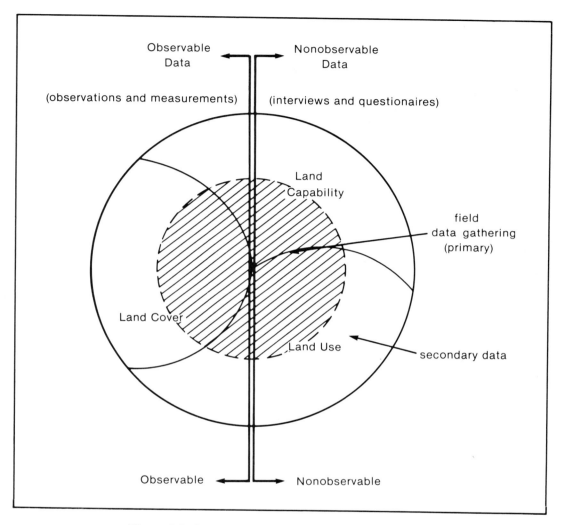

Figure 5.3. Data acquisition and methodological model.

In addition, there are many other sources of data published by business firms, banks, industry, non-profit organizations, foundations, special groups or commissions, and service clubs or fraternal organizations. Frequently such published sources are more difficult to track down than those published by public agencies and professional groups.

All of these agencies or organizations may also yield vast quantities of unpublished materials. Documents on file within government agencies at all levels, within private corporations, and within other organizations form the basis for in-house decisions and research. These data, after once used, are filed and available in manuscript form at local offices where the work was accomplished. A land use analyst is well advised to interrogate various local officials to ascertain if any data of this type are, in fact, available. It should be borne in mind, however, that these data are considerably different from published information. Published information is available to the public by design. Unpublished sources are available at the discretion of the individual who is responsible for the data. Therefore, great care must be taken in handling and storing these data. Such action insures a friendly reception when similar information is again needed.

When acquiring secondary land use data, problems of data storage and organization are often ignored. Data storage and organization depend to a large degree on the background of the researcher and the methodology to be employed in analysis. If computer techniques are to be used, it is often helpful to encode information in a form that is computer readable and to develop a data bank with short time data storage and retrieval capability. To do so may not be cost effective for small amounts of data, but large masses of information, particularly on regional and national scales, are cost effective. Data banking can lead to the efficient use of computer graphics routines discussed in chapter 6 as well as statistical and other sophisticated analysis and synthesis techniques.

Acquisition of Primary Land Use Data

Experiential or field derived information is of two types: observable data and non-observable data. Figure 5.3 shows a double line bisecting the land systems model. The area to the left of the line represents observable data that are directly measurable by the researcher. The area to the right of the line represents data that are not directly observable, but can be gleaned by questioning persons living or working within the area of interest.

Mapping

Information directly observable or measurable in the field may be located and mapped in three ways: single-feature mapping, multiple-feature mapping, or dimensional mapping. Single feature mapping includes locating a phenomenon on existing maps, correcting distributions, and creating base maps.

Multiple-feature mapping records raw materials, land use and land cover through the use of fractional codes. The numerator of the fraction records cultural and land use information; the denominator, natural site information (fig. 5.4). Individual features may be documented through the use of field sketches or photographs made at ground level or from an elevated location either on an airborne platform, or on hilltops or structures.

Dimensional mapping is mainly an urban form of recording data. Land use activities and other pertinent information are recorded by floors of a building. The result is a series of maps, one for each floor.

Ultimately any documentation or mapping may be compared with data acquired earlier. These previous sources of data are considered secondary sources of information and may be used to generate sequential comparisons over long or short time periods. A wide variety of observations may be taken which may ultimately be mapped. Some measurements are primarily used for locating phenomena or producing spatial controls.

Instrumentation

Instruments may be used for obtaining information about a wide variety of environmental and cultural phenomena. It should be noted that measurements obtained with the help of instru-

Numerator = Land use coding of the site $\dfrac{123}{12\text{-}5142}$
Denominator = Physical aspects of the site

The area shown has the following characteristics:

1—Cropped land
2—Tobacco
3—Poor quality
12—Very shallow, moderately heavy and moderately permeable, well drained silty clay loams derived from tuffaceous rocks; Mucara and Picacho series.
5—Steep to very steep (40%-60% slope), serious management problems, may be used for pasture or left in trees (natural)
1—Well drained
4—Relatively severe sheet erosion present 75%+ of topsoil removed
2—Moderately stony, scattered small stones only slightly impeding cultivation.

Figure 5.4. Fractional code mapping system. This system was employed by the Tennessee Valley Authority and was also used in the Puerto Rico Rural Land Classification Program. This photo at a scale of 1:10,000 of Puerto Rico demonstrates the use of the fractional code system.[5] This form of notation culminates in the land use and land cover classification for use with Remote Sensor Data developed by the U.S. Geological Survey,[6] U.S. Department of Interior.

ments are not necessarily more valid than estimation or personal observations. A well-trained field person can deliver extremely accurate and useful data at a considerable saving in time and money through the use of subjective measurements. Depending on the nature of the research, non-instrumented measurements even may be necessary.

In addition to instruments used in providing locational data, such as plane tables, alidades, transits, and theodolites, other instruments are used to determine surface configurations. These include stereoscopes, binoculars, compasses, altimeters, levels, range finders, and all forms of measuring devices from pedometers through measuring wheels, tapes and chains. Measurements of meterological, hydrological, geological, edaphic and botanical phenomena as well as land use may also be made by instruments.

Aerial Photography and Remote Sensing

Aerial photography and remote sensing constitute valuable field tools for acquisition of observable land use and related data. Air photos, or any source of remotely-sensed data, may be employed as base maps and have the advantage of being current at the time of image acquisition. Depending on the scale, the images contain an infinite number of control points allowing extremely accurate location of various field phenomena. Air photos form an invaluable tool for land use determination. By examination of image components such as shape, size, texture, tone, color, shadow pattern, extent and three-dimension configuration a great deal of information may be gathered about the imaged area.

When these data obtained from imagery are checked carefully against ground observations and their significance to existing land raw materials, land use, and land cover types are established, it is possible that the remaining analysis of the data may be done in the office rather than in the field. In order for such analyses to be valid, however, adequate knowledge of areas within the image is required to confirm the information obtained from imagery.

Vertical and oblique aerial photographs may be used in preparing maps; however, these items are not planimetrically correct unless properly rectified. Even in vertical photography, a variety of distortions exists in the image. These include tilts and swings from unstable camera platforms, lens distortion, radial distortion from parallax, variations in scale due to varying relief, and differences in processing. One of the most disturbing problems is the radial distortion which has the effect of showing objects in the correct line from the center or nadir of the photo outwards but in an incorrect position along this line. Accurate location may be difficult unless the phenomenon can be located on existing planimetrically correct maps of the same area. Distortions of this type can be resolved through three-dimensional or stereoscopic plotting. Rarely do field researchers have available planimetrically correct or controlled photography to use as base maps.

In addition to the conventional aerial photography, modern remote sensing technology allows areas to be viewed by a variety of wave lengths created by (1) film or various film filter combinations, or (2) systems employing scanners recording specific frequencies of emission from the surface. With additional information such as this, it is possible to develop precise signatures of particular activities. If the remote sensing platform is an orbital system, the view presented may be somewhat generalized since exact parcels will be below the level of resolution of the imagery. This has the advantage of integrating information over a large area and forcing the researcher to take a regional view of the data. The lack of the ability to determine exact land use and cover for specific parcels, however, dictates that great care be taken in ground observation, and in the development of classification schemes for land use and related information.

Coordination and Data Gathering Precision

Whether or not a standardized system is employed, the research team must be coordinated so that all individuals understand the basic definitions and are able to distinguish land use and other categories in the same way. In fact, this type of consistency is necessary for all primary data gathering procedures. Sufficient training must be given so that all individuals document the same phenomena in the same way. The levels of precision and methods of data measurement should be comparable, whether land capability, land use, land cover, or the basic natural attributes of the land itself are being evaluated. It is inconsistent to make extremely precise land resource and raw material measurements but be loose or unconcerned about land capability rating or land use classification. All are part of the complex system and should be considered equally. If research methods call for estimations and subjective measurements of site capability and activities, the accuracy of estimation or measurement should be the same throughout the project.

In considering land use changes the use of existing standard classifications and categories may not adequately explain the current or future situation. The rates, types and direction of change must be well documented. It may be helpful to simulate scenarios in order to understand what is actually occurring in a particular parcel or study area. Change rates may be so rapid that the casual observer might overlook critical intermediate steps. It may be necessary to view an entire sequence of events much in the same way that vegetation changes leading to particular vegetation associations or climaxes are observed. In other words, a sequence of land use changes or events may give rise to a particular type of land use or cover. Modelling the occurring sequences will aid in understanding overall processes. It is possible that in certain areas all parcels may be undergoing change, and that no final or stable land use and land cover will occur. The researcher should be aware that similar situations may exist with respect to the evaluation of natural resources and raw materials. These may also undergo changes, the rates of which are dictated by other environmental parameters. Thus classifications of climaxes, so to speak, in land use/land cover, perhaps even land capability, might be useful additions to standard observational classification procedures.

Acquisition of Non-observable Data

Within the land systems model shown in figure 5.3 are data that can not be documented directly by observation or measurement. These data must be obtained through interviews or questionnaires and may include attributes of current or past phenomena. Acquisition of these data is a highly technical process with specialized requirements. Since the researcher is dealing with human beings, a great deal of care must be exercised to prevent respondents from giving incorrect or biased information. A large amount of time should be alloted therefore to the design of the questionnaire and to the way in which questions are posed to the respondents. Two types of questions are used in questionnaires: closed response questions which require the respondent to choose among a series of responses provided by the interviewer, and open response questions which allow the respondent to answer questions in his or her own terms.

The closed response is more highly controlled. Open responses, however, often make it possible for the researcher to obtain data which are not anticipated. On the other hand, closed responses are more easily handled statistically than open responses since ranking, intensity, and other options are known and may be coded precisely.

The closed response form of questionnaires, although more efficient from the standpoint of administration in terms of time, requires less skill on the part of the interviewer. They do have some disadvantages, however. For instance, they may produce answers when none really exist. This is particularly true when the respondents have no information concerning the question being asked. Also, closed forms may induce responses which were not anticipated in the questionnaire design.

To avoid misunderstandings, questionnaires must be carefully worded and sequenced. Responses may be either "yes" or "no", or "agree" or "disagree." Questionnaires may also include check lists, intensity scales, frequency scales, distance scales, or personal preference rankings. The sequence of questions commonly proceeds from the general to the specific.

Other rules should also be followed. For example, it is important to gain the interest and confidence of the respondent so that more detailed and adequate information can be gathered. Also, questionnaires should be designed to provide for adequate coding. Since data are generally statistically analyzed, the degree of quantification sometimes depends entirely upon the forms of coding developed for the questionnaire.

Not all non-observable data can be obtained by structured and rigid questionnaires. Informal discussions with a farmer concerning former land use practices, such as "what it was like in the past" may be very informative although not easily quantified. In actuality, a combination of both types of data gathering is frequently necessary in order to analyze a land use problem properly.

A final practical consideration in designing questionnaires and in other methods for acquiring non-observable data relates to the administration by telephone, by mail, by personal interviews, or by group interviews. The selection of any one of these four types will depend on economic and time constraints. Lowest cost questionnaire administration is by mail and telephone. Telephone interviews may be expensive, especially, if computerized prompting is used, or if long distance calls must be made in order to acquire data. The presence of the interviewer, either in a group or a personal interview, provides stimulus and positive support for the respondent. The presence of the interviewer may be more costly, however, than other interview techniques. In all cases when obtaining non-observable data and when sampling techniques are employed, a representative sample is required. Some form of random respondent stratification should be made prior to the interview or questionnaire distribution in order to select representative economic, social, employment, and other groups and to prevent excluding or biasing a particular group.

When dealing with controversial land use and related issues, a great deal of tact and care in administration of any questionnaire is required. Such issues are often volatile and concern the economic well being of the respondent. In such cases it is necessary to be extremely careful in order to obtain responses which represent the full range of opinions within a particular area. Care should be taken not to ask leading questions.

Scale

The scale of the research situation determines the manner in which data are acquired. Regional views, in which information display scales are small, result in high levels of generalization and the obscuration of individual land parcels. The minimum areal units used for such mapping tend to be quite large and only a generalized complex of information may be viewed. Frequently the scale and minimum areal unit size are related to economic and time constraints associated with a particular project. Thus regional study areas are commonly handled at small scales. The decision of the minimum area to be used in land use research is an important one and should be made prior to the acquisition of primary or secondary data.

Also associated with scale is the problem of sampling. As a study area gets increasingly large and the complexity within it increases, the cost of making a 100 percent assessment of relevant phenomena becomes quite high and it is necessary to deal with a small percentage or a sample of the area being studied.

Sampling

Two forms of sampling may be associated with land use data acquisition. The first is a sample designed to obtain information from particular levels or strata in society (interest groups, social levels, economic levels, etc.). This form of sampling is necessary if attitudes, issues or any questions involving classes of phenomena are important. No effort is made to make the samples spatially representative—only topically representative. In addition to this type, which is the standard form of statistical sampling, geographers and land use analysts must be capable of obtaining spatially unbiased samples.

All phenomena vary in their distribution in space and the traditional forms of sampling, based on randomness, tend not to be areally representative. For this reason, combinations of a stratified and random procedures are required; either a systematic sample with a random start or a random sample taken from particular matrix squares are most desirable. They result in even distributions which are unaligned.

Four types of spatial samples may be differentiated on the basis of intensity and type of information initially available within an area. These types are exploratory spatial sampling, reconnaissance spatial sampling, extensive spatial sampling, and intensive spatial sampling. Exploratory spatial sampling is a preliminary data gathering technique used when little information exists and generally no classifications or data categorizations systems are available. The chief purpose for exploratory spatial sampling is to document what exists within a particular area. Frequently no base maps or other ground control exist.

Reconnaissance spatial sampling is the second type. This is used for areas that have more information existing for them—ground control and base maps and even air photography are available. In such instances classification schemes exist, as does sufficient information to formulate research problems. Reconnaissance spatial sampling is a time efficient scheme. It utilizes large aerial units and covers large territories. Mapping units of one square mile or larger are frequently employed. Thus, portions of states or entire small states may be the focus of such reconnaissance spatial sampling.

The two remaining spatial sampling schemes are those which involve extensive and intensive spatial samples. The former, extensive spatial sampling, is used for smaller regions and specific locations where broad base land use problems and issues may be handled. Mapping scales may be as large as 1:24,000. Extensive spatial sampling is ideal for large urban environments where the land use character of the urban region is of greatest importance. Intensive spatial sampling looks at individual sites, local issues, and questions. The minimum mapping unit is typically a parcel of land. In many instances at this particular scale of consideration complete coverage rather than a sample may be obtained.

One additional approach to spatial sampling does exist. This is the technique of "parcelle" mapping. In fact, this technique is not a form of sampling at all, but simply a generalization of information. Parcelle mapping consists of identifying the minimum mapping unit size for the study area and covering the entire area with mapping units placed edge to edge. For example, an entire study area might be gridded with sections or townships and data gathered for each entire township or section. No data are sampled, but data are abstracted or generalized at the township or section level. Often the dominant activity is identified and the entire section coded with that activity. Aerial reconnaissance is often employed to gather data for parcelle mapping.

Of concern to the research project is the form of the sampling design. Depending on the sampling design, point samples, linear samples (transects), or area samples (quadrats) may be employed. The type of sample unit used is to some extent dictated by the form of data being considered. Areal sampling is popular, but not the only choice for land use analysis.

Plotless sampling methods may be used when there is concern for possible biasing of the data which may result from using specific shapes of sampling areas. Such plotless techniques include the point center quarter method, the closest individual method, and others. In all cases, the choice of sampling should be related to cost and time considerations and the type of information being gathered.

Summary

Land use data encompass a wide range of information including the natural attributes of a parcel of land, its inherent and perceived capability, the use to which it is ultimately placed, and the structures and modification of the land which result from human occupance. The researcher who is involved in land use studies must be aware of the great diversity of data necessary to deal successfully with current problems and issues.

Some land use data exist in the form of secondary and even tertiary source materials. Other information, however, does not exist in a suitable form, is outdated, or has never been gathered. Such data must be obtained by the researcher through first hand field acquisition. These are primary data. There are many methodologies and philosophies which guide the acquisition of primary data. The choice of technique depends on the problem at hand, the nature of the phenomena to be measured, and the constraints, such as money or time, imposed on the researcher. There is no single technique or group of techniques that can be used in all situations. Modifications must be made to fit the problem at hand. In most instances a simple approach is more practical and reliable than a complex approach, except when the nature of the data are such that a complex methodology is required.

Finally, in all data gathering it is necessary to make pilot or test runs to insure that the expected information can be obtained and to train the field research crews properly. The acquisition of land use and related information is a dynamic and challenging part of the spatial analysis of land use process. It should be approached with creativity, innovation, and enthusiasm.

Notes

1. C. E. Kellogg and J. K. Ableiter, *A Method of Rural Land Classification* (Washington, D.C.: U.S. Government Printing Office, 1935).
2. U.S. National Resources Planning Board, *Land Classification in the United States* (Washington, D.C.: U.S. Government Printing Office, 1941).
3. M. Clawson and C. L. Steward, *Land Use Information* (Baltimore, Md.: Johns Hopkins University Press, 1965).
4. F. T. Aldrich, J. F. Lounsbury, and L. E. Zonn, "Applied Geographic Research and Data Sources," in *Directions in Applied Geography* (Englewood Cliffs, New Jersey: Prentice Hall [in press]).
5. Department of Geography, Northwestern University, *The Rural Land Classification Program of Puerto Rico.* Northwestern University Studies in Geography No. 1. (Evanston, Illinois: Northwestern University, 1965).
6. J. R. Anderson, E. E. Hardy, J. T. Roach, and R. E. Witmer, *A Land Use and Land Cover Classification for Use with Remote Sensor Data,* Geological Survey Professional Paper No. 964 (Washington, D.C.: U.S. Government Printing Office, 1976).

Selected References

Aldrich, F. T. "A Survey and Evaluation of Land Resource Classification Systems in the United States." M.S. Thesis, Oregon State University, Corvallis, Oregon, 1976.

Aldrich, F. T.; Lounsbury, J. F.; and Zonn, L. E. "Applied Geographic Research and Data Sources," in *Directions in Applied Geography.* Englewood Cliffs, New Jersey: Prentice Hall (in press).

Anderson, J. R.; Hardy, E. E.; Roach, J. T.; Witmer, R. E. *A Land Use and Land Cover Classification for Use with Remote Sensor Data.* Survey Professional Paper No. 964. Washington, D.C.: U.S. Government Printing Office, 1976.

Department of Geography, Northwestern University. *The Rural Land Classification Program of Puerto Rico.* Northwestern University, Studies in Geography No. 1. Evanston, Illinois: Northwestern University, 1952.

Lounsbury, J. F., and Aldrich, F. T. *Introduction to Geographic Field Methods and Techniques.* Columbus, Ohio: Charles E. Merri Co., 1979.

U.S. Urban Renewal Administration. *Land Classification in the United States.* Washington, D.C.: U.S. Government Printing Office, 1941.

Chapter 6

Cartographic and Graphic Presentations

Robert I. Wittick
Michigan State University

Introduction

It is difficult to imagine a land use study that does not contain one or more maps depicting land use patterns. In fact, graphics, particularly maps, are so basic to land use investigations that all land use analysts must have some familiarity with their use. The old adage, "a picture is worth a thousand words," says it all. A well-designed map immediately conveys a message about the spatial arrangement and association of the phenomena being discussed. The same information presented in a table or verbally in the body of a report is very difficult to comprehend, and the spatial patterns are completely hidden from the reader.

Graphics are not only indispensible as modes of presentation, they are also extremely useful as tools of analysis. For example, once a particular set of data is mapped, the resulting spatial pattern may suggest hypotheses pertaining to the factors related to producing the pattern. Another use for maps is in the comparison of two or more sets of phenomena. By comparing or overlaying two maps of the same area portraying different data, it is easy to identify those areas containing varying combinations of the two data sets. For example, assume you are interested in identifying those land parcels zoned R-2 residential with well-drained soils. By overlaying a zoning map with a soils map, it becomes readily apparent if such parcels exist and where they are located. On the other hand, it is also possible to create a map to give a simple visual impression of where features are located. Maps, then, can perform many useful functions for the land use analyst.

It is the purpose of this chapter to present the basics of map design and to discuss automated methods for the production of maps and other graphics. The chapter begins with a discussion of the components of a map. It then discusses how these components should be put together to create a readable and aesthetically pleasing map. The chapter concludes with a section on computer graphics with particular emphasis on the requirements for computer mapping. All illustrations included in this chapter were generated using a computer. This was done to demonstrate both the variety of map types possible with this method of production and some of the advantages and disadvantages of computer-generated maps. After reading the first half of this chapter, you should be able to decide which illustrations are acceptable cartographic products and which are not.

Necessary Components of a Map

A map is a means of communication. Its purpose is to convey a message. If the map is to be effective in that function, it must clearly indicate exactly what the message is. Unfortunately, it is all too frequent that we find maps whose message has been obscured or totally lost by a lack of careful design, an inappropriate production method, or a choice of symbols unsuitable for the intended audience or for the information being presented.

The reader should be able to look at a map and immediately understand the theme of the message. The message, itself, should then be easily discernible by a careful study of the map. The emphasis of this section is on the necessary components of a good map. However, many of the concepts presented here are equally applicable to other graphic forms such as scatter diagrams, pie charts, and time-trend charts.

Title

A very important component of any map is its title, which conveys the theme of the map. Without a clear, easily understood title, a map is next to useless. When choosing a title for a map, wording should be short and concise yet it should clearly indicate the map's theme. An ambiguous title can create more confusion for the reader than any other single aspect of a map. For example, a map depicting recreation land may be titled "Recreation Lands." However, if the map is actually depicting the percentage of total land area devoted to recreation, that title is very misleading. A better title would be "Percentage of Land Area in Recreation."

A common error made when titling maps is to give primary emphasis to the location rather than the theme of the map. Unless the map is a general location map, in which case a title such as "Thompson Reservoir" or "Regal County" is acceptable, the title should first indicate the principal purpose of the map. For example, a map of Goshin Township depicting agricultural land use categories should be titled "Agricultural Land Use" or perhaps "Agricultural Land Use in Goshin Township." The latter title would be appropriate if the geographic area being mapped is not obvious from the map or accompanying text. If the map appears in a report devoted to a township, the name is not needed for the title. However, if the report deals with an entire county or other regional area, then the name of the township may be necessary to read the map.

The title should be placed within the outside border of the map where it will be immediately noticeable, without overpowering the map itself. All too often the map title is included among the legend, scale, and other cosmetics, and it becomes hidden. The reader should be able to glance at a map and pick out the title, and from that have a clear indication of what the map is depicting.

As with all components of a map, the title should be suitable for the intended audience. For instance, if the map is to be presented to an audience of lay persons, the use of technical jargon or obscure abbreviations should be avoided. A title of few words is generally preferable to a longer one, particularly if the intended audience is not a sophisticated one. A title should (1) catch the reader's eye, (2) inform the reader of the theme of the map, and (3) stimulate the reader's interest in studying the content of the map.

Class Intervals

Assuming that the map is a thematic map, that is one depicting a single set of data (e.g., land use categories, soil types), it is important that the data be divided into appropriate class intervals and that a suitable legend defining these intervals be included. The selection of class intervals is dependent upon whether the data are nominal, ordinal, interval, or ratio scaled. Nominal data are divided into qualitative classes such as male and female, or Caucasian, Black, and Native American. Ordinal data are also qualitative, but with an implied order to the classes

such as small, medium, and large farms; or lower, middle, and upper income groups. Interval data are quantitative in that they use numerical values for measurement. For example, population of census tracts or the number of acres in various crops are interval scaled data. Ratio data are very similar to interval data; however, the measurement scheme has a specifically defined zero point. Distance from the center of town would be an example of a ratio scale as would percentage of land area in recreation.

When depicting nominal data types (such as land use categories), the class intervals are dictated by the data categories; that is, there is usually a different class interval for each category. There are situations, however, when the categories can be aggregated, and the map can still contain the desired level of information. For example, the data source may use a two-digit land use classification, but for the purposes of the map one may only need to display major land use categories by the first-digit classification. Regardless of whether the data are aggregated or not, the problem of class interval selection is minimal for nominal or ordinal data.

Interval and ratio data, however, are more difficult to divide into classes. Since the data range along a continuous scale, but the map must depict discrete classes, it is necessary to choose a set of class intervals that accurately and objectively portray the data. Although space is not available here to discuss fully all possible methods of class interval formation[1], a few basic concepts will be mentioned to aid the reader in making class interval determination. First, one should try to avoid visual skewing, that is placing a majority of the observational units at either end of the class interval scale. For example, in a map depicting percentage of substandard housing, it is possible to divide the data into intervals so that a high percentage of the observations fall into the highest class interval. A casual reader of that map could then easily infer that the area being depicted consisted largely of substandard housing, where in fact that may not be the case at all.

Frequently, when arranging the data values into ascending order, natural breaks occur which suggest logical places for class interval boundaries. There may also be logical places to divide the data based on definitional characteristics. For example, in mapping population data by county it may be appropriate to have a class break at 50,000 since that is the minimum size for a SMSA county.

When using computer mapping programs in land use analysis, it is usually advisable to avoid using a default method available for class interval definitions. These default methods frequently divide the data range into equal-sized intervals or occasionally divide the number of observations into equal-sized intervals. The first method is particularly inappropriate if the data are skewed, and both methods tend to make irregular class interval boundaries, such as "11.78 to 23.14 people per square mile," when "10 to 25 people per square mile" would be a more easily understood set of boundaries. Therefore, when using computer mapping programs, the user should generally define class intervals rather than rely on the computer program to do it.

Regardless of how the intervals are determined, it is mandatory that they be clearly defined in a legend placed somewhere within the outer border of the map. A map in which the symbols used are not defined is of no value to the reader. When preparing such a symbol legend it is important to include the unit of measurement, if appropriate and not defined in the title, and to place the legend so that it is clearly visible and of a size which can be easily read, yet does not overpower the map.

Documentation

Another important component of any graphic is documentation. This includes both the date of the information displayed and the source of this information. Frequently the date is included in a title or subtitle; if it is not, it should be included somewhere on the map. This is not necessary if the date is apparent from the context of the map. For example, if the map is included in a report discussing newly acquired data, and the date of the data is given in the beginning of the report, the date can be omitted from the map or maps in the report.

In placing the date on a map, it is preferable not to include it with the other documentation because it is not apt to be seen easily. Since the date is such an important component, it should be placed in a location by itself, usually somewhere along the lower border, but should not be of such a size as to distract the reader from the map itself.

If not obvious from the accompanying text, the source of the map should also be included either within the map border or immediately adjacent to it. This documentation should indicate the names of those who collected the data if they are primary data, or if they are secondary data the source documentation should cite the publication containing the data. This citation should contain sufficient detail for the map reader to locate the publication cited.

Scale

Every map should have some indication of its scale. This can be a numerical scale such as "1:62,500" or "1 inch equals 10 miles," or it can be a graphical scale where a linear symbol represents a certain length in the area being mapped. An indication of scale is particularly important if the reader is unfamiliar with the study area. When a reader examines a map and attempts to understand the spatial arrangement and association of the phenomenon presented, it is very disconcerting not to know the actual size of the area and the relative distances involved. In a publication containing many maps of the same area at the same scale, it is only necessary to include the scale once, usually on the first map. Whether graphic or numeric, the scale is usually placed near or at the lower border of the map.

Other Components

If there is a chance that the area being mapped will be unfamiliar to the reader, an indication of north (usually with a simple arrow) should be included on the map. This is especially useful for very large-scale maps that depict small areas having few familiar landmarks for reader orientation; north arrows are also useful if the map has an unusual orientation due to rotating or sectioning.

Since most maps associated with land use studies are relatively large scale, the concern for the most appropriate map projection is less than it would be with the construction of small-scale maps. However, it is not uncommon to indicate the particular map projection on which the map is based. This is particularly useful if an unconventional projection is used.

A map will have a neater appearance if it and the components discussed above are all framed within a rectangular border, called a neat line. The border acts to tie together the map's various parts. The reader's eye is less apt to wander over the page or onto an adjoining page if a frame is provided to focus his attention. Just as a picture frame can enhance the appearance of a painting, so too can the frame or border of a map.

Figure 6.1 illustrates many of the components just discussed. Note that the map includes a clearly visible title, a legend explaining the symbols used on the map, a documentation citation complete with date, a small north arrow, and a simple border. One of the weak points of this map is that the class interval boundaries are not even integer boundaries. The map would be improved if even boundaries for the class intervals were used.

Considerations Related to Reader or Audience

When designing a map it is imperative that the purpose of the display and the intended audience be considered carefully. Who is going to read the map? How much are they expected to know about the study area or about the data displayed? Is the map to be presented before an audience? If so, how large is the audience and what size is the meeting room? If the map is to appear in a publication, what printing method is to be used? Is it possible to include color? All

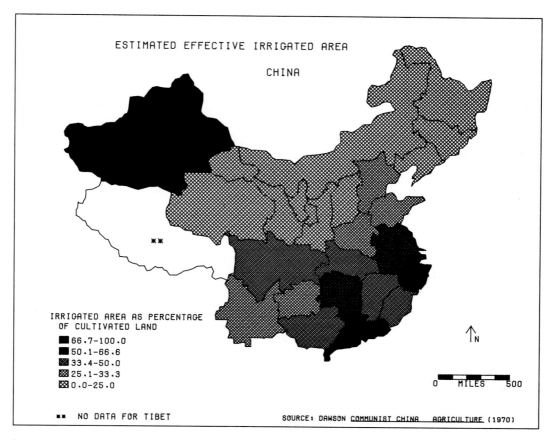

Figure 6.1. A computer-generated choropleth map drawn on a pen-and-ink plotter. The CALFORM program was used to produce the map.

of these questions have a bearing on the design of a map and should be considered before it is constructed.

If a map is to be used only as a working document, such as for hypothesis generation or map comparison, a highly polished final product is not needed. It may be that a neatly sketched pencil diagram will suffice or perhaps a simple inked line drawing or a computer line printer graphic. However, even with this type of construction, accuracy is important as is a consideration of the audience or readers of the map.

When preparing maps related to land use studies, the cartographer must remember that the maps may have two very different types of audience. One is the layperson audience, which may have only minimal familiarity with the study area and no knowledge whatsoever of the information being presented. The second type is the professional audience, which is probably familiar with both the study area and the data being portrayed. The degree of sophistication of the audience is an important consideration in the choice of maps to be used. If it is a layperson audience, a very generalized map depicting major trends is more desirable than one containing excessive detail. For example, if a map is to be constructed showing variations in local relief, a block diagram (such as in fig. 6.2) or a shaded contour map (fig. 6.3) is preferable to a normal isoline map (fig. 6.4 or 6.5), which is more detailed but also more difficult to read. If the audience is relatively

PERCENT OF LAND AREA IN FORESTS: MICHIGAN COUNTIES

Figure 6.2. A block diagram of a choropleth surface drawn using a pen-and-ink plotter with the SYMVU computer program.

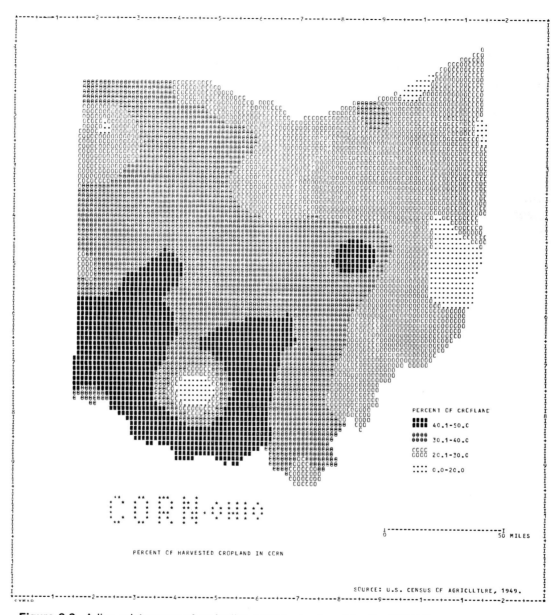

Figure 6.3. A line printer map of an isoline surface produced by the SYMAP computer program.

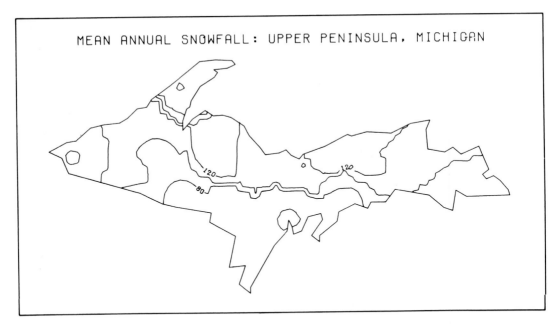

Figure 6.4. A pen-and-ink plotter map of an isoline surface created using the SURFACE II program. Compare this figure with Figure 6.5 which depicts the same data using a different program.

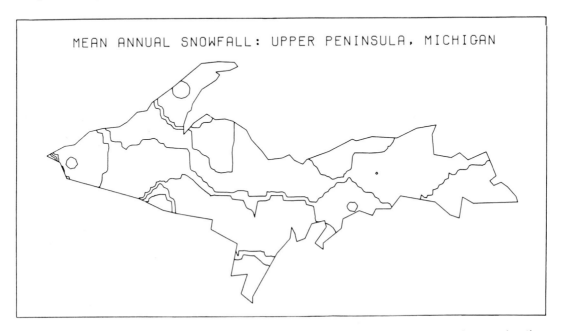

Figure 6.5. A pen-and-ink plotter isoline map without annotations. This map was drawn using the GEOSYS program. Note the difficulty of interpreting the map when the isolines are not labeled.

sophisticated with respect to its knowledge of the study area and the information being portrayed, a wider variety of map possibilities exists. In the relief example, for instance, a traditional isoline map may be appropriate in that it will provide the greatest amount of detail about the relief of the study area.

A similar type of problem exists in the choice of observation units for a map. For a transportation study the greatest detail may be achieved by mapping the data at the traffic zone level. However, such zones have little meaning for a layperson. Aggregations of the data to more familiar units such as townships or other minor civil divisions may better convey the intended message, even though detail is lost in aggregating the data.

Another case where generality versus specificity in a map is preferred is when the map is to be presented before a large audience (a town meeting or public hearing, for example). In such an instance a map with much detail would be impossible to decipher, particularly for someone at the rear of the room. If such detail is important for the intended audience, then several maps should be prepared which either partition the data into several subsets or divide the study area into several smaller regions. In such a case, the proper use of color can greatly improve the readability of the map. In fact, the appropriate use of color always improves the appearance and readability of a map. If only one copy of the map is needed, such as for presentation before an audience, the added time and expense involved in using color may be justified. However, if the map is to be reproduced for distribution or inclusion in a document, then the question of color is a bit more difficult to answer. Preparation and printing may well exceed both available time and dollar budgets. Frequently, in maps designed for publications, shaded patterns are substituted for color because of the substantially higher costs involved in producing and printing color plates.

In summary, before the choice of style is made for a map representation, the intended audience should be considered so that the choice is appropriate for that particular group. Consideration should be given to both the form of presentation and the sophistication of the intended audience.

Types of Displays Commonly Used in Land Use Studies

There are many different types of maps and other graphics used in land use studies. This section describes several of the more frequently used graphics and the types of data that should be used with them. Detailed methods of construction are not included because of limited space. This information can be found in any standard cartography textbook.[2]

Area Data Portrayals

One of the most commonly used types of maps for land use studies is the choropleth map. For this type of map specific area units are delimited and shaded or colored according to a single-data set. The mapped data can be nominal, ordinal, interval, or ratio. A map depicting land use classifications is a typical example of a choropleth map. Since these data are nominal, the categories represented by the shading simply differentiate various land use categories.

The geographic areas delimited on a choropleth map may be well-recognized political boundaries such as state, county, or school district boundaries, or they may be very irregular boundaries conforming to the natural distribution of the data being portrayed. In either case the units of observation are polygons; each polygon is shaded according to its corresponding data value, with the values divided into class intervals, if interval or ratio data are involved. If the map is to be constructed as a black and white map, the number of class intervals should be restricted to only a few (two to seven preferably). With more than eight class intervals it is increasingly difficult for the reader to distinguish between the various shadings used. If the map is produced in color, the maximum number of intervals can be increased slightly. Large numbers of class intervals, however, will always be confusing to the reader. It is not uncommon for land use data to contain more than eight to ten nominal categories, as in the United States Geological Survey land use classification system. Rather than attempt to depict all of the land use categories on one map, it is preferable under most circumstances to depict only a portion of the data (such as various residential categories or only the first-digit categories) on any given map. A specific occasion when this practice might not be followed is when a planning office needs a large comprehensive land use map containing complete detail for the planning area. Such a map may contain all categories. It should be realized, however, that this type of map is not appropriate for general presentation. Figures 6.1 and 6.6 are examples of choropleth maps. In both cases the observational units are easily recognized political units: provinces of China and states of the United States. Note that in both cases ratio data are used and have been divided into a small number of class intervals.

Point Data Portrayals

When portraying data distributed as points, three common methods are used: (1) the dot map, (2) the point symbolic map, and (3) the surface representation map. Before any of these methods can be discussed, it is necessary to differentiate between discrete and continuously distributed point data. If the data are interval or ratio data and can be considered as occurring, to some extent, everywhere within the mapped area, those data are continuously distributed. If, on the other hand, the data occur only at selected point locations within the area, they are discrete. Occasionally it is necessary to consider the scale of the map when determining if a point data set is discrete or continuous. For example, a map of population by minor civil divisions for a rural county is a discrete distribution because the data only occur at selected locations. However, population by minor civil divisions for the entire United States may be treated as continuous. At that scale the data would appear to occur everywhere, assuming approximately the same size for both maps.

It is also possible to transform some discrete data sets into continuous distributions. If, for example, we change population to population density by dividing the population figures by the area of the observational unit, we can consider the resulting data continuous since population density occurs everywhere (even though it may be a zero density). Continuously distributed data are most appropriately portrayed by surface representations while discretely distributed data are portrayed using dot patterns or point symbolic maps.

Surface representations

Continuously distributed data are most frequently depicted by surface representations. The two methods most commonly used for representing surfaces are isoline maps and block diagrams. Isoline maps depict surfaces using lines that pass through points having equal data values. Block diagrams represent surfaces as perspective views that give a three-dimensional appearance to the

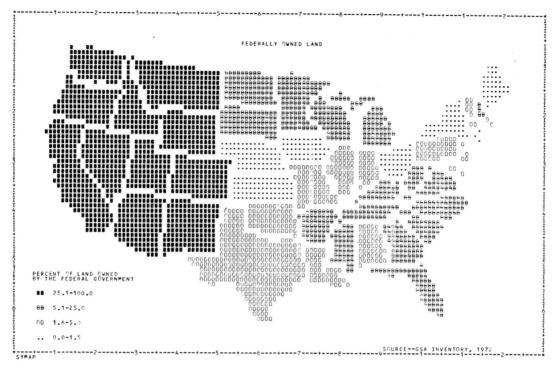

Figure 6.6. A line printer choropleth map produced on the computer using the SYMAP program.

surface. Block diagrams are more appropriately used when a generalized portrayal of the surface is desired, an eye-catching map is called for, or laypersons are the anticipated audience.

Isoline maps are better suited for situations calling for detailed graphic description or graphics designed for further analysis. When constructing isoline maps, it is important to consider the data interval carefully. The data interval, frequently called the contour interval, is the distance in data units between consecutive isolines. A data interval that is too coarse will hide the detail of the surface, and an interval too fine will make the map more difficult to read. The interval should remain constant throughout the entire map. While occasionally there is a need for varying the data interval, such as when constructing a relief map of an area containing both flat areas and steep bluffs, the practice should be avoided whenever possible because it also increases the difficulty of interpreting the map. When preparing isoline maps every fourth to sixth isoline should be annotated with its data value (see fig. 6.5). Occasionally, isoline maps, particularly computer-generated maps such as that shown in figure 6.4 are drawn without annotation. Such maps, unfortunately, are even more difficult to read.

Block diagrams are used to give a generalized view of the surface. While block diagrams are somewhat awkward to construct manually, they are very easy to create using a computer and thus in recent years have become a very popular form of surface representation. Before constructing a block diagram, a decision must be made as to the view from which the surface is to be portrayed.

The angle of inclination for the block (everything from horizontal, which approximates a cross section to near vertical, which minimizes the local variation of the surface is possible) should also be determined. Since the surface is shown as a continuous variable, there are no data intervals. However, the height of the diagram (the vertical distance representing the largest data value) must be chosen. That choice can greatly influence the appearance and, more importantly, the readability of the diagram. Figure 6.2 is an example of a block diagram depicting a discontinuous (choropleth type) surface.

Point Symbolic Maps

For data that are not continuously distributed, the options of point symbolic mapping and dot mapping are available. Point symbolic mapping involves the use of symbols to represent data values or types at discrete locations. If the data are nominal or ordinal, the symbols of different styles (for example, triangles, squares, and circles) are usually chosen to represent the various data categories. If the data are interval or ratio, the symbols are usually of the same shape (commonly circles) with size proportionate to the data values. For such proportional circle maps it is common to base the radii of the circles on a linear relation of the square root of the data. This insures that the areas of the circles are in proportion to the gradation in data values.

Dot Maps

An alternative method of depicting discrete point distributions is the dot map. The dot map with equal-sized dots is used to represent interval or ratio data. The number of dots in any area varies with the magnitude of the data value in that area. A dot map is an excellent technique to use for depicting the general patterns of the data. If, on the other hand, the specific relative sizes of the observational units are of primary importance, then the point symbolic map is more appropriate.

Dot maps are relatively easy to construct by hand, but have proven to be much more difficult to program for computers. When designing a dot map the density of dots and the size of dots are important considerations. If the dots are too small or the spacing is too sparse, the spatial patterns do not emerge and the map's message has no impact. If the dots are too large or the spacing is too dense, the dots will tend to coalesce and the pattern will disappear in a blur of black.

Corridor or Flow Maps

In addition to area and point data, flow data are also occasionally mapped for land use studies. These are data whose locational observations depict linear or curvilinear features. Such things as stream discharge rates, highway traffic volumes, and sewer capacity are all examples of flow data. These data can be either nominal or ordinal in which case different styled lines (solid or dashed, for example) are used for portrayal of data types, or they can be interval or ratio in which case line widths or corridor shadings are frequently used techniques. Figure 6.7 is an example of a flow map depicting interval-scaled data.

Other Graphics

There are other types of graphic displays used in land use studies besides the map. Some of the most common are the histogram, scatter diagram, and pie chart. Scatter diagrams are particularly useful to represent the relationship between two intervally-scaled variables. If one of the

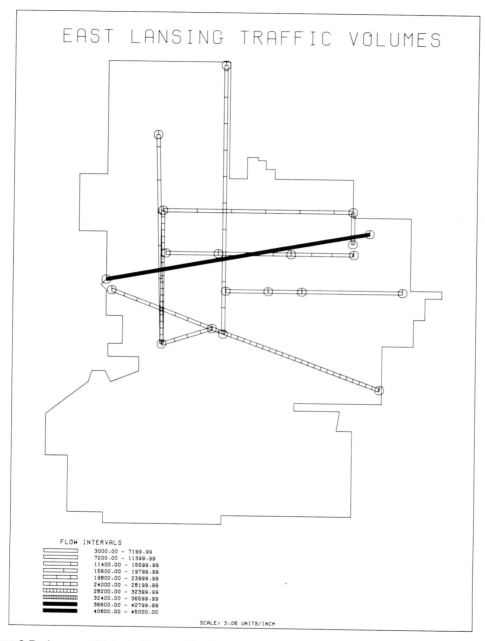

Figure 6.7. A pen-and-ink plotter map depicting flow volumes produced using the FLOW program.

variables is nominal or ordinal, then a histogram is the appropriate graphic to use. Frequently it is useful to be able to depict three variables on a histogram if two of the variables are nominal or ordinal. For these applications the construction of a three-dimensional histogram such as in figure 6.8 is possible. Histograms, representing either two or three variables, are especially appropriate for data that vary over time. In such cases the nominal axis represents the various time periods and the other axis (or axes) represent the data values. Pie charts are appropriate for representing percentage data that total 100 percent or data that represent proportions of a total.

Using the Computer to Produce Graphics

The majority of the map and graphic types discussed in this chapter can easily be produced using a computer. In fact all of the illustrations in this chapter were computer generated. Computers can provide tremendous savings of time in the production of certain graphic applications. If not used appropriately, however, computer processing of graphics can be an incredible waste of time. It is the purpose of this section to discuss the basic requirements for computer mapping and to explain when it is appropriate to use the computer in graphic production.

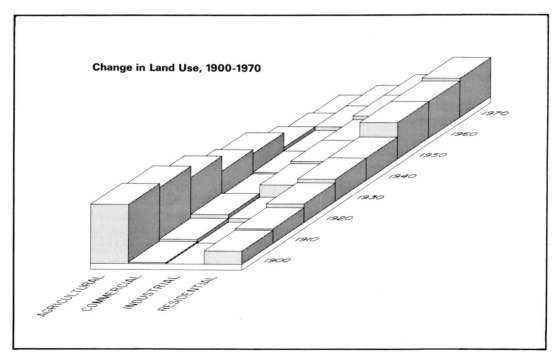

Figure 6.8. A three-dimensional histogram produced on a pen-and-ink plotter using the GEOSYS program. The data presented are hypothetical.

Requisites for Computer Mapping

Before a map can be produced using a computer system four items must be available or created: (1) a computer, (2) a computer mapping program, (3) a geocoded base file (GBF), and (4) the data to be mapped in a machine-readable form. The first requirement, a computer, is the most obvious. It is frequently not realized that the computer need not be at the work site; that is, even though an organization does not own a computer, it may still be possible to produce computer graphics. There are many computer service bureaus available that can be used, or a computer at a related organization may be available.

Once a computer has been found, the next requirement is a computer program designed to produce maps of the type desired. One alternative is to write a program or hire a programmer to do so. This is not usually needed, however, because computer programs already exist for producing all of the commonly used maps and graphics such as isoline maps, block diagrams, choropleth maps, cartograms, dot maps, point symbolic maps, flow maps, scatter diagrams, bar graphs, pie charts, and histograms. An excellent source of information on availability of computer mapping programs is "Computer Software for Spatial Data Handling" (1976), an annotated listing of the computer programs available for manipulating, analyzing, and mapping spatial data. Two sources for purchasing computer mapping programs are the Geography Program Exchange at Michigan State University[3] and the Laboratory for Computer Graphics and Spatial Analysis at Harvard University.[4] Both these organizations have a wide variety of computer mapping programs available for sale.

The third requirement for computer mapping is a geocoded base file, sometimes referred to as a cartographic base file. The geocoded base file (or GBF) is the numerical description in machine-readable form (punched cards, magnetic tape, or computer disk) of the study area and the observational units within it. For example, a GBF for a choropleth map may contain all the X-Y coordinate pairs necessary to define the outline of each observational unit (polygon) within the study area. Preparing a GBF is a tedious and time-consuming task. Automated digitizing equipment is available to expedite the geocoding process although the editing of GBFs prepared with digitizers is frequently more time consuming than the intial geocoding process.

A GBF need only be produced once for any given study area. For instance, a land use map is defined by geocoding the outlines of all land parcels in the study area. Once the parcels have been defined the GBF need not be altered, even when land use changes occur, unless the parcels are subdivided. That is, while the data are apt to change frequently, the size and shape of the observational units are not apt to change as frequently. An alternative geocoding method that eliminates the possible parcel subdivision problem is to superimpose a regular lattice (mesh of the lattice dependent upon resolution required) over the study area and to assign to each lattice cell the data value or type that occupies the greatest portion of the cell. This type of GBF need never to be altered although the information content is less than with the parcel definition method.

For certain types of applications it is possible to purchase existing GBFs for the study area in question. For example, the United States Bureau of the Census[5] can supply geocoded base files for all metropolitan areas (DIME—Dual Independent Map Encoding—files) and county outlines for the entire United States. Unfortunately, land use studies frequently require very individualized and specialized GBFs because of the large scale of the maps and the unique character of the observational units.

Finally, before a computer map, or any map for that matter, can be produced there must be data to be mapped. For a computer map data should be in machine-readable format. Each observational unit, whether it is a point, line, or area feature, has a data value associated with it. Normally, for each geocoded base file there are several data sets of interest. These may reflect the same data item over several time periods, several data elements for a single-time period, or a combination of the two. If only one data set is to be mapped, it is doubtful that automating the mapping process can be justified, unless the software, GBF, and data are already prepared and readily available.

Output Modes

When using the computer to produce graphics, several different output devices are available. The choice may be limited by the computer program or programs available or by the hardware installed at any given site. Each mode of output has its own advantages and disadvantages; thus, there is no one best mode for graphics. The choice largely rests on the availability of modes, the particular graphic application, and the time and monetary constraints on the project.

There are six commonly used modes of output for computer graphics: (1) standard line printers, (2) dot matrix line printers, (3) pen-and-ink plotters, (4) electrostatic plotters, (5) microfilm plotters, and (6) cathode ray tubes. Standard line printers are the most frequently used modes of output for graphic applications because they are always available at computer sites. Historically they were the first output mode used for graphics. For these reasons, a proportionately large number of computer graphic programs are designed for line printer output. The advantage of using a standard line printer for graphics is that it is relatively inexpensive and the output is produced rapidly. The major disadvantage is that the resolution is very poor given the constraints of the character matrix on the printer (approximately 88 rows by 130 columns for one computer page) and the variability of the density due to aging of the print ribbon. Figures 6.3 and 6.6 are examples of maps produced on a standard line printer. The dot matrix printer solves the first of the disadvantages of standard line printers because it uses a matrix of dots to form characters. These dots can also be addressed individually to create graphics with significantly better resolution than with a standard line printer (up to 100 dots per inch).

Pen-and-ink plotters provide the best quality and highest resolution of any computer output device. Many such devices have multiple pen capabilities for varying line widths and ink colors on one graphic. In addition, large flatbed plotters can be used for scribing. Unfortunately plotters are expensive to purchase, relatively expensive to operate and maintain, and much slower than printers. However, any organization that is serious about computer graphics should consider a pen-and-ink plotter for creating manuscript quality maps and graphs. All of the figures in this chapter except 6.3 and 6.6 were produced on a pen-and-ink plotter.

Electrostatic plotters can produce output that looks similar to that produced by a pen-and-ink plotter. The quality, however, is not as high nor is the resolution as good. On the other hand they are faster than pen-and-ink plotters and much less expensive. Microfilm plotters produce the graphic image on microfilm, which can then be photocopied or stored in very little space. They are faster than either the pen-and-ink plotters or electrostatic plotters, but they do not offer the versatility of paper types, pen widths, and ink colors available with pen-and-ink plotters.

The final mode of output, the cathode ray tube (CRT), is quite different from the others mentioned in that a hard copy of the graphic is not produced. Rather than generate a piece of paper with the graphic on it, a CRT draws the image on a television-like screen. The primary advantage of the CRT is that it allows the graphics user to edit the image by adding, deleting, or modifying portions of the graphic simply by using a special electrical device to point to those features on the screen that are to be edited.

It is not uncommon for CRTs to have peripheral hard copy units attached so that once the image has been edited, a copy can be made. In an ideal computer installation, designed with graphics in mind, several of these different devices should be available. Graphics users can choose the one that best suits their needs for each particular application. Examples are the use of a printer or electrostatic plotter for rough graphics, a CRT for editing the graphics, a pen-and-ink plotter for manuscript copies of the graphics, and a microfilm plotter for generating copies to be filed for future reference.

Data and Geocoding Requirements

The type of data and the form of the geocoded base file are dependent upon the particular computer program used and the type of map to be produced. When using the computer to produce choropleth maps, the GBF typically contains X-Y coordinate pairs that define the vertices outlining each observational unit or polygon. The exact manner in which the vertices are defined varies from program to program, but the basic concept is the same. The data for these maps are usually interval-scaled values, one per observational unit. It is possible, of course, to use nominal or ordinal data by assigning a numeric code to each data type and then defining the class intervals such that each data type is in a separate interval.

When constructing surface representations—isoline maps and block diagrams—on the computer, there is a problem in that most of the programs available for this type of representation require regularly spaced or gridded data. This type of data consists of a matrix of data values where the position within the matrix represents the spatial location of the data value; that is, the (7,8) element in the matrix (seventh row and eighth column) is northeast of the (8,7) element. Since the point data collected for surface representations are usually samples that are randomly located rather than uniform in their distribution, it is necessary to transform these random spatial locations to regularly spaced locations. That transformation process is called spatial interpolation. Although the substance of spatial interpolation is well beyond the scope of this book, it should be noted that this additional step is usually required before a computer can be used for depicting surfaces. A few of the surface representation programs include an interpolation capability, but if they do not the data must be interpolated before the mapping program can be used.

Computer programs used for mapping flow data vary greatly in their data requirements. Some of them use a graph theoretic connection matrix or a cost matrix for defining node interconnections in the network. Others require coordinate definitions of all nodes and a table of direct linkages to those nodes. Those programs usually provide the capability of including flow volumes or other quantitative measures related to the linkages.

Point symbolic maps drawn with the computer require a geocoded base file defining the locations of the observational units and the outlines of the study area, and a data set containing values for each observation. Such a GBF is the easiest to create and probably the most useful because it is also the form used for many dot map programs. It is also the form of data required for those surface representation programs that include interpolation capabilities.

Summary of Commonly Used Computer Mapping Programs

It is the purpose of this section to summarize the capabilities of some of the more commonly used and readily available computer mapping programs appropriate for use with land use data. This set of programs is not exhaustive. However, those mentioned here are all well-established, supported, and maintained by organizations that specialize in spatial analysis software, and they are all moderately priced (between $175 and $800 to non-profit organizations).

SYMAP

One of the first computer mapping programs to be developed was the SYMAP program. SYMAP is maintained and distributed by the Laboratory for Computer Graphics and Spatial Analysis at Harvard University. SYMAP uses the standard line printer to produce various types of maps. The two types most appropriate for land use studies are choropleth maps (fig. 6.6) and isoline maps (fig. 6.3). The program has many options for controlling class intervals, symbolization, size of maps, and other stylistic variables. SYMAP is an excellent product to use for working maps or other non-published applications. Because it uses the line printer, the resulting maps are not as suitable for publication as are pen-and-ink plotter produced maps. However, for the installation on a limited budget that has only line printer output facilities, SYMAP is an excellent program to use for depicting either area or point data. It is also possible to use SYMAP for depicting quantitative flow maps, but resolution and thus readability are very low since the line printer is used for creating linear features.

SYMVU

Using the pen-and-ink plotter to create block diagrams, SYMVU is a companion program to SYMAP. It is also maintained and distributed by the Laboratory for Computer Graphics and Spatial Analysis at Harvard University. SYMVU uses a data file created by SYMAP to draw a block diagram of the map created by SYMAP. As a result, SYMVU can depict the same type of data that SYMAP can. Either continuous or discontinuous surfaces may be portrayed with a great degree of flexibility in the style of the diagram. An example of area data originally drawn by SYMAP as a choropleth map is depicted by SYMVU as a block diagram in figure 6.2.

CALFORM

This program uses the pen-and-ink plotter to produce choropleth maps. An example of a CALFORM map is shown in figure 6.1. Because of the nature of land use data and the high quality of maps possible through use of CALFORM, it is the preferred method of land use mapping by computer. The program is extremely flexible in terms of adding cartographic cosmetics, classifying the data, annotating the map, and varying the scale. Perhaps its only serious drawback is that the input structure is very rigid, and the control card interface is awkward and outmoded. It is more typical of a program written twenty-five years ago. CALFORM is also maintained and distributed by Harvard's Laboratory for Computer Graphics and Spatial Analysis.

GEOSYS

This is a general purpose mapping and spatial analysis system designed for use with point data. This system includes graphic capabilities for line printers, plotters, and cathode ray tubes. It can produce point symbolic maps, isoline maps, and block diagrams. It can also produce three-dimensional histograms (fig. 6.8), which, as noted earlier, are useful for portraying data that vary along two nominal or ordinal scales and one interval scale. GEOSYS also includes several spatial interpolation routines as well as a variety of other analysis capabilities. It and the following program, FLOW, are the only ones mentioned designed for either batch or interactive usage; others are strictly batch oriented. GEOSYS is available from the Geography Program Exchange at Michigan State University.

FLOW

The FLOW system is similar to GEOSYS except that it is designed to map and analyze spatial flow data. The mapping capabilities include the ability to portray the flow volumes by corridor shading (such as in fig. 6.7) or linkage annotation. The maps can also depict nominal or ordinal variations in the nodes and interval node variations. A minimum amount of cosmetics can be added to the maps. FLOW is also available from the Geography Program at Michigan State University.

SURFACE II

The SURFACE II program is used for surface representations. It can construct isoline maps on either the standard line printer or pen-and-ink plotter (fig. 6.5), and it can draw block diagrams on the plotter. The program can draw isoline map pairs as stereo pairs, and it can draw anaglyphs using two colors of ink. To view an anaglyph the reader needs glasses with lens of the two colors. SURFACE II also contains a wide variety of spatial interpolation routines. The program is maintained and distributed by the Kansas Geological Survey.[6]

Summary

This chapter has discussed the basic elements of a good map, the importance of considering the intended audience of the map, and some essential considerations related to computer-generated maps. The aim has been to aid the land use analyst in the preparation of graphic displays by providing a check list for the design of a readable map and by suggesting some alternatives available for producing a map.

All illustrations in the chapter were computer generated to illustrate some of the advantages and disadvantages of this method of map production. Note that not all of the maps illustrated contain all the components mentioned at the beginning of the chapter. This is a weakness of the particular computer program involved and not of the production method or mode of output.

Notes

1. A more extensive treatment of this topic may be found in A. Robinson, R. Sale, and J. Morrison, *Elements of Cartography,* 4th ed. (New York: John Wiley, 1978), pp. 171–176.
2. See, for example, Robinson, Sale, and Morrison; or F. S. Monkhouse and H. R. Wilkinson, *Maps and Diagrams: Their Compilation and Construction,* 2d ed., (London: Methuen, 1967).

3. For more information write to the Geography Program Exchange, 510 Computer Center, Michigan State University, East Lansing, MI 48824.
4. For more information write to the Laboratory for Computer Graphics and Spatial Analysis, Room 520, Gund Hall, Harvard University, Cambridge, MA 02138.
5. For more information write to the Bureau of the Census, Washington, D.C. 20233.
6. For more information write to the Kansas Geological Survey, 1930 Avenue Campus West, Lawrence, KS 66044.

Selected References

Braud, D.; Wittick, R.; and Stenger, D. *FLOW: A Computer System for the Analysis and Graphic Description of Spatial Networks.* Technical Report 74–51. East Lansing: Computer Institute for Social Science Research, Michigan State University, 1974.

Calkins, H. W., and Tomlinson, R. F. *Geographic Information Systems, Methods and Equipment for Land Use Planning.* Ottawa, Ontario: International Geographical Union, Commission on Geographical Data Sensing and Processing, 1977.

Davis, J. C., and McCullagh, M. J. eds. *Display and Analysis of Spatial Data.* New York: John Wiley, 1975.

Dougenik, J. A., and Sheehan, D. E. *SYMAP User's Reference Manual,* 5th ed. Cambridge, Mass.: Laboratory for Computer Graphics and Spatial Analysis, Harvard University, 1975.

International Geographical Union, Commission on Geographical Data Sensing and Processing. *Computer Software for Spatial Data Handling.* New York: Geographic Information Systems Laboratory, State University of New York at Buffalo, 1976.

Latham, C. A., and White, D. *CALFORM Manual.* Cambridge, Mass.: Laboratory for Computer Graphics and Spatial Analysis, Harvard University, 1978.

Monkhouse, F. J., and Wilkinson, H. R. *Maps and Diagrams: Their Compilation and Construction,* 2d ed. London: Methuen, 1967.

Muehrcke, P. *Thematic Cartography.* Commission on College Geography Resource Paper No. 19. Washington, D.C.: Association of American Geographers, 1972.

Peucker, T. K. *Computer Cartography.* Commission on College Geography Resource Paper No. 17. Washington, D.C.: Association of American Geographers, 1972.

Robinson, A.; Sale, R.; and Morrison, J. *Elements of Cartography.* 4th ed. New York: John Wiley, 1978.

Sampson, R. J. *SURFACE II Graphics System.* Lawrence, Kansas: Kansas Geological Survey, 1975.

Wittick, R. I. *GEOSYS: A Computer System for the Description and Analysis of Spatial Data.* Technical Report 74–53. East Lansing: Computer Institute for Social Science Research, Michigan State University, 1975.

Chapter 7

Quantitative Techniques in Land Use Analysis

Leo E. Zonn
Arizona State University

Introduction

The number and sophistication of quantitative techniques available for the analysis of spatial problems have increased in recent decades along with a growing acceptance of quantitative analysis. Graduate and undergraduate students in geography are being exposed to techniques that were virtually untried within the discipline only a few years ago. Although the increased scope and acceptance of quantitative techniques have allowed for more rigorous land use analysis, changes have not occurred without problems. Quantitative analysis, for example, has often been characterized by incorrect assumptions, inappropriate techniques, inadequate means of operationalization, and invalid inferences. The acceptance and development of quantitative analysis has been accompanied by an inadequate consideration of fundamental issues.

Problems associated with the use of quantitative techniques are found in varying degrees among the many research directions of geography and related fields. The kinds of techniques employed should vary according to the intent of the respective researcher and the character of the phenomena under study. For example, the intent of the historical geographer usually is not to make generalizing or nomothetic statements that are characteristic of the scientific method. As a result, quantitative analysis, which is closely allied with this method, may not provide an acceptable research framework. Also, the character of the data used by the historical geographer may not be precise enough to justify use of quantitative analysis or even require it. Some researchers may criticize historical geography, to continue use of this example, for its lack of quantitative precision and thus imply that its development is below that of other more "sophisticated" research emphases. This implication is unfair. The use of quantitative analysis does not mean that a research area is more or less developed than another. The point here is that quantitative techniques should be used when appropriate, given the nature of the problem under consideration. To use them when they are not needed or to fail to use them when they are needed are grave errors in research that may produce distorted or incomplete results. Thus, the task of the subspecialists within geography, and as a result the task of members of the discipline as a whole, is to develop a set of quantitative techniques that is appropriate to the nature of the particular research.

This chapter is concerned with the use of quantitative techniques in land use analysis. The intent is to outline selected fundamental quantitative techniques that are appropriate to this newly emergent research direction and to show the manner in which they can and should be applied. Particular emphasis is given to descriptive statistical techniques.

Two general characteristics of land use analysis should be recognized before a discussion of the value of quantitative techniques to land use analysts can be undertaken. First, the study of land use is a newly emerging research area, although geographers and planners, in particular, have been concerned with different aspects of land use for several decades. The energies of these researchers, however, have commonly been confined within other major systematic areas of research, such as urban geography. As a result there is no organized and coherent body of literature that might insure continuity of analysis or justify land use analysis as a distinct research entity. This lack of development has been a major roadblock to the evolution of a set of appropriate quantitative techniques, although the techniques used by systematic research areas such as urban geography often have sufficed for the individual tasks at hand.

The second major characteristic of land use analysis that should be recognized is the general inclination of its practitioners toward applied research. The recent emergence of applied geography has been accompanied by controversy within the discipline. In fact, the legitimacy of applied research as a distinct entity has been questioned by many whose research areas are less-applied. There is no single reason, however, why applied research and, in this particular case, land use analysis should not be recognized as a distinct and legitimate research area. Such a research direction serves to expand the scope and value of the discipline and yet does not threaten the discipline's philosophic tenets. The reader must recognize, therefore, that a unique set of quantitative techniques should be a concomitant of this distinctly applied flavor of land use analysis.

The term technique is used throughout this chapter. It should be distinguished from methodology, which refers to a framework of analysis. Methodology is an outline of the sequence of steps by which research is undertaken. Methodology usually includes the means of data acquisition and organization, the particular tools of analysis, and the process by which the results of the analysis are used to answer the initial problem of study. Technique is a more specific term that refers to the particular tools used in the analysis. In the case of this chapter, technique refers to the specific quantitative tool(s) employed within the overall methodology. Occasionally, the quantitative technique used in a particular problem may be the organizing point for the whole analysis. In such a case, the technique becomes virtually synonymous with the methodology. The quantitative approaches discussed in this chapter, however, shall be called techniques, because that is the form that they usually will assume in research.

This chapter is an introduction to the use of statistical techniques in land use analysis. As a result, only the most fundamental techniques that are most likely to have value for the land use analyst are considered. Furthermore, the intent of the paper is to introduce the reader to particular techniques rather than to provide an indepth description of them. Appropriate texts should be consulted and courses taken before the techniques are used in analyzing land use problems.

Quantitative Analysis, Statistical Techniques, and Land Use

Quantitative analysis is a broad term that refers to the use of mathematics in the study of numerical data. Unfortunately, the term is used frequently, and incorrectly, as a synonym for statistics. The former term is far more encompassing than the latter and, in fact, includes statistics. Statistical techniques are used (1) to summarize information so that it can be more comprehensible and thus useful to the researchers, and (2) to make generalizations about a group of phenomena from a sample drawn from the same group. Thus, there are many quantitative techniques that may be important to the land use analyst that are not innately statistical, such as graph theory, the great realm of mathematical models, including spatial allocation models, and perhaps even many graphic portrayals. This chapter emphasizes statistics in land use analysis primarily because they include most techniques used in basic methodologies employed by land use analysts. Other quantitative approaches are considered, however, when appropriate.

Statistics may be dichotomized as being descriptive or inferential. Descriptive statistics are used to summarize data. By substituting select measures for raw data, the researcher is able to consolidate the information into a form that is probably easier to interpret. Typical descriptive statistics include the mean and standard deviation, percentage and proportion, and various correlation coefficients. Inferential statistics are far more complex than descriptive statistics, at least as a group, and in most research areas have proven to be far more valuable. Inferences are made from a sample to a larger group from which the sample was taken. The use of inferential statistics is more complex than the use of descriptive statistics because far more detailed decision making on the part of the researcher is involved. The technique selected, the size of the sample vis-à-vis the population under study, the probability of making an error in the inference, and the precise meaning of the results are areas where a mistake might be made that conceivably could distort the study results.

The advantages of using inferential statistics outweigh the disadvantages. Most important is the fact that quite often the numerical size of the group under study is so large that the researcher cannot study every unit. For example, if the researcher were analyzing the journey-to-work patterns of a suburban population of 100,000 persons, the cost of interviewing each individual becomes prohibitive. Thus, a sample that is representative of the population is carefully selected. Inferential statistics are used to make statements about the population from information derived from the sample.

Statistical techniques may also be dichotomized according to the spatial character of the data involved. Location is the only element common to geographic data. Information about rainfall, household income, and agricultural productivity, for example, would be of limited use in a geographic analysis unless some spatial element was included. This spatial element may be the specific location of the data set on the earth's surface, or it may be the location of a set of data relative to the location of other sets. An example of this latter possibility is the aforementioned journey-to-work data, in which information might be given for the distances between places of origin and the destination. Whereas the data available to the geographer are virtually infinite in character, their locational possibilities are limited. In fact, most geographic data are available in only one or two of three geometric forms: points, lines, and areas. Spatial statistics, therefore, are concerned with the spatial properties of data. Aspatial statistics center upon the arithmetical character of data, independent of the location of the phenomena under study.

The descriptive-inferential and aspatial-spatial approaches to the use of statistics may be combined to form four statistical types. The reader should be comfortable with definitions of their characteristics before proceeding into the remainder of the chapter. The first type, descriptive-aspatial statistics, includes commonly accepted descriptive statistics such as the mean, median, standard deviation and several types of correlation coefficients. They are certainly valuable to the land use analyst, at least in a very rudimentary form. Yet their importance and use in land use analysis are not very different from other research areas for which numerical data are available. They will, therefore, not be treated here. Descriptive spatial statistics, however, are uniquely important to land use analysis because of their emphasis on locational or spatial data and because of the strong spatial character of land use analysis. Furthermore, the land use analyst may be more apt to need descriptive statistics than researchers in other research areas because of the strongly applied character of land use studies. Nevertheless, inferential statistics are essential in nearly any research that is characterized by numerical data. They are, therefore, considered briefly in this chapter. Inferential-aspatial statistics are treated in detail in many texts, however, and so a few examples are discussed in general terms only as they may apply to land use analysis. Finally, inferential-spatial statistics are considered to be important in land use analysis because of its spatial character, but few techniques fall into this category. Consequently they are treated very briefly.

Descriptive Spatial Techniques

Descriptive spatial techniques have no powers of inference and are by definition limited to summary measurements of the location of phenomena. Furthermore, they tend to be rather simple and quite often have distinct counterparts among descriptive aspatial statistics. Nevertheless, these techniques may be extremely valuable to the land use analyst.

Mean Center and Standard Distance

Centrographic measures are descriptive spatial statistics that measure the central tendency of an areal distribution. A centrographic measure is usually a particular point that represents a central location among a set of observations. The mean center is one such measure that should be given serious consideration because of its simplicity and yet substantive descriptive power. Directly analogous to the mean of an arithmetical distribution, the mean center is a point that represents the minimum possible sum of squared distances to all other points for the study area. No other point can provide a smaller sum of squared distances.

Calculation of the mean center is not complex, although it can become tedious in the case of a large number of observations. Two coordinates (ordinate-abscissa) are constructed so that every observation may be given a value according to each of the two coordinates. The two axes are then scaled, say from 0–100. The mean of all the observations is calculated for the Y axis (ordinate) and then for the X axis (abscissa). The intersection of the lines drawn perpendicular from the mean value on each axis is the mean center. A notation for the calculation is:

$$c\overline{X} = \frac{\sum_{i=1}^{n} x_i}{N} \quad \text{and} \quad c\overline{Y} = \frac{\sum_{i=1}^{n} y_i}{N}$$

where $c\overline{X}$ is the mean value for all observations (x_i) on the X axis and $c\overline{Y}$ is the mean value for the same observations (y_i) on the Y axis. The mean center is the point of intersection for the two lines drawn from the points $c\overline{X}$ and $c\overline{Y}$.

The mean center is not a mapping technique, although it can be presented on a map. The visual comparative value of the mean center vis-à-vis the plotted set of observations is often great. Also, mean centers can be compared with one another for different sets of phenomena at a point in time or for the same phenomenon at different points in time. Furthermore, the distances between the resulting mean centers can be presented in arithmetical forms, independent of their specific locations.

Transportation research frequently relies upon the mean center, because the point provides a central location that is, at least geometrically, accessible to all points of the distribution. Thus, the process of locating a community hospital, for example, might consider the mean center of the area's population as an important variable. Almost any distribution of points or areas, however, can be described with the mean center. In the case of areas, the geometric center of each area may be used as a point for computational purposes.

Suppose the researcher is examining for a medium-sized metropolitan area the distribution of vacant land that is in corporate reserve, which means that it is being held for future development. Each parcel of this type of land can be represented on a map by a point. A visual perusal of the resultant distribution may or may not reveal a distinct pattern. An attempt to distinguish a pattern, however, is enhanced by the placement of the mean center within the distribution. Such a point provides an important generalization in the same way that the mean provides an important overview of an arithmetical distribution.

The mean center of the distribution of corporate reserve land could be compared with other centers that represent other relevant distributions, such as different types of vacant land, developed corporate land, and corporate reserves for earlier points in time. In this latter case, the researcher could document any directional shifts in the location of corporate reserve land. Thus, if corporations began to acquire numerous parcels on the western fringes of a city while neglecting other areas, then the mean center of all such land would begin to shift to the west.

The mean center assumes equal value for each observation when in fact certain subgroups may be more significant than others. Fortunately, the mean center can be weighted to reflect variations in the size or character of each observation. The notation for the weighting is:

$$c\overline{X}w = \frac{\sum_{i=1}^{n} x_i w_i}{w_i} \quad \text{and} \quad c\overline{Y}w = \frac{\sum_{i=1}^{n} y_i w_i}{w_i}$$

where $c\overline{X}w$ is the mean center for all weighted observations ($x_i w_i$) on the X axis, and $c\overline{Y}w$ is the mean value for the same observations ($y_i w_i$) on the Y axis. The weighted mean center is the point of intersection for the two points drawn from points $c\overline{X}w$ and $c\overline{Y}w$. The weights chosen are, of course, up to the discretion of the researcher. This ability to weight gives the mean center a greater flexibility and thus value in terms of its potential use.

In the case of corporate reserve land, the researcher could weight each point, which represents a parcel, according to the size of the parcel. The size factor could be important, because it might reflect more accurately the potential tax base and the capacity for development. The resultant weighted mean center may or may not be located near the original center. If the many parcels on the western fringes of the city tend to be small whereas those on the eastern side are fewer in number but larger in size, then the weighted mean center would be to the east of the original center.

Like the arithmetical mean, the mean center is subject to distortion by extreme values. Also in both cases one has no idea as to the level of dispersion around the mean. In the case of the arithmetical mean, there is the standard deviation, which measures the distribution of observations around the mean. The areal equivalent to the standard deviation is the standard distance. The mean center gives a central location; the standard distance gives an indication as to the degree to which the individual observations are clustered around the mean or are substantially separated or dispersed. The measure represents the value of one standard deviation about the mean center, and is presented in the form of a radius (from the mean center), which would inscribe a circle that would encompass a standard deviation of observations.

Calculation of the standard distance is analogous to that of the standard deviation, only both axes are used in the former calculation and thus two deviations are calculated. The deviation of each observation from the mean center on the Y axis is determined and then squared. The squared deviations are summed. The procedure is repeated for the X axis. The two totals are added. The new total is divided by the number of observations, and the square root of the total is then taken. The value is the radius of a circle emanating from the mean center. The notation for the calculation of the standard distance is:

$$SD = \sqrt{\frac{\sum_{i=1}^{n} (x_i - c\overline{X})^2 + \sum_{i=1}^{n} (y_i - c\overline{Y})^2}{N}}$$

The standard distance is usually used in conjunction with the mean center in the same way that the standard deviation is associated with the arithmetic mean. Nevertheless, the standard distance may be presented separately from the mean center and still provide a valuable contribution. This measure, as with the mean center, may be presented graphically or arithmetically. In the former case it is shown on a map encircling the mean center and in the latter case the numerical value of the distance of the radii are used for further analysis.

In the case of corporate reserve land, a mean center and standard distance may be calculated for several successive time periods. Shifts in the mean center reflect directional changes in the location of the land, and shifts in the size of the standard distance reflect the degree to which the total distribution is becoming more or less dispersed. Standard distances may be compared for cities of roughly comparable size to determine if corporate reserve land is becoming more or less diffuse. Mean centers and their respective standard distances may also be used to compare other land use types with corporate reserve land for one or more points in time for one city or in a comparative framework for several cities.

Median Center

A second major centrographic measure is the median center. This measure is the point of intersection for two lines drawn perpendicular from the X and Y axes in order to bisect the total number of observations. Like the mean center, the median center is directly analogous to its arithmetical counterpart. Thus, the median center is less sensitive to extreme values that distort the mean center. A major disadvantage of using the median center, however, is that there is no appropriate measure of dispersion accompanying it. Thus, when measures of central location and dispersion are needed for analysis of a distribution, the mean center and standard distance are normally used.

Other Measures of Dispersion

Although the standard distance is a particularly refined measure of spatial dispersion, its use usually is limited to an association with the mean center. When an assessment of dispersion is desired for a distribution surrounding a central location other than a centrographic point, a simple azimuthal (circular) grid may be used. Such a grid categorizes points according to their distances from the central location; that is, the number of observations for each ring is noted. The resultant data may be presented in either tabular or graphic form, in which case a cumulative frequency curve, with cumulative percentage of observations on the Y axis and distance from the central point on the X axis, may be used. Unfortunately, this approach does not yield a single distinctive value of dispersion as does the standard distance statistic.

Measures of central location and dispersion provide valuable insights into areal distributions. If more detail of the character of the distribution is needed, however, the researcher may turn to nearest neighbor analysis. This measure is not location-specific as are centrographic and dispersion measures, in that the results of nearest neighbor analysis cannot be located or mapped. The relative dispersion of the distribution, however, is an important aspect of the measure and in that sense it resembles the standard distance. The purpose of nearest neighbor analysis is to distinguish a point distribution according to one of three possible patterns: (1) random, (2) clustered, (3) dispersed. Furthermore, the numerical result indicates the degree to which the distribution resembles one of these patterns.

Nearest neighbor analysis is calculated by comparing the study distribution with a theoretical random distribution. The nearest neighbor value (R) is the ratio between the actual and hypothetical random distributions:

$$R = \frac{\bar{r}_a}{\bar{r}_e}$$

where

$$\bar{r}_a = \frac{\sum\limits_{i=1}^{n} r_i}{N}$$

In this case, r represents the distance from each point to the nearest point among all others, or its nearest neighbor. Thus, $\bar{r}_a$ is the mean value of the nearest neighbor distances. The denominator of the initial formula is the mean value of the nearest neighbor distances in a random distribution, and is represented as:

$$\bar{r}_e = \frac{1}{2\sqrt{P}}$$

where

$$P = \frac{\text{number of points, N}}{\text{area}}$$

The R score that results from the ratio of the observed pattern to the theoretical pattern is used to classify the real distribution. Obviously, as the value of $\bar{r}_a$ approaches that of $\bar{r}_e$, the distribution becomes closer to one. In a situation where all observations are located at one point, the mean distances between neighbors is zero, and thus the R score is zero. Finally, when the distribution is similar to a dispersed pattern in which the points are regularly spaced, the R score nears a value of 2.15. It should be noted that although nearest neighbor analysis is presented as a descriptive technique, it can also be used as an inferential tool. In this latter case the hypothesis to be rejected is that the real distribution is random.

There are several limitations to the use of nearest neighbor analysis that should be recognized. First, the measure does not distinguish between single and multiple clusters, because only the nearest neighbor is calculated. Second, selection of the nearest neighbor is arbitrary. If the second or third neighbor were chosen, the results could be different. Third, one cannot infer that a distribution is by chance simply because the measure indicates that it is random. However, if these limitations are considered and the technique is used discriminately, it can prove to be a valuable tool of land use analysis.

The nearest neighbor value (R) can be used to compare the spatial patterns of groups of phenomena. Commercial activities, for example, can be broken into several categories such as food stores, convenience markets, variety stores, and hardware stores, and the R values can then be calculated for each group. Substantive variations that might exist between groups could be used in a discussion of the spatial structure, and thus land use patterns, that constitute the commercial activities of a region.

In the case of corporate reserve land, comparisons could be made between this vacant type and others commonly found in the metropolitan area. The researcher might contend, for example, that corporate reserve land is less dispersed than land held for speculative purposes. Such a case might arise when the former type is likely to be somewhat clustered on the fringes of the metropolitan area, whereas the speculative land is apt to be more evenly distributed throughout the region. Actually, the two parts of the contention may be examined with a comparative framework or on independent bases.

Measure of Shape

Geographic studies concerned with the use of space are often concerned with its boundaries. These boundaries give distinctiveness, or shape, to segments of space which in essence may be considered regions. The focus upon regions within land use analysis justifies at least a brief discussion, therefore, of the indices of shape. There exist several measures of shape, although only two such measures are presented here. They are the most rudimentary, and yet they are the most likely to have value to the analyst of land use.

The first of the two indices is the length-breadth ratio. This measure evaluates the level of compaction, or the degree to which a shape approaches the most compact form, that is, a circle. In order to calculate the index, the length of a line drawn between the two points on the boundary that are the farthest apart is established. This value is divided by the length of the longest line that can be drawn perpendicular to the first line *and* that connects the two points that are the farthest apart on the boundary. The minimum value of the length-breadth ratio is one. A circle has a value of one, although a square, which is certainly less compact than a circle, also has a value of one. In general, the less compact the shape, the greater the value of the ratio.

The second measure, the compaction index, is a more sophisticated technique than the length-breadth ratio, although its primary concern is also with the level of compaction of an area. The basic formula for the index is:

$$\text{Compaction Index} = \frac{\text{area of unit being measured}}{\text{area of smallest inscribing circle}}$$

The smallest inscribing circle is the smallest circle that can be drawn around the areal unit. The index value is one if the area unit is a circle. The minimum possible value is one, so the less compact the shape the lower the index value.

These indices can be used to compare the spatial extent of two sets of phenomena at a point in time, or one or more sets of phenomena over several points in time. Isopleths of land values, as an example, may be compared for areas surrounding shopping malls of three different size classes. The impact of one class upon land values may be more linear than the impact of the other classes. Furthermore, each class can be examined in terms of changes in the land value isopleths over time. This approach gives the researcher valuable information in terms of the processes by which land is assigned value.

Inferential Statistics

The descriptive spatial techniques discussed above, most of which are statistical, are directly concerned with the location of phenomena, and thus are of immediate importance to the researcher interested in analyzing spatial relations. Conversely, nearly all inferential statistics are aspatial and thus statements about spatial relations must necessarily be limited. Nevertheless, inferential statistics are powerful analytical tools. Furthermore, inferential statistics are an integral building block in the formation and assessment of theory, an essential goal in all research. Thus, the researcher of spatial relations, in this case the land use analyst, must recognize the limitations of inferential statistics in drawing conclusions about spatial relations, and at the same time must recognize the significance of these techniques to research in general. Certainly, *inferential statistics may be appropriate for research of the processes and relations that are manifest in spatial distributions.* The following discussion of a few select inferential techniques is relatively brief because of this chapter's focus on the direct analysis of spatial phenomena.

Application of inferential statistical techniques involves the testing of a hypothesis, which in essence is a statement about a population that is being questioned on the basis of information taken from a sample of the same population. The statement may prove to be incorrect because of the researcher's errors in data collection, organization, and application of the technique with which the hypothesis is tested, and because of chance variations in the selected data. The possibility of erroneous statements can be minimized, therefore, by the careful selection and application of the methodology. Nevertheless, a chance for error always exists because only a segment of the study population is being used to make statements about the larger group. As a result, inferential statistics are very directly concerned with probability theory.

The statistical technique used depends upon the character of the data set and the goals of the researcher, but the size of the sample and the arithmetical form of the data are essential considerations. Inferential statistical techniques are usually divided into parametric and nonparametric types. Techniques of the former group tend to be more powerful and thus more valuable. The requirements to use them are also more stringent. Parametric statistical techniques usually require a normal distribution, a larger sample size and interval data, whereas nonparametric techniques may be used with smaller sample sizes (occasionally less than twenty observations) and with ordinal or nominal data. Two particular techniques are discussed here. The first, Chi-square, is a nonparametric test, whereas the second, analysis of variance, is parametric. These two examples are among the most valuable and widely used techniques within their respective categories.

Chi-Square

Chi-square is a technique that is used often in the analysis of two nominal scale variables. Very simply, the technique uses a matrix of cells, which represents a cross-classification of the study variables, and compares the actual distribution of observations within the cells with the expected distribution, which is the number of observations per cell that would be encountered if there is no relation between variables. The matrix of cells for a particular study is shown below:

		Owner Type	
		State	Local
Land Use	Occupied	X_1	X_2
Type	Vacant	X_3	X_4

The question to be answered in this problem may be stated as follows: "Is there an association between government ownership and the use of land?" If there is an association, the observed frequencies will be found disproportionately in some of the cells when compared to the expected frequencies. Fortunately, comparisons of this type can be made when there are an unequal number of observations for the parts of a variable. If there are only 15 observations for the state ownership type and 35 for the local, therefore, the expected number of observations would simply be much higher for the local category.

All study parcels of land are assigned to the appropriate cell of the matrix. The expected frequencies are then derived by assigning the number of observations per cell according to the size of each characteristic (occupied, vacant, state, local). The Chi-square statistic is then calculated:

$$\chi^2 = \Sigma \frac{(f_o - f_e)^2}{f_e}$$

where f_o and f_e refer respectively to the observed and expected frequencies for each cell. If the calculated Chi-square value (χ^2) exceeds a particular value taken from a Chi-square table, then the researcher may surmise that a relation exists.

Use of the Chi-square test may be valuable to the land use analyst because classifications and taxonomies are particularly important, given the nature and character of the research area. Thus, many types of associations between land use characteristics can be tested, even though the data may be in a somewhat rudimentary, in this case nominal, form. Importantly, the Chi-square test only tells the analyst if an association exists. If the degree of association is desired, the researcher must turn to other more sophisticated nonparametric techniques.

Analysis of Variance

Analysis of variance is a more powerful and valuable technique than Chi-square and, as a result, the limitations upon its use are more stringent and the complexity of its computations is greater. Calculation of the test statistic is too complex to be presented here, and so the researcher should consult appropriate texts. An example of a data set for which analysis of variance might be used is shown below:

Governmental Land:

Owner Type

	Federal	State	Local
Assessed valuation of parcel	X_1	X_2	X_3
	X_4	X_5	X_6
	X_7	X_8	X_9
	X_{10}	X_{11}	X_{12}

The question to be answered is: "Does assessed valuation vary according to owner type?" In essence, focus of study is upon an independent variable (assessed valuation), represented by interval data, and upon whether or not such data vary according to owner type. The answer to the question, therefore, is a dichotomous yes or no. The degree of association between variables cannot be distinguished by analysis of variance.

Analysis of variance, like Chi-square, is a valuable technique for analyzing categorized land use data. The notable advantage of analysis of variance is that interval data, which are the most precise data available, can be the focus of study. A more complex version of analysis of variance, two-way analysis of variance, presents yet greater research possibilities. A data set appropriate for two-way analysis of variance is shown below:

Governmental Land:

Owner Type

		Federal	State	Local
	Occupied	X_1	X_2	X_3
		X_4	X_5	X_6
		X_7	X_8	X_9
Assessed valuation of a parcel				
	Vacant	X_{10}	X_{11}	X_{12}
		X_{13}	X_{14}	X_{15}
		X_{16}	X_{17}	X_{18}

In this particular case, the question to be answered is: "Does assessed valuation vary according to owner type and land use?" Such an approach has the value of indicating the relationship between one of the two independent variables and the dependent variable, while controlling for the other. In essence, this means that the influence of the second variable is momentarily ignored. Calculation and interpretation of two-way analysis of variance are more complex than calculation and interpretation of one-way analysis of variance. The reader, therefore, must be familiar with its structure and characteristics before using it.

Multivariate Techniques

The processes of land use change commonly reflect the interrelationships between many factors. Some factors may be extremely important whereas others may have only slight significance. The task of the researcher is to delimit those variables (which represent factors) that are the most influential and, if possible, to show the degree to which they affect land use change. The statistical and other quantitative techniques dealt with to this point are inadequate for such a task. Certainly these approaches are valuable means for distinguishing general relationships, but the number of variables that each technique can accommodate at any one time is in itself a serious limitation in many cases. Fortunately, more sophisticated techniques exist that can provide the simultaneous recognition of several variables. The most popular technique for such a task, multiple regression, is addressed here, as are factor analysis and spatial compositing.

Multiple Regression

Linear regression is the single variable form of the multiple variable case. The basic form of the linear model is:

$$Y = a + bX$$

This model, which assumes linearity of variables, shows the relationship between the variables Y and X. It represents a best fit line that is drawn through the plotted data on a two-dimensional scale. The letter *a* represents the point where the line intersects on the Y axis and *b* represents the slope of the line. The resulting line tells the amount of change in Y given an increase in one unit of X. This value is synonymous with the slope index (b).

Importantly, the Y variable in the above model is the dependent variable, in that it represents the phenomenon that needs to be explained, while the X variable represents the factor that may help to explain the variations in Y. In linear regression, the degree of association between the two variables is calculated, but more importantly, the independent variable is used to predict the dependent variable. For example, the form might be:

$$Y \text{ (land value)} = a + bX \text{ (distance from city center)}$$

In this case, the researcher has a set of land value data, say 200 parcels, and also has the distance of each parcel from the city center. The primary concern of the research is with variations in land values. The question then arises: "What factor is associated with land value that may help to explain its areal variation?" Research of the literature concerned with land values, or perhaps an intuitive grasp of the particular circumstances of the study area, may lead the researcher to choose a specific factor as an independent variable. Finally, computation of this particular model (by computer) will reveal the degree to which distance from the city center accounts for variation in land value, but it will also delimit the degree to which changes in land value are explained by the distance factor.

In reality, there will be several variables that will help to explain variations in the dependent variable. Multiple regression is used in such a case. This model has a slightly more complex form, although in reality it is a simple extension of the linear model:

$$Y = a + b_1X_1 + b_2X_2 \ldots + b_nX_n + e$$

This form of the model also assumes linearity in the variables, and is sufficient for the purposes of this chapter.

The multiple regression model reflects a best fit curve in multidimensional space. As with the linear model, a value of correlation is presented for all variables in relation to one another. In fact, the computer printout usually provides a matrix of correlation values. The more significant aspect of the multiple regression model, however, is that it will show the explanatory value of each independent variable. This means that it will indicate how much of the variation in the dependent variable can be explained by the independent factor. Importantly, the model will show the value for the independent variable, while it controls for other variables. This means that the explanatory value of the other variables is momentarily ignored. Thus, the new form may be:

$$Y \text{ (land value)} = a + b_1 X_1 \text{ (distance from city center)}$$
$$+ b_2 X_2 \text{ (distance from major arterial)} + b_3 X_3 \text{ (zoning of parcel area)} \ldots b_n X_n \text{ (etc.)}$$

Land value is again the dependent variable, while all the others are independent. In summary, calculation of the above equation will provide: (1) a correlation matrix; (2) the relation between the dependent variable and each of the independent variables, while it controls for all others; (3) the amount of variation explained by all the variables present in the equation. Finally, an error term (e), or the amount of variation that remains unexplained, can be included.

Factor Analysis

An analysis of land use patterns may include a large number of variables if adequate data are available. Regression analysis is used to delimit the associations between a dependent variable and select independent variables. In such a case, only one variable is being explained and the variables used to help in the explanation are selected by the researcher according to some rational choice process. A statistical technique is required, however, that can synthesize a large number of variables and delimit general patterns, or dimensions, of similarity, without focusing attention upon any one variable. Factor analysis is one such technique.

Factor analysis is closely related to principal components analysis. The difference is that the latter assumes that the variables will explain all variation within the population defined by the variables, whereas the former does not. As a result, factor analysis is a more flexible technique and thus it is recommended here.

Factor analysis attempts to collapse a group of variables into several common dimensions. Income, education, and occupation, for example, are closely related although they may be termed independent variables. A factor analysis would probably combine these variables, and perhaps several others as well, into a common dimension which may be called socioeconomic standing. The numerical value of the dimension would reflect common aspects of all the variables. Other unrelated variables in the analysis would be combined into other dimensions. In factor analysis, one does not know the number of dimensions until the statistical computations have been completed. A large number of variables could easily collapse into a very small number of dimensions.

Factor analysis may be performed upon point or areal data. Certainly, interpretation and value of the results are dependent upon the characteristics of the data. The latter data type is usually preferred for a factor analysis of land use patterns, as will be explained later. Assuming use of areal data, the general question to be answered by use of factor analysis is: "What kinds of common variations are there among all variables (characteristics) for the study area?" Results of the analysis may be presented in map or arithmetical form, depending upon the intent and purpose of the particular study.

Factor analysis is complex in mathematical terms and thus its computation is accomplished only by a computer. It is not possible in an elementary land use text to explore the details of factor analysis but its value to land use planners is twofold. First, it can delimit associations between characteristics and sets of characteristics that no human eye can discern. Second, it enables the researcher to delimit areal variations in these associations. Such an approach is an important step in explaining the reasons for the particular patterns of land use.

Spatial Compositing

The purpose of multiple regression differs from that of factor analysis in that the former is concerned with the degree to which variations in independent variables explain variation in the dependent variable whereas the latter centers upon general patterns of similarity between a relatively large number of variables. Both techniques are innately aspatial and yet both have clear applicability to spatial problems. Furthermore, both may be valuable tools in hypothesis testing and thus theory building. In general, however, both techniques are somewhat limited in applied research, particularly at the micro scale. The third technique to be considered here, spatial compositing, is distinctly different from the other two in terms of its spatial character and applied value.

Spatial compositing is a technique that is concerned with the spatial synthesis of a data set for the purpose of finding a particular point, points, or area that are characterized by the most notable presence or absence of particular variables. This technique is innately spatial, is not particularly conducive to theory building, and has a distinctly applied value. The spatial synthesis of data allows the researcher to answer questions such as: "Where is the best location for a shopping center? Which sites should be developed for open pit mining processes? On what corner should a fast food restaurant be located? What is the best route for a freeway extension?"

The most simple form of spatial compositing is presented by Ian McHarg in *Design with Nature*. In this approach, an overlay of a map is constructed for each characteristic that has a potential impact upon the proposed project. Characteristics that have a potentially negative impact are darker and those with less potential negative influence are clearer. The shading is graduated according to the degree of potential impact. All overlays concerned with important characteristics are placed upon one another. Those areas of the map that are the clearest indicate areas of the greatest potential for development or location of a phenomenon. The problem with such an approach, of course, is that the value of each characteristic cannot be monitored and the degree of clarity, which represents the potential impact, must be assigned subjectively.

A more sophisticated approach to compositing involves a more detailed set of data and a more complex process of synthesis. Specifically, the area of interest is divided into cells, which are preferably square and are of equal size. Each cell is assigned a numerical value according to each pertinent variable. All variables are weighted according to their significance within the composite system under consideration. The final result of the computer summation indicates areas that are potentially least affected by the respective characteristics. This particular approach has the advantage of adding precision and objectivity to the synthesis process, and yet allows for the incorporation of a larger number of variables.

Conclusion

The use of quantitative techniques in land use analysis is subject to a set of guidelines that should be viewed as a generalized blueprint rather than as a set of rigid constraints. The fact that the analyst must be aware of the general context of the use of these techniques is addressed by this chapter. Thus, the articulation between the research topic, including the intent and purpose of the research, and the quality and character of the data must be carefully considered in the selection, application, and interpretation of the appropriate technique. Failure to recognize such a linkage could provide inappropriate, or even incorrect, results.

The generalized blueprint provided by this chapter is necessarily an introduction. The reader must recognize that he or she should be familiar with the context of each research problem. A fact that is often forgotten, however, is that there is always room for innovation and well-directed experimentation. This is particularly true of land use analysis, because of its increasingly applied character. Thus, the role of imagination and originality may be substantial in the selection of particular techniques and, eventually, in the design of more comprehensive methodologies appropriate for land use research.

Selected References

Blalock, H. M., Jr. *Social Statistics*. New York: McGraw-Hill, 1978.

Hammond, R., and McCullogh, P. *Quantitative Techniques in Geography: An Introduction*. Oxford: Clarendon Press, 1974.

Haring, L. L., and Lounsbury, J. F. *Introduction to Scientific Geographic Research*. Dubuque, Iowa: William C. Brown Co., 1975.

King, L. J. *Statistical Analysis in Geography*. Englewood Cliffs, N.J.: Prentice-Hall, 1969.

McHarg, I. *Design with Nature*. Garden City, NY: Natural History Press, 1969.

Rummel, R. J. *Applied Factor Analysis*. Evanston, Illinois: Northwestern University Press, 1970.

Siegel, S. *Nonparametric Statistics for the Behavioral Sciences*. New York: McGraw-Hill, 1956.

Yeates, M. *An Introduction to Quantitative Analysis in Human Geography*. New York: McGraw-Hill, 1974.

Section C

Laws, Regulations, and Policy

Chapter 8

Regulating the Use of Land

Larry K. Stephenson
Arizona Department of Health Services
Arizona State University
and University of Phoenix

Introduction

The Need for Regulation

In a predominately rural and agrarian society such as existed in the United States in the early nineteenth century there is relatively little need for land use regulations. The economic landscape is fairly homogeneous and the cities small. With increasing industrialization and concomitant urbanization, however, the complexity of land use patterns increases. The agglomeration of large numbers of people into restricted spaces of cities sets the stage for increasing numbers of potential conflicts between land uses, e.g., residential vs. industrial. Certain land uses need to be restricted or constrained as to their location; others need to be protected from encroachments by incompatible neighboring uses.

One solution to these land use conflicts is the rational determination of locations where selected uses are permitted. This allocation process is synonymous with land use planning and is generally implemented by zoning and other regulatory devices. Underlying the paired concepts of planning and regulation is an assumption tending toward cultural determinism: that is, by specifying the spatial design of environments (especially urban environments) it is possible to influence the social, economic, and cultural character of areas in a positive manner. There are, to be sure, a variety of reasons why certain groups may be in favor of particular planning and zoning schemes. From the planning perspective, however, the primary reason for regulating the uses of parcels of land centers about the belief (often implicit or unspoken) that the "natural order" of the economic landscape produces an excess of negative externalities, maladies that can be corrected via design and regulatory processes.

The purpose of this chapter is to provide an overview of land use regulation in order to impart a greater sense of appreciation of the unseen "legal landscape" which is superimposed on existing land use patterns and which influences subsequent land use decisions.

Origins of Land Use Regulations

Explicit regulations concerning the use of land have been in existence for several centuries. Many of the regulations in the United States may be traced back to English common law. For example, in the late 1690s, the colony of Massachusetts passed a law that allowed "the selectmen of the towns of Boston, Salem and Charleston respectively . . . (to) assign some certain places in each of said towns (where it may be least offensive) for the erecting or setting up of slaughter-houses for the killing of all meat, still-houses, and houses for trying of tallow and curing of leather. . . ."[1]

The legal controls on the use of land in the United States today have their origins in each of the three branches of government—legislative, executive, and judicial—on the national, state, and local level. Zoning, for example, is most commonly the result of action by the legislative branch. The zoning requirements and accompanying zoning maps are voted into law as city ordinances by a city council comprised of elected representatives. Occasionally (and where permitted), land use controls are the result of petitions initiated and sponsored by local citizen groups. When such issues are placed on the ballot in this fashion and voted into law by the electorate, the resulting controls are considered legislative in origin.

The executive branch of government, e.g., a city planning department, also issues land use controls, often in the form of rules and regulations developed subsequent to the passage of a law or ordinance.

Decisions handed down from the bench of the judicial branch represent a third source of land use controls. Over time, there has developed in the United States a considerable case law on land use control.[2] Laws, ordinances, rules, and regulations are all subject to judicial scrutiny, if challenged. Those that have been ruled on provide the general set of precedents for later legislative and administrative actions.

Direct versus Indirect Regulation

The legal devices used to regulate the use of land can be categorized into one of two types: direct or indirect. Direct land use controls operate to limit the use to which some particular parcel of land may be put. The best example of a direct control is zoning, for it specifies the exact set of alternative uses allowed on a parcel. Contrasted to these are indirect controls, which are not necessarily spatially linked to particular sites but rather apply to larger areas. The permit is one example of such a control. Prior to the development of many types of facilities or industries, permits for their operation must be acquired from government or quasi-governmental agencies. Few parcels are specifically zoned for, say, a hospital or a sanitary landfill, and both these land uses require permission to be established, permission which usually is based in part upon locational characteristics. There appears to be a trend away from direct land use controls and toward more indirect regulation.

Zoning

Legal Basis

The notion of channeling certain land uses to preselected locations is actually quite old. As a contemporary planning concept, however, zoning is of fairly recent vintage in the United States. The legal bases for zoning are the police powers reserved to the states by the United States' Constitution. The Constitution allows the respective states to pass laws related to the health, morals, safety, or general welfare of the community. The constitutionality of a particular zoning ordinance usually depends upon whether it is a reasonable exercise of police power. The police power is specifically reserved to the states, not local governmental entities. Thus for a local government to have a lawful zoning ordinance, there must have been an expressed delegation from the state of this authority. Although this delegation may take several forms, the most common is the passage by a state legislature of an explicit zoning enabling act.

Typical Restrictions

A zoning ordinance can be as simple or complex as a community desires. There are several common elements, however, in most ordinances, all of which combine to exercise control over the general spatial and economic landscape. The first element in zoning is the explicit portrayal of land use categories or types in the form of a zoning map. In the typically zoned community, detailed zoning maps are prepared depicting the uses allowed for each parcel.

A second element of a zoning ordinance is a set of areal restrictions. These note the minimum parcel size necessary for selected uses. A single-use type, e.g., single-family residential, may have several areal categories associated with it. Thus certain parts of the community may be zoned for single-family houses on lots of 5,000 square feet minimum, whereas other parts of the community may be restricted to lots of 10,000 or 20,000 square feet. The areal restrictions are used to regulate the density of development.

A third element is a set of restrictions relating to bulk. These specify the minimum front, side, and rear yard setbacks as well as height limitations for buildings. "For high rise structures (where allowed) bulk regulation may be expressed through a 'floor area ratio' (F.A.R.) by which the total floor area in a building is limited to a certain multiple of the site area on which it stands. An F.A.R. of ten allows a structure of ten floors covering the entire site, or of twenty floors on half the site."[3]

The concept of zoning has evolved in the direction of decreasing rigidity, while an effort has been made to maintain control over development. One particularly interesting notion from the spatial perspective is that of the "floating zone," a use classification not found on the zoning map. The floating zone "in theory floats above the landscape in anticipation of being brought down to earth. . . . It is a use classification which is not employed until needed nor pinned down to any area until the necessity arises."[4] The purpose of the floating zone is to reserve flexibility for new kinds of uses or demands that cannot be accurately anticipated, or for selected types of uses that can be foreseen but for which no locational decisions have been made, e.g., regional shopping centers.

To circumvent some of the inflexibility of a fully operational zoning ordinance, provisions are made for exceptions. One way is to rezone a parcel of land (usually at the request of the landowner) from one use type to another. Another is to permit a variance from certain of the restrictions, e.g., the height limitation for some parcel. A special or conditional use permit is yet another means providing exceptions.

Diffusion of Zoning

The first comprehensive zoning ordinance was adopted by New York City in 1916. The New York City zoning ordinance, upheld by a New York State Court in 1920, served as a model for other community ordinances as the concept of zoning diffused rapidly throughout the country.[5]

One such community was Euclid, Ohio, a suburb of Cleveland. It adopted a zoning ordinance in 1922, subdividing the city into six use classes ranging from single-family residential to heavy industrial. A local firm and landowner, Ambler Realty Company, challenged the reasonableness of the ordinance, charging that it deprived the firm of a great part of the value of its land, i.e., the zoning was equivalent to confiscating their property for certain uses. In 1926, after a long period of litigation, the United States' Supreme Court ruled in Euclid v. Ambler Realty Co. that such zoning provisions were a legitimate exercise of the police power.[6] This case has provided the legal rationale for zoning since 1926.

Although there was much interest in and some adoption of zoning prior to the Euclid decision, it was in the period immediately following that zoning diffused most widely. Part of the ease of diffusion was related to the availability of a "Standard Zoning Enabling Act," sponsored and prepared by the U.S. Department of Commerce in the 1920s. This enabling act served as a model states could easily adopt or adapt without having to devise one of their own.

The Taking Issue

As noted in Euclid v. Ambler, at the heart of zoning (and most other land use controls) is what is referred to in the legal and land use literature as "the taking issue."[7] The Fifth Amendment to the United States Constitution contains a provision that private property shall not be taken for public use without just compensation, a provision that also applies to the states through the Fourteenth Amendment. When government needs particular lands for specified uses, e.g. for a new highway, it may obtain them through either direct purchase or the process of eminent domain. In either instance, the landowner is compensated for property taken by the government. The direct acquisition (and hence control) of land by government is viewed as legitimate.

When government, however, begins to limit the nature and intensity of use allowed on a parcel, how restrictive may this be before government effectively "takes" the property, i.e., preempts virtually all uses? This question has vexed legal scholars since the inception of zoning and is one that courts have periodically been called upon to decide. The general consensus of the courts has been to allow governments fairly tight regulatory controls over the uses of land so long as each individual landowner is provided some reasonable use or uses for their parcels. As noted in *The Taking Issue*[8] there is a trend toward resolving the taking issue in favor of environmental protection and land use control.

Planning and Zoning

Planning and zoning, often spoken of as an inseparable pair, are two distinct activities. Planning is a process whereby goals are articulated, objectives defined, desired land use patterns specified, and the mechanisms for attainment identified. Zoning, on the other hand, is a process centered about limiting the uses allowed on various land parcels. Ideally, planning precedes zoning in temporal sequence. The planning activities synthesize a variety of objectives related to community growth and development. Zoning in turn provides a means of attempting to assure that these are attained.

Despite the close logical linkage between them, it is possible to have planning without zoning and zoning without planning. In the former instance, the planning may be carried out as an intellectual or administrative exercise with little impact on the community, or it may be implemented by a variety of policies and tools other than zoning. In the absence of planning, zoning becomes synonymous with planning. Since the zoning maps and regulations are not based on a more general plan, they become the de facto planning documents guiding land use decisions in the community. Thus, there occasionally appears to be confusion between planning and zoning, and which has precedence over the other.

Zoning should thus be subsumed under the general plan, except when no such plan exists. Recent court decisions have strengthened the role of the comprehensive plan by noting that zoning decisions must be consistent with it. For example, in Oregon a court found that "the zoning decisions of a city must be in accord with that plan and a zoning ordinance which allows a more intrusive use than that described in the plan must fail,"[10] while in New York a court ruled that "the comprehensive plan is the essence of zoning. Without it, there can be no rational allocation of land use."[11]

Zoning As Regionalization

From the spatial perspective, zoning may be thought of as a form of regionalization. In formal regionalization, the intent is to maximize the degree of homogeneity within areal units while at the same time maximizing the differences between regions. With zoning, the individual building block is the land parcel, a unit of real property enclosed by a "legal description."[12] The areal size of a parcel may vary from a few hundred square feet (e.g., a small urban lot) to several thousand acres (e.g., a farm or ranch). Each parcel is classified as to its perceived best possible uses, given the goals of the community. The parcels are then aggregated into approximate regions. For example, parcels classified for use as single-family residences are generally contiguous to one another, forming a residential region. Parcels zoned for industrial or other purposes are likewise usually clustered together in space.

As in most delineated regions, there is some variation within each one. In the case of zoning-regionalization, the degree of variation is controlled not by individual researchers but instead by community decisions surrounding the planning and zoning processes. Many of the regionalization methodologies employed by geographers and others may have utility in zoning applications.

Limitations of Zoning

Zoning, the most common and important land use control tool, suffers from some serious shortcomings which have led critics to search for other regulatory devices. One major problem with zoning is that although it specifies *where* certain types of developments may occur, it does not indicate or control *when* development should occur. Thus, land use planners dependent upon zoning to implement plans have some influence in the spatial dimension but very little in the temporal dimension.

Planning is generally considered a rational process, based on objective analyses by unbiased, professional planners. In reality, planning is politicized and perhaps not as objective as many might desire or like to believe.[13] The administration and implementation of zoning, on the other hand, is an explicitly political process, subject to all the pros and cons, benefits and costs, and biases inherent in the American political system. The politicalization of zoning has often been noted by observers and critics.[14] It is important for land use planners to realize the explicit political process of zoning and its role in the negotiation and reconciliation of conflicting land use goals between and among the various groups concerned.

Other criticisms against zoning include the argument that it is used primarily to protect the value of private property rather than to benefit the community as a whole. Related to this is another which states that zoning, as applied at the local level, is used primarily to assure and enhance the local tax base of the community instead of guiding the pattern of urban expansion. The fact that urban sprawl has continued unabated despite the presence of zoning is a further criticism of it.

Some communities have been accused of using zoning to exclude certain classes of people and land uses, a practice which has given rise to the concept of exclusionary zoning. Central to the criticism of exclusionary zoning is the claim that it severely restricts the amount of low and moderately priced housing which may be constructed. The legality of exclusionary zoning is often questionable and must be decided by the judiciary on a community-by-community basis.

Related to exclusionary zoning is the issue of regional needs as addressed in individual local zoning schemes. If each of the respective communities in an area adopted an exclusionary stance toward certain facilities needed by the entire region (e.g., a correctional facility or low-income housing), then the larger region suffers.

Beyond Zoning

A range of other regulatory tools for controlling and directing land use developments have been developed. Subdivision regulations, for example, provide local governments with control over the way the land is subdivided and prepared for building. Subdividers are often required to install public improvements such as streets, sidewalks, curbs and gutters, sewers, and street lights; to dedicate land for parks, schools, fire or police stations; and to impose selective covenants on deeds. Just how demanding local communities can be of land developers depends upon several factors. Many of the subdivision ordinances in the country could perhaps not withstand rigorous judicial scrutiny.[15] As long as developers can pass along the costs associated with subdivision regulation to the home buyer, there may be few legal challenges.

Planned Unit Developments (PUDs) are a form of regulation used for large parcels of land. While zoning seems to apply best to large numbers of small parcels, it has limited applicability for large parcels. A developer of a sizeable parcel may desire the flexibility to design a mix of land uses, or a community may be interested in limiting development on part of a parcel and thus be willing to accept higher-than-usual densities on the remainder of the land. PUD regulations generally require the developer to submit proposed plans to the community for approval. Resultant approved plans are often a compromise between the desires of developers and the community as a whole.

The requirement of a permit for certain types of developments represents another form of regulatory control, one more often utilized at the state level than the local level. To obtain a permit successfully, the applicant or developer must satisfy certain locational criteria. The requirement of a "Certificate of Need" for construction of a new hospital is one such example of a permit.

Most regulatory devices for land use are site-specific, i.e., they apply to particular parcels of land. One of the more interesting and innovative controls from a spatial perspective is the concept of "transferable development rights" (TDR). This control allows splitting of development or use from the site itself.[16] Initially devised to provide protection for historic buildings and sites, TDR is still in formative stages. The concept of TDR is based on the *right* of each parcel to be developed to its highest and best use, given the usual constraints of zoning. What is unique about this device, however, is that those development rights cannot be utilized at that site but rather can be transferred to other specified sites in exchange for monetary consideration. The TDR mechanism thus provides a means of compensating landowners who, due to community values or other factors, are not allowed to develop their land to its maximum while simultaneously recouping from other developers some of the benefits from allowing greater-than-normal density.

To be fully operational, TDR assumes a market exists for the development rights. The market may either be private, in which supply and demand are the determining factors of price, or it may be public, in which case a governmental agency would both buy and sell the rights and establish their value.[17]

Perhaps one of the more interesting land use alternatives is lack of zoning. Houston, Texas, is often cited as a classic example of lack of land use controls. Houston does not have zoning; however, it does have a variety of other controls, e.g., subdivision regulations.[18] What is unique about Houston is its reliance on deed restrictions as a regulatory tool. The importance and utility of these restrictions is determined by the willingness of local government to enforce them.

Zoning and most of the other regulatory tools are designed to regulate development at the *parcel* scale, even given the vagaries of parcel size. In the past few years, there have emerged a series of attempts to control the magnitude of development at the *community* level, using a mixture of land use controls. These growth control policies and techniques have been both innovative and controversial. Recent court decisions have given approval to certain forms of growth control that are firmly based on a rational land use and community development plan.

Historical Inertia

The legal authority to control the use of land, based upon the police power doctrine, rests with the individual states. Although the *power* to regulate is at the state level, most land use regulation is carried out at the local level, e.g., city or county, as a result of special enabling legislation. Land use control in the United States is thus primarily a function of local government and at a spatial scale which both yields benefits and creates problems.

The proponents for local land use control claim that regulation at this scale is beneficial because planners and enforcers are closer to and more familiar with land use problems and can thus be more responsive. The externalities generated by various uses of land tend to be fairly localized, an argument used to depict the necessity of control at the local level. Yet another reason put forth for local regulatory power stems from the large number of land parcels that must be dealt with. Dividing the regulatory labor among the respective local communities in a state is seen as a rational response to this problem.

Despite the benefits of local land use control, there is also strong criticism of it. Begun at a time when the level of urbanization, degree of sprawl, and level of spatial interdependence were all much less than present, local control is seen by some as antiquated and in need of being replaced by metropolitan or regional planning and land use regulation.[19] Arguments against local control include parochialism, exclusionary zoning, insensitivity to regional needs, incompatibly zoned uses along either side of a political boundary (e.g., city limits), and insensitivity to land use needs of the larger region. Related to this last point is the siting of regional facilities, which have themselves increased in size over time due to both technological changes and scale economies. "To the extent that the regional facilities are economically misplaced, a misallocation of resources occurs and the costs of the misallocation must be borne by the residents of the metropolitan area as a whole."[20]

Toward Regional Planning

The problems resulting from the patchwork of local land use policies and patterns in a metropolitan area have been used to rationalize the need for land use planning and control at the regional scale. Proponents of this perspective believe that it offers the most realistic approach for complex metropolitan areas comprised of a traditional central city surrounded by a host of sub-urbs.[21] Regional planning ideally allows for a systemic view of such an area, with controls exercised so as to allocate the various land uses equitably throughout the region. Especially important from this larger scale viewpoint are those locational decisions concerning region-shaping developments such as airports, regional shopping centers, power generating facilities, and highways. The siting of such a development by one community near another community could greatly alter the *planned* land use patterns of the latter by generating subsequent developments that conflict with the local plan.

For regional planning to be effective, it must be linked with the regulatory authority; i.e., planning and control should be exercised at the same scale. In the United States, there is much more interest and activity in regional land use planning than in the concomitant exercise of regulatory controls at this scale. The councils of government found at the metropolitan or multi-county level often function as regional land use planning bodies with little or no regulatory authority. There is a fairly clear division of labor between the planning functions of such councils and the power retained by the constituent members of the council to regulate major land use decisions. Regions often receive indirect benefits from land use planning at this scale, but these benefits tend to be derived from information exchange and peer group pressure (from other planning departments) rather than from direct enforcement or implementation of the regional plan.

A few instances can be cited for successfully meshing of planning and regulation at a regional scale. In Vermont, for example, the state strengthened regional planning efforts by delimiting seven district environmental commissions and "conferring upon them the power to regulate the use of lands and to establish comprehensive state capability, development and land use plans. . . ."[22] The primary control mechanism used in Vermont is the permit. Most proposed developments of a substantial nature, e.g., more than ten acres or ten dwellings, are required to apply to a district commission for a permit to develop. Prior to granting the permit the commission must determine that the development "is in conformance with a duly adopted development plan, land use plan or land capability plan."[23]

Rediscovering the Police Power

The Quiet Revolution

The police power was rediscovered by some of the states during the 1960s and 1970s. Whereas in the past they had preferred to delegate the authority to plan and control the uses of land, states began to search for regulatory mechanisms to implement at the state level. This rediscovery of the police power by the states, labeled "the quiet revolution in land use control," may be one of the more significant events in the history of land use controls.[24]

A primary reason for the states beginning to assume an active role in land use policy centers around the failure of *local* controls to deal adequately with siting and development issues of extralocal concern and impact. The responses of states vary considerably in the detail of their statutory design. They can be generally categorized, however, as a) reserving the right to review land use decisions related to large-scale developments that may be of regional impact, b) protecting certain environmentally sensitive areas, or c) providing direct controls at an aggregate level over all land in the state.

In Florida, for example, "critical areas" can be delineated by the state and "developments of regional impact" defined. Local regulatory decisions concerning either of these are then subject to review at the state level prior to being finally authorized.[25]

Hawaii was the first state to initiate and implement a *state* land use plan. Concerned about the conversion of prime agricultural lands to urban uses, Hawaii zoned all land in the state into one of four major land use types: urban, rural, agricultural, or conservation. The spatial considerations mandated in the statutes are explicit. The Hawaii State Land Use Commission "shall set standards for determining the boundaries of each district, provided that:

1. In the establishment of boundaries of urban districts those lands that are now in urban use and a sufficient reserve area for foreseeable urban growth shall be included;
2. In the establishment of boundaries for rural districts, areas of land composed primarily of small farms mixed with very low density residential lots, which may be shown by a minimum density of not more than one house per one-half acre and a minimum lot size of not less than one-half acre, should be included;
3. In the establishment of the boundaries of agricultural districts the greatest possible protection shall be given to those lands with a high capacity for intensive cultivation; and
4. In the establishment of the boundaries of the conservation districts, the 'forest and water reserve zones' provided . . . shall constitute the boundaries."[26]

Once delineated, the urban districts were assigned to the respective county governments for a finer degree of zoning and control. Within an urban district, the decision to allocate certain areas or parcels to residential use and others to commercial or industrial use is entirely a local decision rather than a state one. The state, however, retains primary regulatory authority for the other districts.

In a reflective piece written ten years after *The Quiet Revolution in Land Use Control,* David Callies stated that overall the impact of the "revolution" was to strengthen *local* planning efforts as well as state efforts.[27] Reasons for this included a maturation of local land use planning, responses to court decisions, and both a sensitivity to and reaction against state land use controls.

The National Land Use Policy Bill

The success of Hawaii, Florida, Vermont, and other states with state-level land use planning and control, coupled with disappointing results of regional planning attempts, led some in Congress to believe that *all* states should be encouraged to implement similar measures. This belief resulted in federal legislative attempts to pass a National Land Use Policy Bill, which "proposed that some of the land use regulatory authority traditionally exercised by local governments be shifted to the states."[28] In general, the effort was to try to have states assume explicit regulatory authority for "critical areas and uses." Between 1970 and 1974, there were several attempts to pass versions of such a bill, though in the end this legislative effort was defeated.

The interesting history of this legislation has been recorded.[29]

"Critics charged that 'the bill would give the Secretary of the Interior the right to control every piece of land in the nation,' that it was a 'Federal zoning bill.' More damaging was the charge that the bill's implicit, if not explicit, purpose was to bribe the states to use their police power to prevent development on privately owned land for purposes that, in the opponents' view, were anti-growth, aesthetic and elitist.

The bill's advocates, on the other hand, maintained that the bill was a policy-neutral, states-rights bill which left it to the states to determine what lands should be protected. . . . The limits to the police power . . . were not to be resolved in the national legislation but in each of the separate states."[30]

The issues discussed in the National Land Use Policy bill are notable. "They are, ultimately, questions about growth and development; how much, what kind, where, who shall decide, and how can these decisions be made equitably."[31] The defeat of this bill is a testament to the persistence of *local* land use control in the United States and implies that the federal government perhaps should not be involved in local land use decisions or in mandating direct planning controls by state and local governments.

Uncoordinated Efforts: Federal Impacts on
Local and State Land Use Policies

The lack of explicit federal land use statutes does not indicate a lack of federal impacts on land use controls. Many of these impacts, however, are not the result of a coordinated national land use policy, but result from a series of laws passed over a period of time, each with a distinct land use or environmental focus. "The failure of Congress to pass a National Land Use Policy Act . . . does not mean that the nation has no land use policy. The problem is too many policies. For 200 years, the only consistency in federal policies and actions with respect to land has been their mutual inconsistency."[32]

The federal government has direct planning responsibility and regulatory authority for about one-third of the land in the United States, e.g., national parks and forests and land administered by the Federal Bureau of Land Management. Increasingly, those government agencies responsible for respective federal lands have been required to take cognizance of state and local planning efforts on neighboring lands.[33] This requirement recognizes that decisions on the uses of federal lands have spillover effects on surrounding nonfederal lands.

In addition to the direct regulatory controls on federal lands, the United States Government exercises a myriad of indirect controls affecting the uses of nonfederal lands. These types of controls have been categorized by Mandelker into three major types: Type I, those that implement some state planning policies of federally-mandated programs; Type II, those required to implement national pollution standards; and Type III, those necessary to monitor and evaluate environmental impacts.[34]

Type I legislation "attaches land development control requirements to federal financial assistance."[35] Cited as examples of this type are the National Coastal Zone Management Act and the National Flood Insurance Program. Under these laws, states and communities choosing to participate must devise land use plans and implement controls aimed at limiting land development in coastal areas and in flood plains, respectively. Failure to adhere to federal requirements and expectations result in a denial of federal financial assistance.

"Type II legislation provides for pollution control programs which include land development controls."[36] Initial responsibility for attaining air and water quality standards mandated in the federal Clean Air Act and Water Pollution Control Act rests with the federal Environmental Protection Agency. These authorities may be delegated to state-level agencies if those agencies' (and hence states') programs are "consistent with federal statutory requirements, and the federal agency may reassume control in those instances in which state control is found inadequate."[37] In any event, the goal is attainment of certain environmental performance standards, regardless of level of responsibility or enforcement. To attain these standards, the Water Pollution Control Act repeatedly uses the phrase, "set forth procedures and methods (including land use requirements) to control to the extent feasible such sources of pollution."[38]

The third type of control identified is associated with requirements for environmental impact statements (EIS) for federally funded developments. The intent of an EIS is disclosure of impacts; the effect of an EIS on the siting of a development depends on many factors. The net result, however, is often a change in the proposed developmental decision, and hence may be considered an indirect land use control.

The imposition of order upon the types of federal controls should not be confused with order and coordination at the federal level. As noted previously, these efforts are fragmented. The challenge remains with the land use planner to synthesize the desired range of controls.

Conclusions

The use of land in the United States is subject to a variety of regulatory forms, depending in large part on where the land is located. The lack of a consistent set of federal policies regarding land use coupled with the presence or absence of controls at the state level means that the vast majority of land use regulations are local in origin. From a spatial perspective, this fragmentation presents a paradox. The great diversity of types and degrees of control implies a rich and varied regulatory surface while simultaneously making the understanding of this legal landscape that much more difficult to comprehend fully. From area to area and at the respective levels of governmental control, land use regulations exhibit considerable variation.

Those wishing to become fully versed in land use regulation will want to peruse some of the articles published in law journals. These articles discuss the pros and cons of certain regulatory devices and comment on recent court decisions. The field of land use regulation is far from static; it is changing constantly as new regulations are drafted, current regulations challenged, and old regulations implemented.

In addition, those interested in the application of land use regulations may want to become familiar with the planning and regulatory policies, programs, and tools currently being utilized in their respective state, county and local community.

Notes

1. "An Act for Prevention of Common Nuisances Arising by Slaughter-houses, Still-houses, etc., Tallow Chandlers, and Curriers," 1692–3, reprinted in J. H. Beuscher, R. T. Wright, and M. Gitelman, *Cases and Materials on Land Use,* 2d ed. (St. Paul: West Publishing Co., 1976).
2. See Beuscher, Wright and Gitelman, *Cases and Materials on Land Use,* for example.
3. R. H. Platt, *Land Use Control: Interface of Law and Geography,* Resource Paper No. 75–1 (Washington, D.C.: Association of American Geographers, 1976), p. 21.
4. Beuscher, Wright, and Gitelman, *Cases and Materials on Land Use,* p. 21.
5. For a comprehensive account of the development of zoning in New York City, see S. Toll, *Zoned American* (New York: Grossman Publishers, 1969).
6. 272 U.S. 365 (1926).
7. See especially, F. Bosselman, D. Callies, and J. Banta, *The Taking Issues: A Study of the Constitutional Limits of Government Authority to Regulate the Use of Privately-Owned Land without Paying Compensation to the Owners.*
8. Bosselman, Callies, and Bante, *The Taking Issue.*
9. D. L. Callies, "The Quiet Revolution Revisited," *Journal of the American Planning Association* 46, (1980) p. 142.
10. Callies, "The Quiet Revolution Revisited," p. 139.
11. Ibid.
12. For a discussion of legal description, see Platt, *Land Use Control: Interface of Law and Geography,* p. 4.
13. P. Davidoff, "Advocacy and Pluralism in Planning," *Journal of the American Institute of Planners* 31 (1965): 331–338.
14. R. M. Babcock, *The Zoning Game* (Madison: University of Wisconsin Press, 1966). R. R. Linowes and D. T. Allensworth, *The Politics of Land Use: Planning, Zoning and the Private Developer* (New York: Praeger, 1973); R. R. Linowes and D. T. Allensworth, *The Politics of Land Use Law: Developers vs. Citizen Groups in the Courts* (New York: Praeger, 1976).
15. Beuscher, Wright, and Gitelman, *Cases and Materials on Land Use,* p. 372.
16. For a collection of articles dealing with TDR, see J. G. Rose, ed., *The Transfer of Development Rights: A New Technique of Land Use Regulation* (New Brunswick: Center for Urban Policy Research, Rutgers, 1975); F. J. James and D. E. Gale, *Zoning for Sale: A Critical Analysis of Transferable Development Rights Programs* (Washington, D.C.: The Urban Institute, 1977).
17. See James and Gale, *Zoning for Sale,* p. 7.
18. For a description of land use control in Houston, see B. H. Siegan, *Land Use Without Zoning* (Lexington: Lexington Books, 1972).
19. For a pair of classic critical statements on regional planning, see C. M. Haar, "Regionalism and Realism in Land Use Planning," *University of Pennsylvania Law Review* 105 (1956–57): 515–37; W. J. Bowe, "Regional Planning Versus Decentralized Land Use Controls—Zoning for the Megalopolis," *DePaul Law Review* 18 (1968–69): 144–66.
20. Bowe, "Regional Planning Versus Decentralized Land Use Controls," p. 162.
21. Ibid.; Haar, "Regionalism and Realism in Land Use Planning."
22. "Findings and Declaration of Intent" accompanying Vermont's statutes, reprinted in Beuscher, Wright, and Gitelman,*Cases and Materials on Land Use,* p. 317.

23. Vermont Statutes Annotated, Title 10 (1973), Section 6086, "Issuance of Permit; Conditions," reprinted in Beuscher, Wright and Gitelman, *Cases and Materials on Land Use,* p. 320.
24. This phrase was coined by F. Bosselman and D. Callies, *The Quiet Revolution in Land Use Control.* Also see R. G. Healey, *Land Use and the States* (Baltimore: Johns Hopkins University Press, 1976); N. Rosenbaum, *Land Use and the Legislatures: The Politics of State Innovation* (Washington, D.C.: The Urban Institute, 1976).
25. Platt, *Land Use Control,* p. 13.
26. Hawaii Revised Statutes (1968), Section 205–2, "Districting and Classification of Lands," reprinted in Beuscher, Wright, and Gitelman, *Cases and Materials in Land Use,* p. 323.
27. Callies, "The Quiet Revolution Revisited," p. 142.
28. N. Lyday, *The Law of the Land: Debating National Land Use Legislation 1970–75* (Washington, D.C.: The Urban Institute, 1976), p. 1.
29. Ibid.
30. Ibid., p. 2.
31. Ibid., p. 2.
32. Platt, *Land Use Control,* p. 11.
33. See, for example, regulations developed to implement the Federal Land Policy and Management Act of 1976.
34. D. R. Mandelker, *Environmental and Land Control Legislation* (Indianapolis: Bobbs-Merrill, 1976).
35. Ibid., p. 16.
36. Ibid., p. 15.
37. Ibid., p. 17.
38. The Federal Water Pollution Control Act, as amended by the Clean Water Act of 1977, Section 208 (b)(2).

Selected References

Babcock, R. M. *The Zoning Game.* Madison: University of Wisconsin Press, 1966.

Beuscher, J. H.; Wright, R. R.; and Gitelman, M. *Cases and Materials On Land Use.* 2d ed. St. Paul: West Publishing Company, 1976.

Bosselman, F., and Callies, D. *The Quiet Revolution in Land Use Control.* Washington, D.C.: U.S. Government Printing Office, 1971.

Bosselman, F.; Callies, D.; and Banta, J. *The Taking Issue: A Study of the Constitutional Limits of Governmental Authority to Regulate the Use of Privately-Owned Land Without Paying Compensation to the Owners.* Washington, D.C.: U.S. Government Printing Office, 1973.

Bowe, W. J. "Regional Planning Versus Decentralized Land Use Controls Zoning for the Megalopolis." *DePaul Law Review* 18 (1968–69): 144–66.

Callies, D. L. "The Quiet Revolution Revisited." *Journal of the American Planning Association* 46 (1980): 135–144.

Davidoff, P. "Advocacy and Pluralism in Planning." *Journal of the American Institute of Planners* 31 (1965): 331–338.

Haar, C. M. "Regionalism and Realism in Land Use Planning." *University of Pennsylvania Law Review* 105 (1956–57): 515–37.

Healy, R. G. *Land Use and the States.* Baltimore: Johns Hopkins University Press, 1976.

James, F. J., and Gale, D. E. *Zoning for Sale: A Critical Analysis of Transferable Development Rights Programs.* Washington, D.C.: The Urban Institute, 1977.

Linowes, R. R., and Allensworth, D. T. *The Politics of Land Use: Planning, Zoning, and the Private Developer.* New York: Praeger, 1973.

Linowes, R. R., and Allensworth, D. T. *The Politics of Land Use Law: Developers vs. Citizens Groups in the Courts.* New York: Praeger, 1976.

Lyday, N. *The Law of the Land: Debating National Land Use Legislation 1970–75.* Washington, D.C.: The Urban Institute, 1976.

Mandelker, D. R. *Environmental and Land Control Legislation.* Indianapolis: Bobbs-Merrill, 1976.

Platt, R. H. *Land Use Control: Interface of Law and Geography.* Resource Paper No. 75–1. Washington, D.C.: Association of American Geographers, 1976.

Rose, J. G., ed. *The Transfer of Development Rights: A New Technique of Land Use Regulation.* New Brunswick: Center for Urban Police Research, Rutgers, 1975.

Rosenbaum, N. *Land Use and the Legislatures: The Politics of State Innovation.* Washington, D.C.: The Urban Institute, 1976.

Siegan, B. H. *Land Use Without Zoning.* Lexington: Lexington Books, 1972.

Toll, S. I. *Zoned American.* New York: Grossman Publishers, 1969.

Chapter 9

Economic Policy and Land Use

Glen W. Atkinson
University of Nevada, Reno

Introduction

For more than half a century there has been a general trend toward greater social control
of private land use.[1] This trend is surprising in view of the enthusiasm with which Americans
support the concept of unfettered private property. On the surface it appears that Americans
would want to avoid "government interference" in the use of a resource so vital as land. However,
our actions suggest we want to prevent or modify many of the consequences of private decisions
in land markets. As one resource economist put it " . . . nearly all land, regardless of ownership
has significant public good characteristics. This means that even if land is in private ownership,
individuals, other than the owner, are affected by the way land is used by the owner."[2]

The purpose of land use policy is generally agreed to be the reduction of negative external
effects and the enhancement of positive external effects that result from interdependencies among
land users. More recently there has been a growing concern over the provision and management
of public facilities to serve private land developments.

The discussion in this chapter will be limited to public economic policy that affects private
land use decisions, rather than management policy that affects public land by such agencies as
the Bureau of Land Management and the Forest Service. The focus will be on land use in urban
areas to highlight the spatial approach.

The appropriate level of government to exert social control over land use has been a major
issue of debate. Traditionally local governments have been more involved in the development of
land use policies than either the states or the federal government. State governments have not
been very active in land use planning, but with threats of federal land use planning legislation,
mounting regional as opposed to purely local planning issues, and increased concern for environmental issues, states have taken a more active role during the last decade. The federal government
has also increased its participation in land use planning with the environmental movement. However, some of the most important influences of the federal government on land use are indirect.
For example, taxation laws may have had a more profound effect on land use decisions than direct
land use policies of the federal government.[3]

Externalities as the Rationale for an
Economic Policy of Land Use

Economic policy is concerned with the efficient allocation of resources. Resources are means
of producing useful commodities or goods and are typically classified as land, labor and capital.
David Ricardo, one of the nineteenth century classical economists, implied that the quantity of
fertile land could never change when he described the powers of the soil as original and indes-

tructible. Resources are now considered to be a function of our knowledge of how to use them in the production process rather than as original and indestructible. Rivers can flood destroying production, or they can be useful for transportation, irrigation or electrical generation. Petroleum was not considered a resource before we learned how to use it. Thus, our resource base evolves with our knowledge.

Economists distinguish between free resources, which are abundant, and economic resources, which are scarce. If a resource is perfectly abundant its price will be zero causing us to exploit that resource relative to other more scarce resources. Until recently water and air were abundant resources to be used freely in the production of goods. As we exploited these resources, they became scarcer. The rising cost of air pollution regulation and waste water treatment has caused us to conserve these resources.

From the beginning of European settlement in North America until the closing of the frontier, land was an abundant resource. It was abundant relative to land per capita in the Old World and to other factors of production such as labor or capital in the United States. This relative abundance was reflected in the low price of land, and the low price was a signal to exploit the resource. It was responsible for the old adage of father to son, "Boy, by the time I was your age, I had already worn out three farms." Thus, economic resources are best understood in terms of relative rather than absolute abundance or scarcity. The purpose of an economic system is to organize production so that more of an abundant (cheap) resource is used relative to a scarce (expensive) resource.

It would seem then that the disappearance of an abundance of a resource, such as air, water or land, would force economizing through higher prices. With a smoothly working market there would be no need for an "economic policy." Then, why not let the market work to bring about an efficient solution? Many economists have argued that in the case of these basic resources there are market failures caused by *externalities.* Externalities result when significant benefits or costs are not reflected in market prices. In the case of air, no one owns the air so no market prices exist for its use. Thus, people acting in their own self-interest will use the air without concern for the social consequences. Factory owners will economize on the use of labor, but they will dump waste in the air unless public economic or legal action is taken. For water we cannot allow upstream users to reduce water quality downstream without bearing the consequences.

The cause of externalities is incomplete property rights. An example of incomplete property rights is air, which is a common property resource and not privately owned at all. Fisheries are another example of common property resources that are overused. The costs of overfishing an ocean fishery are social as well as private. Thus, international agreements are necessary to prevent excessive exploitation.

All external effects have two properties: interdependency—one person's behavior creates a cost or benefit to other persons; and lack of compensation—the one who creates cost is not made to pay for it, nor is the one who creates the benefit completely rewarded for it.

In every economic transaction, one party incurs costs in order to receive benefits. The other party receives payments and gives up goods and services. This demonstrates interdependence and closes the feedback loop. In an ordinary transaction, the purchaser is expected to pay the full cost of the item and expects to get full and sole claim to its use. For example, a homemaker who buys a loaf of bread expects to pay the cost and to get the full enjoyment from consuming it. Unfortunately, the feedback loops in economics do not always close this completely or this surely. Sometimes those who pay the costs do not receive all the benefits, and sometimes the payments made for an item do not cover all the costs of producing it. An example of the first type is the man who sprays his swampy backyard so mosquitos will no longer breed there. His neighbors receive some benefits (positive externality) even though they have not contributed any payments. An example of the later condition is the factory that dumps raw industrial waste into a nearby stream. It is not paying all the costs of doing business. Those who live downstream suffer the negative externality.

There are two policy approaches to deal with negative externalities. First, regulations can be imposed to limit or prohibit the use of resources. Second, tax penalities, user charges or subsidies can be enacted to provide an incentive to reduce the exploitation. Tax penalities or user charges can be tied to the amount of a resource used to take the place of a price in a private market. Similarly, subsidies can be paid proportionate to the reduction in the use of a resource. Legal regulations to deal with land use are discussed at length in chapter 8. In this chapter the emphasis is on the incentive approach. Economists prefer to rely on incentives rather than regulations. Regulations tend to be rigid and do not let economic actors make their own decisions within cost constraints. Tax penalities can be used to reflect the social costs of resource use. Private decisions can then be made in terms of total social and private costs.

It might appear surprising that an argument for public economic policy for land use is based on the concept of externalities caused by incomplete property rights. Property rights in land are usually thought of as absolute. An extreme example of externalities in land use is the location of a busy commercial airport in a residential neighborhood where surrounding property values will be reduced. In chapter 3 it was suggested that leap-frog developments generate social costs by requiring public infrastructure facilities to be extended to the fringe of the urban area. Positive externalities are often associated with the location of playgrounds or schools in a neighborhood. The costs of such facilities are paid for by general taxpayers, but some of the benefits are captured in the values of surrounding property.

The analysis in this chapter focuses on the development of policies that take into consideration social costs and benefits of land use decisions. This contrasts with much of the literature on land use policy that focuses on zoning regulations. There is the tendency to increase the potential density of a given area with a windfall accruing to the existing owners. However, if zoning is changed to reduce the potential density, property owners will contest the change arguing that their property has been taken. They bought the land at a price that reflected a high use and are no longer able to use the property in that fashion. It may be argued that the legal approach is too rigid, and more effective policy might be developed by using an incentive system.

One innovative approach is to treat zoning rights as collective property rights and to create market mechanisms to allow the developer to compensate the existing owners for the change in the zoning classification. It is argued that the property rights approach would provide more flexibility and less political manipulation.[4]

The property rights approach to zoning is preferred by those who recognize that regulatory agencies created to serve the public interest often end up as captives of powerful special interests.

Public Finance Aspects of Urban Sprawl

Many of the critical issues concerning externalities of land use are related to the changing spatial configuration of cities. This is not to deny that important conflicts exist between alternative uses of land in rural regions. For example, a decision to strip mine rich agricultural land in the western United States may result in a problem with serious public implications. Nevertheless, problems of externalities are most obvious in crowded urban environments. In fact, externalities are often termed "neighborhood effects." The problems of urban sprawl and leap-frog development have been addressed in previous chapters. Urban sprawl entails substantial social costs. Low-density land use causes high land prices, high transportation costs, and high cost for such public facilities as sewage disposal plants. In this chapter it will be shown how private market decisions and public economic action interact to create the urban sprawl, and what public economic policies can be used to slow or reverse the sprawl.

Populations of the central city have been declining for the last several decades. There has been a movement of people from the central city to the suburbs to escape the problems of city living. Many of the early suburban residents have also moved from declining rural areas. As residential growth occurs in the suburbs, business establishments and jobs have followed. When affluent people and business firms move out of the city, the city becomes less desirable causing property values to decline. Then people tend to move before property values fall further. As property values fall and business activity declines, the tax base shrinks and the city can support fewer public services. The quantity and quality of public services are a large determinant of private property values.

The free market model suggests that an equilibrium consistent with an efficient regional spatial allocation will be established because lower property values tend to attract potential users back to the city. However, it is more likely that a cumulative causation process is at work rather than a tendency toward equilibrium. As the city declines the affluent move and the poor remain. It may be argued that this mobility is desirable because it allows people to choose the level of public services they are willing to support by voting with their feet. However, because local governments are so dependent on local property tax revenues to finance local public services, this mobility leads to political fragmentation and tax competition among local jurisdictions, which in turn contribute to the fiscal crisis of some of our major cities. Each local jurisdiction attempts to capture high value property within its boundaries and to leave the social problems to the central city. Some state courts have recognized this trend in school finance and have declared that the education of pupils cannot be a function of the wealth of their parents or the district.

Tax competition to attract industry can be self-defeating for local governments. Tax levels are only one of the factors business firms consider when choosing plant sites. Relative tax levels are more important for intraregional decisions than for interregional choices. This is because the most important variables—resource availability, transportation and energy costs, and market potential—are more homogeneous within a region than between regions. In other words, everything else being equal, tax differentials can be decisive in a location choice. Rather than contributing to an efficient spatial allocation for the region, local tax subsidies are used to capture a tax base. Every city wants clean industry, but no city wants low-cost housing developments. Because each jurisdiction must engage in this competition, the regional tax base is smaller than it would be if the tax structure were to be used as a regional planning tool.

Land values and uses are affected by local government expenditures as well as taxes. One of the main determinants of the value of a particular site is its access to public services, especially public capital facilities. Industry prefers to locate where adequate capital facilities such as roads or sewers exist, but where it does not have to support such social expenses as welfare or education. The benefits from capital facilities are easier to capture in land values than the benefits of education because graduates often move to other labor markets. The decision of where to locate a highway or a sewer interceptor will influence the location of private economic activity and, therefore, land values. It has been proposed that placement of such facilities should not be merely demand responsive, but should be used to guide urban development.

Leap-frog development and urban sprawl result in higher costs of capital facilities than intensive, high-density land use. More miles of roads and sewer lines have to be laid per user. It also takes police longer to respond to a call in a sprawling city.

Private, decentralized market decisions and public actions interact to determine the design of cities. Public decisions of infrastructure development and placement can be made in a way that retains private choice. Private choice is commonly lost in the zoning process, but may be retained by rational public planning. Dick Netzer argues that zoning is not general, but highly specific.[5] It is not continuous as taxes or subsidies, but is a yes or no decision. The timing and placement of public capital facilities is often referred to as urban growth management. It is difficult to determine the ultimate population of a city or an urban region, but it is possible to influence the density and pace of outward spread.[6]

One of the proposed means to curb urban sprawl is to implement marginal cost user charges for the extension of public capital facilities to the urban fringe. The typical arrangement is to charge the average cost for the use of a sewer system. However, if it costs more for the *additional* or *marginal* facility than the existing system because of the sprawl, the new users will be subsidized by the existing users. Privately owned utility firms often use this pricing concept to string wire and poles beyond the mainline. Railroads can also use marginal cost pricing for spur lines, and developers can provide public streets within a development. Why not charge developers to improve access roads to the development? For example, shopping centers and suburban office complexes provide parking for their patrons, but they do not have to pay to solve traffic congestion on the access streets. If they did have to pay, this might encourage them to locate nearer an urban center. They would have to calculate the savings from cheaper land costs in outlying areas against higher costs of access roads. The public decision would not have to be yes or no, but yes if the developer pays the marginal costs of the development.

Such growth management techniques are frequently not employed because of political and fiscal fragmentation of the urban areas. Local jurisdictions have too much to gain from subsidizing by charging average costs rather than marginal costs. These are the same barriers that prevent rational regional planning through zoning.

The Property Tax and the Urban Fringe

Conversion of agricultural land to urban uses on the rural-urban fringe has been a major concern of land use planners in recent years. Transactions in this zone are the key to orderly urban development and the containment of the costs of sprawl. In addition, there is concern over loss of prime agricultural land and green spaces near the city. Historically, property taxes have contributed to the conversion of agricultural land on the fringe. Not surprisingly then, reforms in the administration of the property tax have been proposed and implemented to provide an incentive to maintain fringe land in agricultural use.

Before examining the reforms the logic and administration of the property tax will be explained since the present administration of the tax has been viewed as a substantial cause of sprawl. Because the property tax is a local tax employed in about 70,000 units of local government, many of which overlap, it is difficult to generalize about its administration.

First, property tax is levied on wealth and not income. This is a source of major concern and confusion. Wealth and income are related, but they are not the same thing. Wealth is a stock of assets that can generate a flow of income in the future, but not necessarily in the present. Both wealth and income are measures of the ability to pay taxes, but in extreme cases wealth may have to be liquidated in order to pay taxes. This is more often the case in a zone of transition from low value use to higher value use.

Property value is determined by the assessor to be its highest and best use and not its actual use. A property located in a neighborhood that is in transition from low-density, low-value use to high-density, high-value use is assessed at its highest value. The market determines the highest and best use. A farm located on the urban fringe is a low-density use which will have a higher market value as perhaps a residential subdivision. In other words, the stream of income is greater from the subdivision than from the farm. Thus, the market provides farmers with an incentive to sell. On top of the market force the property tax provides an additional incentive to sell since taxes will be levied on the highest and best use of the land as determined by comparable sales in the neighborhood rather than the actual use of the land. This illustrates the difference between wealth and income. Farmers might be wealthy because they own a valuable asset, but their income from that land is relatively low. They can only realize the potential income if they convert their land to other uses.

Taxes are levied on all property—real, personal and possessory. Real property consists of land and its permanent improvements. Personal property includes business inventories, household furnishings, and livestock. Mobile homes can be treated as real or personal property for taxation. Possessory interests include such valuable rights as leases of airspaces or mineral exploration rights. Some states require uniform assessment of all property, but most have allowed for differential assessment of one sort or another. There is a trend allowing for the exemption or low assessment of all personal property. There is also a tendency to provide special treatment for industries with a high capital to output ratio because property taxes fall heaviest on capital-intensive industries such as agriculture.

One of the most widely used means to decrease the impact of property taxes on agricultural land in the urban fringe is differential taxation of farmland. Maryland enacted the first differential assessment law in 1956, and now more than thirty-five states have some type of special assessment for farmland. With preferential assessment land is valued according to current rather than highest and best use, and no penalty is levied if the land is converted to another use. Under deferred tax law land is taxed according to current use value, but when the land is converted to an ineligible use a penalty tax is levied against the owner. Usually the penalty is the difference between market and use value for a number of years. This provides a payment to local governments when public capital facilities are needed to accommodate the development and serves as a deterrent to convert the land use.

The intent of these laws is twofold. First, there is a question of tax equity. Farms pay a higher percentage of their income for property taxes than most other industries because farming is land intensive. If farmers on the urban fringe must pay taxes as if the land were developed, there would be an incentive to develop the land. Between 1950 and 1972, the nation lost 6.1 percent of its taxable farmland. Although this loss is not substantial for a national land market, the loss is of great concern for expanding urban areas. During this same period, seventeen states lost more than 20 percent of their taxable farmland, nine states lost more than 30 percent, four states lost more than 40 percent, and two states lost more than 50 percent.

Preferential tax laws benefit speculators as well as bona fide farmers. Differential assessment laws attempt to distinguish between the two by levying a penalty payment on conversion. Some of the eligibility criteria used by various states to distinguish between the two are the proportion of the landowner's income from farming, family-owned farms rather than corporate-owned farms, land care practices, and zoning. There is an increasing recognition that two criteria—the proportion of income derived from farming and zoning of agricultural preserves—are the most effective tools for distinguishing between farmers and speculators.

Most observers of differential assessment laws have concluded that they have, at best, a marginal impact on land use. Their effects depend on the amount of tax saved by differential assessment. Tax savings depend on the degree of divergence between use and market value. The greater this divergence, the greater the potential gain from changing land use. In other words, market forces and tax impacts both work to encourage the conversion of agricultural land to urban uses on the urban fringe. Differential taxes merely reduce tax impacts, but do not affect market forces. The greater the amount of the tax saving, the more likely the land will be retained in farm use. However, since most programs are voluntary with respect to the taxpayer, a stiff penalty is likely to limit participation in the program, especially near expanding cities where land prices are being driven up by growth.

A very different approach to the use of the property tax as a tool to reduce urban sprawl was first proposed by Henry George in his classic *Progress and Poverty* a century ago. His solution to the inefficient use of urban land was to tax only land value and not the value of improvements. The logic of George's proposal was derived from the classical economics of David Ricardo and John Stuart Mill. The key to economic growth is the accumulation of real capital such as buildings, machinery and irrigation equipment. Accumulation of capital can be discouraged by heavy taxation of capital. Raw land, on the other hand, is a gift of nature and, therefore, its total value is fixed. Land can be improved by the addition of labor and capital. However, the landowner can withhold his underdeveloped or undeveloped land from the market until the price is right. Advocates of the use of a land value taxation believe withholding of land in the urban center for speculation forces developers to the urban fringe. Moreover, the taxation of improvements discourages the intensive use of central city land. This is one explanation for the existence of slums on valuable land. If land were heavily taxed, landowners could not afford to hold valuable idle or underutilized land in the central city. This would be reinforced by the removal of the property tax from improvements.

This proposal rests on the economists' definition of rent. Economic rent is income in excess of whatever is needed to keep a factor available for use in production. Pure economic rent is a surplus, or a payment greater than required to have the productive resources available. It is not what is popularly meant by rent; that is, payments made to property owners for land and improvements.

Because the total amount of land is fixed, the price of land is determined by shifts in the demand for land. In a growing city, as the demand for land rises the price of land increases. However, this increased price will not bring about a greater supply of land. If the land tax is low the rising price will encourage some people to hold their land idle in anticipation of even higher prices in the future. However, if the increase in the value of land is taxed away there is no reason to hold land for speculative gain. In fact, there would be a penalty for holding land idle. There is also an incentive to develop the land because improvements would not be taxed.

The arguments for land value taxation are based on equity and efficiency of land use. The equity argument is that most of the land value is a consequence of investment in public facilities and population growth rather than individual action; owners realize large increases in land values over time that are not the result of their own efforts. The community can thus justify recapture of this unearned profit by taxation to finance public facilities.

The land use argument for land value taxation is that land value taxation is neutral. It does not change land use incentives compared to no tax at all, because changing the use of the land does not affect tax liability. However, present property taxes applied to both land and improvements are not neutral. They discourage intensive development of land in favor of extensive development. Dick Netzer believes the land value tax would have the following beneficial effects on urban development. He claims that "it is likely that a switch to land-value taxation would encourage development most in two parts of the metropolitan area—in the central sections, on valuable sites where older and smaller buildings are now standing, and on the urban-rural fringe where landowners would be less likely to hold out for future speculative gains. Landowners would generally be under pressure to utilize their land or to sell out to others willing and able to better use the site."[7]

Land value taxation has not been widely used in the United States. It has been successfully practiced, however, in western Canada, Australia and New Zealand. Public officials in the United States fear that the loss of revenue from removing the tax on improvements cannot be offset by land taxes, although it has been estimated that land value tax rates of no more than 6 percent nationwide would replace the entire present tax on land and buildings.

Federal Taxes and Land Use[8]

Less attention has been directed toward the indirect effects of federal taxes on income and wealth on land use than has been focused on the effects of local property tax on land use. Federal taxation has indirectly affected land use patterns, although the various forms of taxation were specifically designed to raise revenue, not to alter land use. At the federal level these indirect policies are perhaps more important than the direct attempts to regulate private land use. Income tax law provisions tend to place a premium on a high valuation of buildings and improvements, which are depreciable, and a low valuation on land, which is not depreciable. Property taxes inhibit intensive land use where land is taxed relatively less than the structures on it. Federal taxation, however, has contradictory effects. The deductibility of property tax for income tax purposes reduces its inhibiting nature, whereas depreciation, mortgage interest deduction, and capital gains all tend to encourage expansive land use.

Depreciation

Accelerated depreciation methods stimulate construction through the conversion of ordinary income into long-deferred capital gains. These methods also encourage instability of tenure by causing turnover of properties so that the next owner, having reestablished the depreciable basis at the sale price, can repeat the process.

Depreciation tax laws result in "simultaneously encouraging slum deterioration in the cities and encouraging urban sprawl in the suburbs."[9] Depreciation tax savings create built-in incentives for quick turnover and minimum maintenance. They increase the supply of new building but prolong the life of the old.

Homeowner Benefits

Federal income tax laws that provide important concessions to the homeowner generally increase housing consumption (land consumption) relative to other less subsidized types of shelter. These tax advantages comprise three interrelated elements:

1. The exclusion from the concept of taxable income of the net imputed rental value (gross rental value less repairs, maintenance, insurance and depreciation)
2. The deduction from this narrow income concept of mortgage interest payments
3. The deduction of property tax payments

Capital Gains

Tax concessions in this area were designed primarily with the fluidity of organized capital markets in mind. This tax structure gives substantial incentives to land speculation when compared with other economic activities that generate ordinary income taxed at regular rates.

Internally inconsistent and inadvertent effects of the capital gains tax rules further complicate their impact on land use. The lower rate is designed to encourage market fluidity and willingness of owners to realize speculative gains once they have materialized and their rate of accrual no longer justifies further holding. But the potential exemption of unrealized gains means that it becomes advantageous purely for tax reasons to hang onto property beyond the otherwise advantageous time of sale. "The capital gains tax preference is thus brought into a competitive juxtaposition with a zero alternative rate rather than the higher ordinary tax rate."[10]

The freezing of land holdings for income tax-exempt transfer to heirs may block normal patterns of land use and community development for decades, creating artificial scarcities, higher land prices, and irregular patterns of sprawl and leap-frog growth.

Federal Taxes and the Urban Fringe

The two major federal taxes on wealth, capital gains and estate taxes may influence the timing of farmland sales for development on the urban fringe. The period following retirement is an opportune time to realize capital appreciation in order to avoid capital gains taxation. It is widely held that the federal estate tax forces farm families in metropolitan areas to liquidate their holdings at the time of death of the owners to pay their estate tax liability. If this is true it would be a factor in leap-frog development. Farmland sales do tend to occur between retirement and death. However, a recent study of the Baltimore metropolitan area concluded that personal reasons other than federal taxation determined the timing of land conversion.[11] In interviews with farmers it was found that although farmers are very knowledgeable about tax laws, the reason for selling was that their heirs were not interested in farming.

Concluding Observations

This chapter has not covered the economics of land use comprehensively. Instead it has illustrated how economic analysis can be applied to land use policy, and how economic policies such as taxation can have substantial unintended effects on land use patterns. Economic policy that directly affects land use is based on the principle of market failure due to incomplete property rights which generate negative externalities. These are negative effects on neighboring property as a consequence of the way a particular parcel of land is used. Zoning regulations are attempts to reduce negative externalities by preventing nonconforming uses. It has been argued that zoning laws are the creation of collective property rights to enhance private property rights. Since there is no mechanism to transfer the collective property rights created by zoning, zoning laws cannot adequately cope with land use problems in a dynamic community. This is perhaps the major difference between the economic approach and the legal approach to land use policy.

Land use can also be directly affected by planning the location of public facilities such as roads, sewer interceptors, or airports. Growth management advocates are paying a lot more attention to the interrelationships between private land use patterns and public capital facilities. One means to relate these two factors more directly is through user charges to finance the public facilities. The benefits to growth are obvious in their effects on employment, income and land values. However, many of the costs of growth have been hidden in our tax payments.

The property tax is still the major local tax, and its administration has major effects on land use patterns. Several property tax reforms have been proposed or enacted to reduce the effect of the tax on urban sprawl. One approach is to tax agricultural land at a lower ratio than other land as an incentive to maintain agricultural land on the urban fringe in its existing use. Another approach is to tax land at a higher rate than improvements to force intensive rather than extensive land use.

Federal environmental legislation adopted in recent years has had substantial impact on local land use patterns. This legislation has been supported by those who are concerned about the negative effects on the environment resulting from private land use decisions. Air and water are common property resources, but they are affected by how private land resources are used. On the other hand, the federal government has other policies that indirectly affect land use patterns that run counter to their direct policies. This was illustrated in this chapter by provisions of the federal income and estate tax laws. A serious evaluation of land use policy requires understanding of these indirect effects.

Notes

1. M. Clawson, "Economic and Social Conflicts in Land Use Planning," *Natural Resources Journal* (July 1975), p. 482.
2. E. N. Castle, "Every Body Has to be Some Place: The Role of Land in a Changing Economy," Paper presented at the Northwest Regional Economics Conference, Portland, Oregon, May 3, 1980, p. 5.
3. Ibid., p. 7.
4. R. H. Nelson, *Zoning and Property Rights* (Cambridge, Mass.: MIT Press, 1977).
5. D. Netzer, *Economics and Urban Problems* (New York: Basic Books, Inc., 1974), p. 169.
6. R. Wells, "Impact Zoning: Incentive Land Use Management," *Management and Control of Growth,* Vol. 4 (Washington: The Urban Land Institute, 1978), pp. 43–47.
7. Netzer, *Economics and Urban Problems,* p. 257.
8. Discussion in this section is based on R. E. Slitor, "Taxation and Land Use," in *The Good Earth of America: Planning our Land Use,* ed. C. L. Harriss (Englewood Cliffs, N.J.: Prentice Hall, 1974), pp. 67–87.
9. R. A. Levine, "San Jose, The Urban Crisis and the Feds," Paper presented before the Legislative Action Committee, U.S. Conference of Mayors, San Jose, California, May 15, 1972. Quoted in *Ibid.,* p. 79.
10. *Ibid.,* p. 83.
11. G. E. Peterson, "Federal Tax Policy and Land Conversion at the Urban Fringe," in *Metropolitan Financing and Growth Management Policies,* ed. G. F. Break (Madison: University of Wisconsin Press, 1978), pp. 51–78.

Selected References

Atkinson, G. W. "The Effectiveness of Differential Assessment of Agricultural and Open Space Land." *The American Journal of Economics and Sociology* 5 (1977): 197–204.

Clawson, M. "Economic and Social Conflicts in Land Use Planning," *Natural Resources Journal* 15 (1975): 473–489.

George, H. *Progress and Poverty.* London: K. Paul, Trench, 1889.

Hardin, G. "The Tragedy of the Commons." *Science* 162 (1968): 1243–1248.

Nelson, R. H. *Zoning and Property Rights.* Cambridge: MIT Press, 1977.

Netzer, D. *Economics and Urban Problems: Diagnoses and Prescriptions.* New York: Basic Books, Inc., 1974.

Peterson, G. E. "Federal Tax Policy and Land Conversion at the Urban Fringe." In *Metropolitan Financing and Growth Management Policies: Principles and Practices.* Edited by G. Break. Madison: The University of Wisconsin Press, 1978.

Slitor, R. E. "Taxation and Land Use." In *The Good Earth of America: Planning our Land Use.* Edited by C. L. Harriss. Englewood Cliffs, New Jersey: Prentice-Hall, Inc., 1974.

Social Sciences Course Team of the Open University. *The City as an Economic System.* Bletchley Books, Great Britain: The Open University Press, 1973.

The Urban Land Institute *Management and Control of Growth.* 4 vols. Washington: Urban Land Institute, 1978.

Chapter 10

ENERGY AND LAND USE

Martin J. Pasqualetti
Arizona State University

Introduction

Energy and land are two of the fundamental elements of human life. Survival and progress have long required a constant and continuous use of both. Moreover, the two resources are closely interrelated. Except in theoretical constructs, virtually all aspects of energy development and utilization have a land use component.

In earliest human times the development and use of energy resources took place in the same general location as their consumption. Examples of such patterns may still be found in the tropics and elsewhere. As industrialization has continued and cities have become larger and more complex, however, the distance between energy development and utilization has increased. As a result, the public tends to forget where energy comes from, and this is partly responsible for a dimmed awareness of the environmental repercussions of the energy quest.

Authoritative and compelling writings on environmental sensitivities and responsibilities have appeared through the years, but it was not until the recent environmental movement reached the public that an awareness of the land-based impacts of continued energy development and utilization developed. Energy supply and demand and energy dependence became key issues. Most countries redoubled their efforts at domestic energy development. These efforts are now being scrutinized by environmentalists.

The focus of much of the newly heightened awareness of energy and environmental matters in the United States has been in the western states. Boom towns in association with energy resources have developed in many previously unsettled areas of the West. Many of these developments are considered "intrusions" and unwelcomed threats to a way of life which has long been based on few people and plenty of open space. The number of clashes between those with dissimilar ideas about land use has increased. These clashes have played a role in publicizing many of the close interrelationships between energy and the land.

The public is now finding examples of the energy-land interrelationship almost everywhere. This relationship may be found during all phases of development and is most apparent in energy consumption. The fight over the Alaskan pipeline, the cancellation of the proposed Kaiparowits coal burning power plant in southern Utah, the relocation of the Inter-Mountain Power Project, the development of boom towns, the question of solar "rights," and the development of mass transit are just a few of the energy-land issues that have gained attention over recent years.

The interrelationship between energy and land can be complex because both energy and land are so fundamental to human activities. In order to simplify discussion as much as possible, the topic is divided into two principal parts. The first part describes energy development in all its phases. Most of the examples have been taken from the western states because the West is receiving the most attention in terms of energy and land, and because the West also presents the most promising opportunities to effect meaningful changes of policy toward energy and the land. The second part addresses utilization and focuses on the city because its basic form and function is a reflection of conscious and unconscious decisions about energy use, and because cities are the primary focal point in solving many of the energy-land conflicts, particularly through conservation.

Present Energy/Land Use Interrelationships

Resource Development

Several factors contribute to the amount of land required to develop a particular source of energy. An examination of each factor provides an organized way to discuss many of the relationships between energy and land, and serves to illustrate how much land is being committed to energy developments.

Energy Phases.

Energy reaches the consumer after seven phases of development (fig. 10.1). Each phase produces some impact on the land. Exploration produces the most widespread, if not the most significant, impact on the land because it takes place in so many areas. The impacts of exploration are particularly noticeable in the ecologically sensitive cold, dry, and coastal locations. In such areas the effects of exploration are long lasting, and even though the local scale of disruption may be small, these effects are often long standing.

Regardless of the method of resource removal, the extraction phase usually produces the most apparent impact on the land. With regard to oil and gas many of the impacts of extraction are a larger scale and more intense version of the effects of exploration. Extraction of coal and uranium, however, require completely different techniques than those used in the exploration phase. For all four resources, the impacts of access are much the same as the impacts of exploration.

The overall impact of the extraction phase depends on the resource and the area. Well pumps for obtaining oil require only a few hundred square feet, although the drilling rig, mud tanks, and other equipment temporarily require more land. Nevertheless a densely drilled well field may preclude some land uses. In the relatively isolated oil fields of Texas, Oklahoma, and the San Joaquin Valley of California there is little competition with the oil companies for the use of the land. In the Los Angeles Basin, however, urban expansion has overrun the wellfields, and both uses coexist in several areas such as at Seal Beach and Beverly Hills.

Coal is mined both underground and on the surface. The number of surface mines has steadily increased and the number of underground mines has steadily decreased over the past ten years. This trend has resulted from the development of shallow, low sulfur western coal mines. Substantial attention has been given to the environmental effects of strip mining in these arid and semiarid western lands, but underground mining as practiced in such places as eastern Pennsylvania and the Cumberland Plateau has also degraded the surface severely. Around Wilkes-Barre and Scranton, Pennsylvania, hundreds of piles of waste materials (generally slate and shale) called culm banks cover the landscape. In the Cumberland Plateau, devastation by mining and related activities is readily seen and has found clear expression in the writings of Harry Caudill.[1]

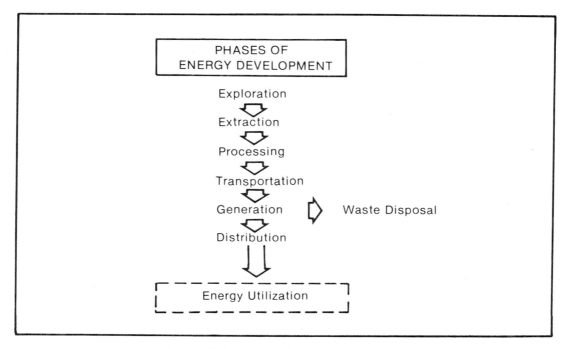

Figure 10.1. Phases of energy development.

Oil extraction and underground mines have often produced problems of subsidence, particularly in densely settled areas. For example, hundreds of insurance claims have been filed in eastern Pennsylvania because of structural damage to residences as a result of subsidence.[2] Although damage has been small in southern California, land surface atop the Wilmington oil fields subsided 28 feet as a result of oil extraction.[3] New techniques and remedial efforts have reduced but not eliminated the impact from such energy-related subsidence.

Probably the single most significant factor in establishing the long-term effects of energy development on the land will be the success and public acceptance of reclamation. Even with mandated reclamation procedures, which include separately removing, stockpiling and replacing topsoil, recontouring, revegetating, fencing, watering, and monitoring reclaimed land, hope for reclamation in western states is marginal at best. The National Academy of Sciences has concluded that in most areas receiving less than ten inches of rain each year, reclamation is impossible.[4] In those areas where some success has occurred, the revegetated species usually have not been native. This can be a critical consideration to people such as the ranchers in and near the Powder River Basin of southeastern Montana because their cattle-based livelihood is founded on native grasses.

Processing, which varies with the type and quality of fuels, is necessary before most fuels can be used commercially. Processing of coal and natural gas is relatively cheap and requires little land, but processing of oil and uranium is expensive and necessitates large land commitments. Refineries require land and access to supplies of crude oil. Larger facilities are located along coastlines and must compete with other potential users of shoreline sites. In addition to the land actually occupied by a refinery, odors, lights, flarings, and other common characteristics substantially affect surrounding land uses.

Uranium milling usually takes place at the mine site, but enrichment occurs at only three places: Oak Ridge, Tennessee; Paducah, Kentucky; and Portsmouth, Ohio. Enrichment facilities require tight security and prodigious amounts of electricity, which must be imported. Numerous transmission lines and facilities to generate the electricity both require land.

Transportation is important to several energy types. Large port facilities are needed for much of today's shipments of fuel. Oil and gas can be transported overland by pipelines. Railroads are also used to transport coal and liquid fuels. Construction and operation of most of these facilities preclude other land uses. In the case of pipelines, the land along rights-of-way may be used in nonpermanent ways, such as for grazing or agriculture.

Railroads have long affected land use both in rural and urban settings. In northern Arizona the 78–mile Black Mesa and Lake Powell Railroad from the Kayenta Mine to the Navajo Generating Station at Page passes through land owned by the Navajo Indians. Construction and operation of the railroad has disrupted the Navajo way of life. At least once the train has killed several dozen sheep, an almost sacred possession of these Indians. When trains pass through settled areas, they tend to affect urban forms and functions. Segmentation of cities by railroad rights-of-way is commonplace.

The amount of land disturbed at the site of generation again depends largely on fuel requirements. Power plants fueled by natural gas have the smallest impacts because the fuel is piped to the plant continuously. Oil-burning power plants usually require on-site storage tanks. Large areas are needed at coal plants to accommodate the blending of coals of differing characteristics. These areas are also used to store several weeks' supply of coal in the event supply from the mine is interrupted. Often this reserve is sufficient to fuel the power plant for 90 to 120 days. At the Navajo Generating Station near Page, Arizona, land for fuel storage and the rest of the plant totals 1,050 acres.

At nuclear power stations excess fuel is held on site only during refueling operations, but there are mandatory "exclusion zones" around the plant that tend to increase land needs. In addition, there are low-density zones beyond security fences. The site of the Palo Verde Nuclear Generating Station west of Phoenix, Arizona, encompasses about 4,000 acres although actual construction is confined to about 2,600 acres. Arizona Governor Bruce Babbitt, a member of the President's panel investigating the March 1979 accident at Three-Mile Island nuclear plant, has suggested an additional ten-mile "buffer zone" around nuclear stations such as Palo Verde.

Land use impacts from waste disposal are restricted primarily to coal and nuclear plants. Coal ash does not burn. The Black Mesa coal contains 10 percent ash. At full load the plant burns 23,000 tons of coal per day; thus 2,300 tons (minus about 10 percent, which is emitted through the stacks) must be removed to a disposal site. Because of its low value, ash is disposed of as close to generating stations as possible. At a mine mouth operation such as Four Corners, ash is dumped in the spent mine pits. At the Navajo plant (78 miles from the mine), the ash is trucked one mile to a 745-acre box canyon and dumped. A small portion of it is sold to a firm which uses it as pozzolen in making hydraulic cement.

In contrast to coal ash, which has only small proportions of intrinsically harmful agents, nuclear waste consists of materials that must always be handled with great care. The well-publicized absence of a waste disposal or reprocessing program in the United States means that the spent fuel assemblies are currently stored on site at each plant. There is a 17-year storage capacity at Palo Verde Plant (3810 mw). When the capacity here and elsewhere is reached, another plan needs to be made operational. Wherever the nuclear waste depository is finally located, surrounding land use will be directly affected because of necessary security measures and public apprehension.

Distribution corridors often involve more land than any other energy phase. In Arizona, two adjacent 345 kv electric transmission lines require a 330–foot right-of-way. This amounts to a disturbance of 40 acres per mile. The routing of high voltage transmission lines has for many years encountered public opposition. With the Clean Air Act and its amendments, the power plants are being located farther from load centers than ever before. In the case of the Navajo station, the total length of transmission lines is about 800 miles.

Time/Scale

The process of site selection for power plants involves the concomitant shortening of the list of possible sites while increasing the degree of data specificity needed for each site (table 10.1). In site selection, fuel, water, and land are the "classic" first-stage requirements. There is some flexibility in finding a balance between supplies of each, but tradeoffs cost money. Ideally, one would want a location that optimizes access to all three, such as a land parcel near a coal mine and a river. The Four Corners Generating Station in northwest New Mexico is an example of that situation. It is called a "mine-mouth" operation because the coal mine is immediately adjacent to the power plant. The San Juan River supplies cooling water.

After the first stage areas have been identified, a more detailed analysis is undertaken. Meteorological stations are established for air pollution studies, promising routes for transmission lines are determined, and the area's topography and demography are studied. The number of acceptable sites is reduced once again, and detailed ecological studies are conducted on these sites. Such a process usually yields more than one acceptable site, and the sites not chosen for a particular plant are kept in unofficial reserve as possible future sites. The realization that these alternate sites represent a valuable investment has led to the formulation of the concept of "site banking." Site banking is a means of shortening the lead times necessary to move from demonstration of need to on-line power.

Recent, Local Issues

Time-scale factors for facility siting have recently been influenced more strongly by several issues. These matters primarily involve air quality and nuclear safety, and in Arizona, water. Clean Air Act and Clean Air Act Amendments of 1977 designated certain areas as having Class

Table 10.1. Considerations in Siting of Power-related Activities

Time/Scale	Recent Issues
1. Fuel, water, land	1. Air quality
2. All of 1. + meteorology, accessibility, transmission lines, demography, topography.	2. Geology
3. All of 2. + ecology	

I or pristine air. Such lands include National Parks and Wilderness Areas. Some of these areas are actually below the Class I standard; therefore, they must be brought into compliance. Nothing may be done that will adversely affect air quality in these areas. Air quality, thus, is a critical siting issue. Even before the Clean Air Act Amendments, air quality had an impact on facility siting; for example, the Kaiparowits project was abandoned because of air quality concerns.

Another result of the Clean Air Act and its amendments is that coal-burning power plants are not permitted in smoggy metropolitan areas because these areas are usually classified as being "nonattainment" areas. This designation (from the Environmental Protection Agency) means that they do not meet certain standards set for any of several pollutants. According to the law, no further degradation is allowable in such areas. Such concerns for air quality have resulted in coal plant location ever farther from the load centers with longer and longer unit trains and transmission lines being required.

The construction of any additional polluters must be met by an off-setting decrease from another source at more than a 1:1 ratio (to allow for a gradual clean up of the air). The off-set provision of the Clean Air Act was exercised in the proposed location of the Long Beach (California) terminus of the SOHIO oil pipeline. The pipeline consortium agreed to reduce the emissions from an oil and gas burning power plant also located in the South Coast Air Basin. The issue became moot, however, when the pipeline was abandoned in early 1979 because of what was termed a "gauntlet" of required permits.

The Clean Air Act also requires a reduction of sulfur dioxide emissions, a goal that is usually met by the use of scrubbers. Such scrubbers require the mining of carbonate rocks. New lands will also be needed for the disposal of sludge produced in the scrubbing process.

Air quality issues are for coal plants what geological concerns are for nuclear stations. For a nuclear site, one must be able to *prove* that any nearby fault has not moved in 500,000 years. If this cannot be demonstrated conclusively, the site cannot be used. Together, the two issues of air quality and geology have become the most important factors in siting power plants. Their specific significance varies with location.

In Arizona and other western states a third consideration in power plant siting is the availability of water. Nuclear-generating stations have thermal efficiencies substantially lower than fossil fuel plants; 32 to 33 percent for PWRs (Pressurized Water Reactors) and 33 to 34 percent for BWRs (Boiling Water Reactors) compared to 40 percent for coal. Lower efficiency translates into greater cooling water needs. A typical PWR, such as the Palo Verde Nuclear Generating Station (PVNGS) under construction west of Phoenix, requires about 1,000,000 gallons/min/1,000 MW. In the arid and semiarid West the water requirement for a power plant is critical to the location of the facility. In the case of PVNGS, water is supplied by the Phoenix 91st Avenue sewage treatment plant and is transported to the site through large concrete pipes. It would not have been feasible to locate the power plant at its present location without such a source of water. A longer distance from the treatment plant would not have been within a practicable delivery distance.

The site for the coal-fired Navajo Generating Station in northern Arizona was chosen because of its nearness to Lake Powell. To have located the power plant at the coal mine would have required pumping water 78 miles. All such siting considerations affect the amount of land required by the power plant and the amount of nearby land that is affected.

Resource Types

Each individual resource has different land use implications (table 10.2). For example, neither solar electric nor geothermal energy requires traditional extraction, processing, or transportation. As a result the location and intensity of their impact on the land are substantially different from other types of energy. Even at individual sites of power generation, land use differences in fuel source are apparent (table 10.3).

Company Policy

Utilities have different policies affecting land use. All of them are required to adhere to applicable laws (e.g., reclamation), although reclaiming land mined before regulations became effective is a matter of company policy. Company policies also determine the size of coal stockpiles at power plants. In turn these policies affect the amount of land needed at the site. Many utilities (e.g., Union Electric of St. Louis, Missouri) have some power plant sites much larger than needed for their present equipment. Such land may be leased to farmers and will come within the fence of the power station only when expansion is required. Other companies follow a limited policy of "stockpiling" or "site banking" of potential sites by obtaining land or options on the land ahead of time.

Table 10.2. Resource-specific Land Use Considerations

COAL	Mining (surface, subsurface), Surface Transport, Ash and Sludge Disposal, Air Pollution, Storage Areas, Bulk of Fuel
OIL	Source (foreign, domestic), Ports, Refineries, Pipelines, Air Pollution
NUCLEAR	Complexity of Cycle, Safety Considerations/Regulations, Low Bulk Fuel, Waste Disposal, Security, Greater Cooling Requirements
SOLAR	Inefficiency, Pollution Free, No Extraction or Processing or Transportation, Site Flexibility, Variable Insolation, Concentrated Land Use, Storage
GEOTHERMAL	Site Specific for Electricity Production, No Extraction or Processing or Transportation, Concentrated Land Use, Dispersed Production/Injection Fields, H_2S Production, Subsidence, Induced Seismicity

Table 10.3. Land Uses at Generation Sites*

COAL	Storage, Mixing, Ash Disposal, Sludge Disposal
OIL	Fuel Storage
NUCLEAR	Exclusion Zones, Waste Storage
GEOTHERMAL	Production/Injection Fields
SOLAR	Panels, Storage

*All have generation equipment and cooling systems

Ease of Acquisition

Site acquisition may be affected by jurisdiction, ownership, price, and legal constraints. Examples of legal constraints are (1) zoning might not allow power plants or refineries; (2) the company may not own the mineral rights; and (3) the land may be federal or state owned.

Site Competition

Where the land is already developed or has been committed to a use such as wilderness, there may be severe constraints on the amount of land available. At the Navajo power plant, the size of the plant is completely constrained because additional, adjacent land is unavailable. In New York City where competition for land is keen and land prices high, the configuration of power plants is vertical rather than horizontal. Many federal lands, such as the national parks, are altogether off limits to energy development, although there is constant pressure to change this policy.

Demand

The demand for electricity stimulates reactions from those responsible to supply it in terms of base and peak loads, location, and concentration. Base load refers to the generation capacity always needed, that is, for refrigerators, clocks, safety lighting, and the like. This base load produces the minimum generating demand. Peak load often occurs in the summers and may be two to three times the base load. Generating capacity must include these peak demands plus a reserve margin. Other, lower peaks occur daily, usually in the morning and early evening hours. If the peak demand can be lowered, so too will the use of the land for several phases of electrical generation notably generation and distribution.

Utility companies must supply electricity where the demand is located. The location of demand in a general way influences where generation will take place. When the generation is close to areas of scenic or ecological sensitivity, the impact of supplying this power can increase. Demand in the Southwest and the concentration of electrical generating facilities in the scenic Four Corners area are testimony to that fact. In close proximity are the Four Corners, San Juan, Navajo, Hunington Canyon, and Craig power plants. The electricity generated by these plants is transmitted out of the area although the impacts of producing it are concentrated locally. Many of the recent battles over power plant siting have taken place in this region.

Site Characteristics

Because of the need for leveling and access, hilly construction sites usually result in more disruption of the land than flat sites, although restrictions of topography can sometimes mean a more efficient use of the actual land disturbed (e.g., building compactness in a mountain valley). In terms of local climate, a lower wet bulb temperature will reduce the area necessary for a cooling lake because evaporative cooling is more efficient under such climatological conditions. Development of energy resources on any ecologically-sensitive or ecologically-unique site will require careful planning. For example, a power plant to be located near a redwood forest usually stimulates more concern and adjustment than a site in a nondescript area of creosote bush.

Power Plant Operations

The primary mission of multipurpose hydroelectric facilities such as Glen Canyon Dam in northern Arizona is to control water. After this responsibility is met, power can be generated, but generally only during peak demands. Therefore, the capacity of the plant is never fully utilized. It takes two 1,000 MW Glen Canyon power plants to equal one conventional 1,000 MW coal-burning power plant. A power plant fueled by uranium also produces fewer kilowatt hours during a year than, for example, a sub-critical oil-burning power plant of the same rated capacity simply because nuclear plants are shut down more often.

Socioeconomic Factors

Energy-related socioeconomic impacts on the land result from boom town conditions. If, for example, a construction project requires 4,000 employees, most of whom will live near the construction site, this can mean 800 acres will be needed for housing (assuming five houses per acre and no other available housing). Land will also be required for school expansions, sewer facilities, streets, and other support needs.

One additional socioeconomic impact that has received no attention is migration *away* from an energy development facility. Some of these migrations can be called "forced," for example, those resulting when houses are within an area to be inundated by a hydroelectric reservoir, or a surface mining company owns mineral rights under houses, or subsidence occurs from fuel withdrawal, or a subterranean mine fire makes it necessary to remove all structures and dig out the burning coal. "Induced" migration occurs when people become displeased by the placement of power lines nearby or when they perceive some danger (e.g., radiation near a nuclear power plant). Many people have actually moved for all these reasons.[5] These migrants do not generally relocate in run-down, old, vacant buildings, but rather they relocate in other reasonably acceptable residential areas. In other words, additional housing is required in cases that occur either in sparsely settled land or a settled area that is gaining population. Such migrations involve land condemned at the beginning of the process and land required for resettlement. These land needs can be attributed to the development of energy resources.

Time Factors

An accurate assessment of land use impacts of energy developments must include more than appraisals at a given time. These impacts must also be viewed temporally. Energy-related land use may be considered as being concurrent, sequential, or precluded.

Concurrent land use occurs in Texas oil well fields where cattle are allowed to graze. In Beverly Hills, California, oil wells are camouflaged by false-front buildings. Electrical generation from geothermal resources in California at the Geysers and in Italy at Larderello continues concurrently with grazing and agriculture. The intense agriculture in the Imperial Valley of California faces little disturbance from the concurrent development of geothermal resources.[6] Grazing or cultivation beneath transmission lines and the use of power plant cooling lakes for recreation are two common additional examples. In such cases it is obviously difficult to calculate the actual amount of land that will be disturbed. In the aggregate the land actually is being utilized to a higher degree than if it were used for one purpose only. Neither activity hinders the other significantly. If it did, one or the other would presumably have to cease.

Sequential land use is possible with several phases of energy development. Some energy activities allow other uses once the energy activity has ceased. Sometimes this is termed "temporary" vs. "fixed" land use, and it depends on the time frame involved. The most common example is strip mining, which disturbs thousands of acres each year. However, the term "sequential" is applied when reclamation has been effected or is possible. The land overlying a coal reserve might be in forest, range land, agriculture, or housing. During the mining operation, all other uses cease. Upon reclamation, however, other uses, perhaps the original use, may be resumed. One of the difficulties about reclamation centers on the feasibility of recreating an environment identical with that which preceded energy development. In terms of appearance this is impossible because something has been removed, but some type of use, be it grassland, agriculture, or forest, can begin again. Sequential use for residential, commercial, or industrial purposes is easier. The greatest hesitation about the efficacy of strip mine reclamation lies in the West where ecosystems are fragile and slow to recover and in the Midwest (e.g., Indiana) where some of the country's best agricultural land is underlain by huge quantities of coal at shallow depths. This land is important in producing grain for export and is thus useful in countering balance of trade deficits. A policy decision must resolve the question: Should we grow crops for overseas sale to help offset our purchases of oil, or should we mine the coal to reduce our oil purchases in the first place?

In southeastern Montana many ranchers are opposed to strip mining of coal because of what they believe to be the impossible task of reestablishing native grasses, which are the keystone to the local cattle ranching economy. The coal companies do not claim success in such fine-tuned reclamation, although they have had some success coaxing the growth of other grasses. Without native grasses, ranchers claim their way of life, and the way of life of generations before them, is doomed.

Ancillary to the issue of native grasses in Montana is the general impact that mining has on the socioeconomic condition of the region. Mines and coal plants require workers. They in turn require land, services, roads, and the like. In many areas, such as around Colstrip, the once sparsely settled, open land is now covered with modular homes, roads, power lines, restaurants, taverns, and people. Sequential land use is possible there in a technical sense, but to many of the old timers, such land is ruined forever.

From the perspective of several decades, other types of energy-related sequential land use are possible. All land used for facilities such as power plants, refineries, and transmission corridors can be put back into full nonenergy utilization if the time frame is long enough and if no caustic or dangerous materials have poisoned the land. Thirty to thirty-five years is often given as a presumed life time of a power plant, and capital investments are amortized over this period. Presumably the facility could be dismantled and the land cleared for some other use. This has happened in the East, particularly in cities where land values are very high. On the other hand, it has happened rarely if ever in the West even though some of the generating facilities are older than four decades. The 30–35 year period is based on assumed refinements in equipment technology, equipment fatigue, and the law of diminishing returns on maintenance; but these facilities can still be serviceable, however inefficiently. Some old power plants, which are very inefficient to operate, may be utilized in times of unusually high demand.

Precluded land use occurs when land is removed from other possible uses essentially forever. Energy processes involving dangerous materials are usually at the root of such permanent removal. Nuclear-related activities are the most obvious. Uranium mines and mills, enrichment and fabrication plants, power generation facilities, waste disposal sites, and reprocessing equipment usually preclude any future use of the land. Nuclear waste depositories are the clearest example. Decommissioning of power plants and land clean up have actually occurred for test facilities. In general practice, however, these sites will probably be shunned for other uses.

Examples of nonnuclear activities that further preclude use of the land include the disposal of scrubber sludge or other hazardous materials, land destroyed by acid drainage, or slopes subjected to contour mining.

The complexities of determining the land impacts of our energy activities and decisions are summarized in figure 10.2. Each factor is important for understanding the interrelationship between land use and energy.

Resource Use

The previous section concentrated on the various processes and consequences of bringing energy to the consumer. The other half of the equation, energy use, also has significant impact on the land. Nowhere is this more apparent than in the urban landscapes.

The city may be conceived as being concentrated energy. Rural visitors feel the pulse of that energy as soon as they approach an urban area. It is more than their personal excitement. Automobiles, air-conditioned buildings, machinery of every description, scurrying time-is-money activities exude an excitement which is lifeblood to some and anathema to others. Little attention is given to the role continuous energy supplies plays in the daily lives of the millions of urbanites who eschew country life for the conveniences, the excitement, the energy of the city. Nor do many city dwellers often think about the source of the energy they use. The mines, wells, refineries, enrichment plants, and generating stations which give the city its life are usually out of view or at least out of mind. What is important to city dwellers is continued high levels of productivity.

If few ever wonder about the source of the city's driving force, fewer pause to consider the influence energy has on city configuration or form, house types or population density, sprawl or transportation.

Transportation, particularly the automobile, often receives blame both for urban sprawl and high energy consumption. However, one cannot place the entire burden of our energy problems on transportation. It is much more complicated than that. Some of the most significant influences are the location of the cheapest and most likely to be developed land, and the location of the nearest freeway. There is no specific causative energy explanation for this pattern of development because there has been no integrated consideration of the land use and energy implications of such decisions on a consistent and meaningful or effectual scale. Planners will, of course, claim that energy, particularly that consumed for transportation, has indeed been considered in locational decisions, but the impact of this consideration has been very minor. Planners, like everybody else, have been used to thinking in terms of unlimited resources.

Even in California, which requires, under the California Environmental Quality Act, the consideration of energy implications as part of every Environmental Impact Report, sprawl continues unchecked and total energy is used in ever more copious amounts. It is doubtful if any project in California has been abandoned because of energy costs. Certainly some projects have received more energy consideration with regard to building design—that is required by California state statute—but little has been done on the smaller-scale problem of population densities, urban sprawl, single-passenger vehicular transport, or anything related to changing city forms or transportation patterns. On the contrary, the momentum of the pre-energy crunch days is still strong.

The "move to the suburbs," almost synonymous with "sprawl," has been motivated by many things, but one of the most significant has been the desire for a greater feeling of space. The farther out one moves, the greater the per capita expenditure for energy.[7] Single-family dwellings

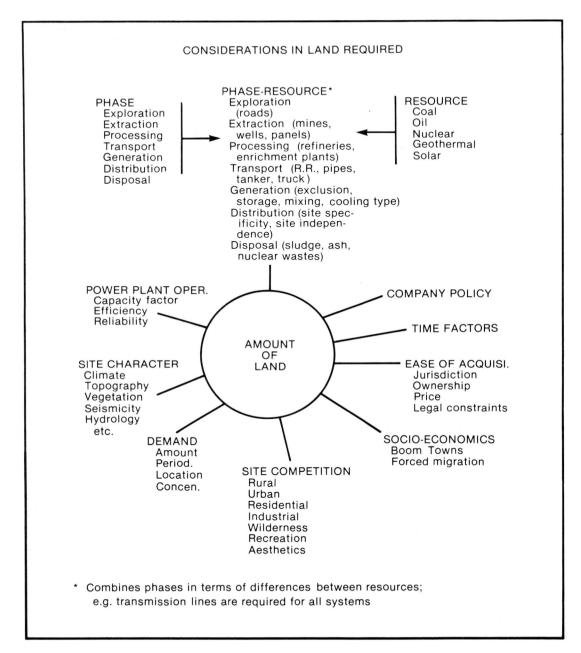

Figure 10.2. Considerations in land required.

with substantial setbacks and large yards are characteristic of developments away from the higher land values of the central city. Lower suburban population densities have been a direct function of this move to more spacious surroundings. Thus, not only is there more energy used commuting to work for those living in outlying areas, there is also more energy consumed fulfilling other daily, nonwork travel needs.

Many of the relationships between sprawl and energy have been documented in a study by Real Estate Research Corporation.[8] It reported that "low-density sprawl" consumed 80 percent more energy than "high-density planned" development (4,059,787 *vs.* 2,257,400 billion Btu/year). Intermediate densities such as "planned mix," "combination mix" (i.e., 50 percent PUB [Planned Unit Development], 50 percent sprawl), "sprawl mix," and "low-density planned" consumed intermediate amounts of energy. Calculations were made for natural gas, electricity, and gasoline. These relationships are graphically portrayed in figure 10.3.

In large measure our high suburban energy consumption and the sprawl itself are representative of an overall tendency toward nonintegrated city functions. Uses of the land for housing, industry, recreation, business, commerce, entertainment, and education are usually disaggregated. This is a result of a combination of planning premises and business practices and can make sense from certain perspectives (e.g., market studies), but does not necessarily make sense in terms of energy. The energy used to get from one function to another can be called "interstitial," and such energy use should be a key factor in deciding whether major land uses should continue to be segregated geographically.

One of the important nonenergy factors in a decision to reverse such a pattern is that of aesthetics. The result "may mean locating industries in areas now reserved for residential and recreational uses."[9] Even in today's world of energy insecurity, such considerations as aesthetics and convenience still carry weight. But this may not always be so.

Means of transportation have played a large part in the establishment and early patterns of many cities. Everyone has seen pictures of linear cities which have grown up along railroads and have spread away from them only later. Although historical studies reveal such a beginning for many cities in the West, all the major cities have gone beyond that by now. The railroad is no longer the noticeable influence on urban form it once was. Its niche is now occupied by the car and truck which have stimulated a very strong tendency for the horizontal spread of many western urban areas.

Urban sprawl of course is found throughout the United States, but it is in the Southwest that one finds its clearest examples. Many of the cities have experienced virtually all their areal growth since World War II, and they have relatively low-density core areas. These cities have grown with the rise in personal transportation. In western cities there are few rapid public transit systems. Western transportation systems are based on the car, and the only limit to how far people might live from work or recreation or entertainment has been the time they are willing to spend driving. With freeways a typical western urbanite might drive 35–40 miles to work.

In the vast Los Angeles Basin spaces between several once isolated and autonomous towns such as Pasadena, Anaheim, Long Beach, Santa Monica, and Los Angeles have been filled with housing in response to the expansion of controlled-access urban transportation networks. Commuters drive to work without worrying about side traffic. A driver need not think about stopping, starting, or turning. The freeway offers both a faster and more relaxed means of commuting. Of

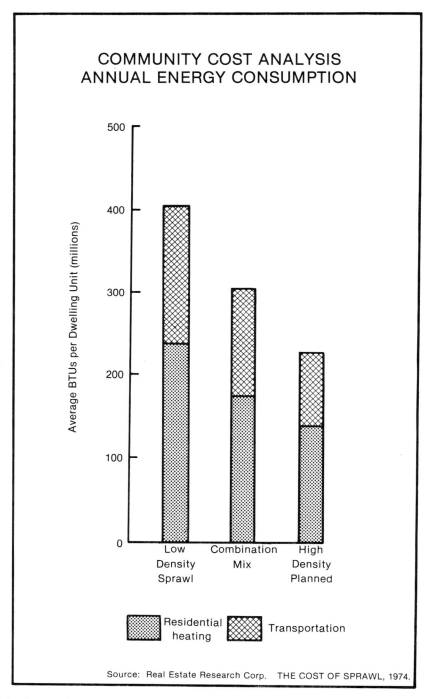

Figure 10.3. Community cost analysis, annual energy consumption. (From *The Cost of Sprawl,* Real Estate Research Corporation, 1974.)

course overuse during rush hours has challenged those advantages. However, even if the car nowadays does not get people very far very fast, it does represent isolation, privacy, and freedom. There are no telephone calls, no questions, no demands. The average driver is loath to abandon such amenities. This is the basic explanation offered for the scarcity and ineffectiveness of car pools. Using private cars has become established, and like all habits it is difficult to break.

Abundant energy has allowed a close dependence on the automobile and the automobile, in turn, has made sprawl possible. Urban expansion has been a product, more than anything else, of cheap and abundant energy. Now with talk of gas rationing and with the cost of energy becoming an ever larger expense to the typical single-car commuter, people in places like Los Angeles are bewildered and angered at the prospect of not being able to get to work or to other destinations.

Ironically, urban sprawl, which cheap energy made possible, has also made it very difficult to justify economically any form of more sensible urban mass transit. Even when rapid transit is available, it is not utilized by high numbers of people. Where it has been tried in western cities, it has generally failed, partly because housing densities are so low and partly because people in such low-density urban areas still have to drive their cars to transit stations. When they arrive, they are faced with finding parking places at the station.

The experience of the San Francisco Bay Area Rapid Transit (BART) system is an example of this response. BART has had troubles from the beginning even though San Francisco is relatively densely populated. Part of the problem has been that few stations are in the city where the highest densities are, whereas the greatest number of stations are in more sparsely settled suburbs.

If the BART system were transferred to a city such as Phoenix, which has a comparable population but seven times the land area, the hopelessness of the situation becomes even clearer. Moreover, San Francisco has no available land to annex while Phoenix continues to add to its landholdings. The problems of moving people within Phoenix and between Phoenix and its surrounding communities are constantly worsening as exemplified by a current bitter dispute over the routing of Interstate 10 through the area. Part of the routing issue involves the fear of some citizens that an ugly scar will be thrust down the middle of their town. Even in the face of rising gasoline prices and falling supply, no one is seriously talking about in-filling or increasing downtown densities.

Transportation is the largest single user of energy in the United States. Over half the oil consumed (one-half our total energy use) goes for transportation. Cutting transportation consumption by one-half would reduce our oil imports by four million barrels per day, an amount equivalent to over $120 million per day or about $43 billion per year. In other words, there is substantial logic in reducing our transportation-sector energy consumption. One way to do it is through the implementation of energy-conscious, publicly-supported land use schemes, for example, cluster housing and taller buildings. Several schemes are needed simultaneously; no single strategy will work.[10]

Future Implications

A heightened awareness of the close relationship between land use and energy will occur in the future. Conflicts will result from a rise in the relative importance of energy matters in our daily lives, development of alternative resources, intensified search for diminishing fossil fuels, development of new types of fossil resources, greater economic cost of energy, concerns about national security, political motivations, limited energy-related resources such as water, larger commitments of land, rising importance of energy matters in industrial location, and promulgation of planning ordinances and statutes.

Changing Emphases

There is no doubt that energy has become the focal point of our society. Whereas in the past energy was only one of many factors in residential, transportation, commercial, and industrial decisions, today it is becoming the most significant factor. We will have to begin to consider the impacts of rising costs of energy, lowered per capita availability, reduced but continued population growth, slowed but increasing energy demands, rising significance of energy matters in all phases of the economy, political implications of an increasing reliance upon foreign governments for fuel, and all the other impacts that result from a rising demand for a finite commodity.

The impacts on rural land have thus far received greater attention than those within cities. Furthermore, the impacts of energy developments have been discussed mostly on purely environmental grounds. This has tended to disconnect them artificially and unrealistically from land and land use. Such perceptional and attitudinal patterns, however, are shifting. In a country based on continued economic expansion the finite nature of nonrenewable resources must be a concern. This is particularly true in the case of an integral resource such as land.

The greater significance of energy for the short term can be adjusted by enforcing "automatic" conservation through development of more efficient appliances and automobiles. Such actions will slow the rate of land disturbance, but each increment of more efficient resource use, whether it be energy or land, renders the next increment slightly more difficult to effect.

Industrial location is another indicator of energy/land considerations. Prior to the Arab boycott of 1973–74, energy was just one of the factors in location decisions, generally ranking behind raw materials, markets, transportation networks, communication, and perhaps a couple of other factors.[11] Except for the very heavy energy users such as the electrolytic industries and paper manufacturers, energy rarely influenced industrial location significantly. Today energy availability, as well as price, is having a heightened impact.

Future Disruptions from Developments

Most plans for new energy supplies involve western energy resources: low-sulfur coal for stripping and liquification and gasification, oil shales, tar sands, solar, and geothermal. Development of any of these resources will affect land that is sparsely populated and that supports much more fragile ecosystems than those of eastern states. A National Academy of Sciences study used the words "national sacrifice areas" to refer to the western resource lands because of their ecological fragility.[12] The same study suggested 140 square miles of the West would be disturbed by 1990 and 300 square miles by the year 2000 because of the development of energy resources. Although this is a relatively small amount of land compared to the over 1 million square miles found in the western states, disruption will be unwelcomed by many of those living in or with a stake in the sacrifice areas.

Two key considerations will be important in determining the type and extent of land impacts resulting from future energy-related activities: (1) the effectiveness of energy conservation efforts, and (2) the type of energy resource developed. Energy conservation is probably the most sensible and direct way to slow the increase in energy demands in the future. In terms of the land resources, more can be preserved by saving a Btu than by developing one. This is true because of the indirect manner by which energy, especially electricity, comes to the consumer.

With regard to the land impacts of two types of future energy sources, neither geothermal nor solar requires traditional mining, processing, or transportation. All the land use impacts (except for transmission) are found at the site of generation. In the case of solar energy there is not even the worry about air pollution that has sometimes plagued the development of geothermal energy. Geothermal power plants must be placed at the site of the resource, whereas solar devices can be placed virtually anywhere. Therefore, in the development of solar energy, facilities can be placed as near an urbanized area as land prices and availability permit. Their location is not constrained by bulk fuel transport, and transmission lines are much shorter than those common for western coal-fired power plants.

Calculations presented elsewhere[13] show that the total amount of land required for the operation and supply of a coal-fired power plant (including coal mine, railroad, power plant itself, evaporation ponds, ash disposal, and transmission lines) need be no greater than for a solar photovoltaic power plant of comparable generating capacity.

If the option is selected for a community solar grid system or an individual solar array (assuming technical and economic feasibility), there is enough roof area in the southwestern cities to accommodate collector/conversion devices. As an example, the United States Army has recently constructed a building on its Yuma Proving Ground near Yuma, Arizona. This two-story, 78,000 square foot building will be completely heated and cooled by solar energy collected from an array of parabolic-trough concentrating devices. The array is equivalent in area to one-half the roof. In other words the system will require one-quarter the roof area of a one-story building or all of the roof area of a four-story building. Most buildings in southwestern cities have less than four stories. Such low density, low-profile housing is, therefore, amenable to the use of solar equipment similar to that installed near Yuma. The urban land use pattern of the southwestern city is an aid to solar energy development and use, while it is the nemesis to development of energy efficient mass transit systems. In addition to concentrators, many other possibilities exist to conserve energy and land such as passive architectural design, ponded roofs, and rock bin storage systems.

Future Energy Resource Development

Large amounts of geothermal energy are found in many areas of the West. Some significant reservoirs underlie Phoenix, Tucson, Las Cruces, and Albuquerque. Direct, i.e., nonelectric, use of these resources for space conditioning should be possible on a large scale. Such technology has been developed and used in many other areas of the world and is now receiving increased attention in the United States. Direct utilization of these resources does not require large amounts of land for mining, processing, generation, transmission, or waste disposal. Of course, the use of geothermal energy would not satisfy needs that are purely electrical, but it would meet the greatest demand for energy. It has been estimated, for example, that about 75 percent of the residential/commercial energy use of Maricopa County (which includes Phoenix) can be supplied by geothermal energy.[14]

Even if geothermal energy is developed for electricity (thus requiring more land for centralized equipment), the land affected per megawatt would not be great, i.e., less than 1 acre/

MW.[15] This level of disruption should be compared to an average of 10 acres/MW of land disturbed directly by the four coal plants in Arizona.[16]

With regard to oil shale and tar sand development, a new device may substantially reduce the impact on the land. Developed for Texaco, it involves the use of radio-frequency electric fields to induce the release of oil and gas without the heat or the water requirements of conventional methods. If this procedure proves to be practicable, development of oil shale resources will not produce the environmental devastation which heretofore seemed inevitable.

Such a process would be *in situ*; i.e., it would take place underground where the rock is located. The trend in the development of coal gasification is also for an *in situ* process. Plans have also been considered to place nuclear stations underground. This tendency toward underground energy developments will have a substantial ameliorating effect on potential land use impacts.

Even fuel transportation in the future may require less land. Coal slurry lines will become more and more common. Currently there are only two in operation in the United States, the longest of which, 273 miles, is in Arizona. Many others have been proposed, and their operation will remove the need for rail lines and will exchange precluded land use for more acceptable concurrent land use. Slurry lines will also reduce air pollution from the blowing coal.

The possible benefit of reduced land use impacts from future energy developments must still be balanced against the realities of future energy demand and the current pattern of large land commitments. Coal mines are increasingly on the surface, power plants continue to be located great distances from load centers, off-shore drilling is increasing, and the need for coastal facilities for docking and refining is on the upswing.

Significance of Urban Planning

The impact of energy-focused land use planning will be most firmly identifiable with regard to population densities, transportation regimes, city form and function, and the implementation of soft and distributed energy technologies. Virtually no lasting process can be expected in cutting energy consumption or reducing impacts on the land without effective attention to these four topics.

In terms of the first three, the focus is on different levels of consumption as a product of different land use patterns. For example, the most common existing urban pattern has the major land use sectors—residential, commercial, industrial, public service, and transportation—segregated geographically. People use a lot of energy just getting from one urban function to another. These facts suggest that the pattern of consumption can be altered by changing the pattern of land use.

Few cities still have abundant vacant peripheral land. Phoenix is one exception, but in Los Angeles most of the land within a reasonable commuting distance has already been developed. The expected emphasis there and elsewhere will be toward infilling. In areas such as Phoenix infilling will occur slowly unless it is required in some way, in which case it will increase residential densities and reduce collective commuting distance and the need for the further expansion of utility distribution facilities. Residential density has increased on a limited scale in San Francisco. The city is completely limited in its lateral expansion. As a result high rise apartment buildings have replaced lower buildings in the downtown areas. This has increased the Btu/acre consumption and reduced automobile commuting.

In a study of Tucson, Arizona, it has been calculated that reconstitution of patterns of horizontal expansion and leapfrogging, plus a move toward higher densities and consolidation of city functions, would result in an energy savings of 40 percent over present consumption.[17] A similarly high savings can be expected for many cities in the Southwest.

Until very recently energy has not been considered important to urban design. Even today it rarely receives direct attention. Given an assignment of designing a city with energy as the primary consideration, such designers address the importance of reducing or eliminating the use of the automobile. Often plans are based on a circle, with main spokes representing mass transit facilities.

Clearly the energy-efficient transport of people in urban areas remains one of the great planning challenges. In order to reduce the amount of fuel consumed, trips must either be made more efficient or shorter. In terms of efficiency, the federal government has mandated a timetable for certain gas mileage improvements. The other primary means of higher efficiency is mass transit. Making trips shorter can best be effected by planning the integration of city functions. Ultimately, higher fuel costs might produce the same results. By that time, however, great unwelcomed adjustment in living styles will have taken place. In such a scenario, most driving will cease and mass transit will be the only solution; distances will be too great for walking and bicycling. Given an alternative, citizens will probably voluntarily live close to work, recreational facilities, and so forth. This change may already be occurring.

Great residential energy savings can be realized by responsive planning. However, reduction of residential energy use suffers from the same restriction as does the reduction of transportation consumption and reformation of urban forms and functions. This restriction can be called the "residential inertia," which means that in the future a vast majority of people will live primarily in those areas where they are now located. No new giant or even moderate-sized urban areas are likely to develop. There may be some expansion of the present areas, albeit slower than in the 1950s, but with few exceptions the expansion will occur in areas already established. This means that any measures or commitments taken to save energy will entail a new "three Rs": Retrofitting, Renovation, and Remodeling.

The first "R" entails the installation of energy-saving materials (e.g., insulation) or the incorporation of equipment to allow the use of newer energy sources (e.g., geothermal). Renovation entails bringing back into more common use those structures with energy-conservation construction. Remodeling is the active restructuring of the architecture of energy-wasteful homes.

The need for the three Rs must be considered when calculating the potential energy savings of "soft" energy technologies. Soft energy paths include renewable (e.g., solar), long-term non-fossil (e.g., geothermal), conservation, and passive (architecture and landscaping) technologies. One additional soft path involves the achievement of greater efficiencies in the current modes of generating electricity. One of the many ways to do this is by cogeneration. Essentially, cogeneration involves the use of waste heat in another turbine for space conditioning or industrial processes. For coal-fired power plants this will usually not be possible because of the great distances between them and possible heat users. Oil, gas, and nuclear generating stations should be encouraged or specifically directed to locate near these plants. To encourage cooperation, the generating station should be planned and designed with the assured useful application of waste heat as a key part of the permitting procedure.

There are many potential stumbling blocks in the way of developing "soft" energy paths, especially in urban areas. Little *et al.*[18] have suggested that one of the great problems in the development of *current* energy resources has been a conflict between Aldo Leopold's "land ethic" (i.e., responsibility for the land) and a desire for energy independence. The implementation of "soft" energy paths should reduce this conflict because it poses less of a threat to the landscape. However, other obstacles would undoubtedly be in evidence. The political, legal, and institutional hindrances are most significant. First, we do not really know the characteristics of future energy demands, nor do we know the extent and the location of new energy and land developments. Secondly, local and state statutes could prevent some of the necessary steps to soft energy utilization. Thirdly, lending institutions may be reluctant to finance structures considered to be "avant garde," even if they are part of an overall, approved plan.

The look of the city could be substantially altered by the large-scale utilization of soft energy technologies. In the case of solar development, access rights should preclude shading of another collector; roofs should be adaptable to the useful installation of solar devices; east-, west-, and south-exposed windows should be shielded from direct solar rays; and the cooling effect of an irrigated landscape should encourage the abandonment of desert landscaping. Street patterns and building design should be primarily a function of average solar positions rather than of maximization of the number of housing units on a parcel. Years of public education and assurance should be an important part of "selling" such structures. Meanwhile, as these processes are underway, old practices will continue to inhibit fulfilling the goal of soft energy utilization.

Because many of these paths require great commitments of land, it has been said that "energy demands have been converted to land use demands. As such, these activities must compete with all present and projected land use activity and become subject to the broad range of economic, political, social, and institutional constraints traditional in governing the use of land."[19] Thus, it appears that even though implementing soft energy sources lends itself to the three Rs, it will only be through proper planning that a meaningful proportion of their potential will be realized.

Without knowing the future energy sources and the land to be developed, or the particular form and extent of consumer demands, or the response of consumers to rising energy costs and decreasing energy supplies, how the changing emphases within the broad category of energy matters will influence city shapes and functions is speculative. However, if we assume that the future will include the exercise of a reasonable amount of common sense, we can suggest two possibilities. The first possibility is that inner cities will continue to experience the slow renovations which began prior to recent concerns about energy. Such trends will continue to be largely motivated by fashion, but they may also be encouraged by practical considerations of energy. These renovations will accompany in-filling and other activities which collectively will increase population densities and reduce interstitial energy consumption.

The second possibility is ironical; that is, the urban form that tends to favor the development of alternative energy sources such as solar will also favor a continuation of the move toward the suburbs and beyond. The rapidly expanding southwestern city is so spread out that it provides ample space for solar collectors both in vacant lands and on low rise housing. Moreover, the technique of retrofitting existing buildings in southwestern cities, in contrast to retrofitting existing buildings in slowly growing urban areas, is relatively less significant to energy conservation than is the simpler procedure of installing devices on all new buildings.

Southwestern cities have two opportunities to adjust land use for energy conservation. Inner city areas can be renovated and filled in, and the areas of rapid growth can be designed to be energy efficient. In areas where neither of these possibilities exists, meaningful energy-land use savings will be low.

Planning Possibilities, Mechanisms, and Encouragements

City planning that integrates energy considerations is still a rarity. Several steps must be taken before it becomes more common. First, there must be a heightened awareness of land-energy interrelationships and their significance. This new awareness is usually not difficult to achieve at the conceptual level. For example, planning directors and energy officials are generally willing to listen to a new approach which promises to make their jobs more effective and efficient. Second, cooperation between these officials and developers, politicians, and private citizens must be obtained. This cooperation may be achieved initially through establishment of an advisory panel.

The subsequent steps are often subsumed under the rubric "realities" or "practicalities." "How," the question usually goes, "are you going to acquire the necessary legal tools to effect any significant change?" The best response suggests two dicta: start early and use existing channels.

Starting early always seems good practice, but such new efforts, at least for the local agency, usually result in a shift of personnel from some other activity. It is always difficult to find funding for new staff. The most likely source for such new funds is the federal government. The Department of Energy, the Department of Transportation, and the Department of Housing and Urban Development are the most obvious sources. They have funded several exemplary planning efforts that are firmly founded on energy considerations. Such funding, if it is directed toward the state or substate level, will eliminate the many problems inherent in an attempt at national planning.

The initial planning should be in cities that are representative of many others in order to allow transfer of methodologies and results. Appropriate first choices include one densely settled northeastern city, with mass transit, and a slowly growing population; and a southwestern city with opposite characteristics.

Planners need to be aware of new energy sources as they are developed. Their plans need to be flexible enough to take advantage of technological breakthroughs as they become available. One example of an imminent breakthrough is the photovoltaic cell. Government timetables seem to be essentially on schedule with regard to producing an economic, commercially viable solar cell by 1987.[20] It is apparent that land use adjustments will be necessary before solar cells can be used on a large scale.

Planning has to begin immediately to resolve some of the inevitable *land use* impediments to the implementation of such devices. For example, many problems will need to be resolved including solar rights, setbacks, roof orientation, uniformity of brackets, standardization of testing procedures, reliability, ordinances requiring their use, city configuration, collector areas, patterns of deployment, scale of use, ownership, utility involvement, and architectural review, to name just a few.

Some states have already passed laws to ensure solar access. Those states are California, Colorado, Connecticut, Florida, Georgia, Idaho, Kansas, Maryland, Minnesota, New Jersey, New Mexico, North Dakota, Oregon, and Virginia.[21] The statutes vary in how they address the specific issue of land use, and of course solar access is a fairly specific problem.

The use of existing legislation may be the only way to effect broad policy actions. Many federal laws already on the books can affect energy developments and land use. Some of the more significant laws are the Clean Air Act and Clean Air Amendments of 1977, the National Environmental Policy Act of 1969, the Federal Aid Highway Act of 1974, and the Federal Water Pollution Control Act Amendments of 1972. Through these and other laws many federal agencies clearly have the authority to affect land use and energy relationships. Often such laws have already been used in this way, but only indirectly. They could become important tools if their full potential were exercised.

Efforts have been made to pass federal legislation dealing specifically with energy and land use, but they have become mired and finally abandoned. For example, the Land Resources Policy and Planning Assistance Act of 1975, S. 984, was designed to make planning grants available to states for establishing statewide land use programs. One section of the bill dealt with energy facility planning. The bill passed the Senate but not the House. Jealousies, fears of outside control, apprehension about lost political powers, jurisdictional disputes, and similar considerations have been at the root of such legislative failures.

Although efforts at national energy planning have not been successful, several states have had limited success passing energy legislation designed to cut consumption. In California, for example, legislation is in force which requires appliances to adhere to high standards of efficiency, insulation, and heat loss and gain.[22] The California energy legislation is only marginally involved with land use; even the procedural pathway to siting a generating station is responsive rather than directive.

All California counties are required to have a land use plan. These plans have resulted in the concentration of different energy users. To redesign such county plans in order to reflect a new energy consciousness will be time consuming at best and overwhelmingly opposed at worst.

Some California counties, for example, San Diego and Imperial, do have energy elements as part of their land use plans. The Imperial County General Plan actually includes a Geothermal Element to facilitate the development of the substantial supply of geoheat which lies beneath the extensive agricultural fields.

Concern for energy as manifested in local and county plans is still unusual. Even if such plans become more popular and effective, they will not replace intercounty, interstate, interregional, statewide, or national policies. Therefore, such plans are severely limited in ameliorating the broader, more common and serious concerns of energy and land use which have arisen in the past and which will probably occur on a more significant scale in the future. An increasing population, a broadened and more frantic search for energy, a constant push to streamline approval procedures and the rising energy demands themselves will make it so.

Many less formal existing mechanisms can be used in energy-related land use planning. Planning departments usually have direct or advisory authority on development plans. Limits to growth may be a result of the difficulty in acquiring new energy sources. Planned Unit Developments (PUDs) offer many potential energy-saving advantages over small projects.

Such attempts to use existing authority are of course subject to political pressures. For this reason education is very important and must accompany a relentless attempt to convey an understanding that energy planning and land use planning must be considered as one issue.

Two cities in California, Indio and Davis, have received national attention because of their implementation of energy-sensitive land use planning. The basis for both efforts was work conducted by a firm called Living Systems.[23] Some of the energy-sensitive planning suggestions included reduced setbacks, more housing clusters, deciduous tree landscaping, narrowed streets, a reduction of sidewalks to one side, more one-way streets, no exposed west- or east-facing windows, safe routes for bicycles, plus standards measures regarding insulation. Many of these recommendations, particularly those which could be required as part of housing construction, have been made mandatory in Indio. Davis has gone even further, and their energy cost reductions have been great.

The federal government will have a large, though indirect role, in energy-based land use planning. The impact will be indirect because all the initiatives, encouragements, requirements, statutes, and restrictions which exist (or may be effective in the near future) are related to energy not land use. The impact upon land use will be because of energy decisions, and not because someone devised a specific energy planning concept or directive. There is a Department of Energy, but there is no Department of Land Use. In truth, the term "land use" makes a lot of people uneasy from the start, especially when they think it means they will be *compelled* to do something to their land.

Conclusions

Land use planning needs to be nationally mandated and energy focused. Some cities are initiating their own plans, but little is being done outside cities where most of the land, and virtually all of the energy development, is found. The little attention such planning has received has been with regard to utilization not development.

So much attention is being paid lately to quick development of energy that little effort has been made to avoid long-term problems. This lack of foresight is particularly true of energy and land use. The evidence of a coming avalanche of problems is everywhere: California has made in-state nuclear siting almost impossible; Eastport, Maine, is resisting proposals to construct a port for supertankers; proposed wilderness areas in Alaska are under vitriolic attack by those who fear the use of resources will be foreclosed within such areas; deployment of photovoltaic cells and solar satellite receiving stations is said to be too land consumptive; the assumed land impact of geothermal energy threatens to curtail its potential before it gathers momentum; oil shale development may threaten large areas of sparsely populated western open space; and the routing of electrical and fuel transmission lines always seems to involve a major fight. The list will continue to grow. There is no concerted, coordinated, or organized plan to stop it.

Certain land-based responses to the energy situation will happen naturally as energy becomes more expensive. For example, higher population densities, slowed horizontal expansion, more numerous multistoried buildings, and less vacant inner-city land can be expected. Exactly how meaningful these adjustments will be is conjectural, but they probably will occur very slowly without focused planning efforts at the local, regional, state, interstate, and federal levels.

The use of existing mechanisms is the safest and quickest way to get something accomplished, but it is still a short-term solution. Other action is needed. The surest way to the integrated consideration of land use and energy will be to take several paths. First, ordinances must be formulated requiring "built in" approaches to energy conservation such as street patterns, window orientation, and architectural features. Secondly, these efforts should be organized through a consolidated energy office instead of through disparate and often competing agencies which exist in states such as Arizona. Thirdly, if a central energy office is not feasible, then each state or community county should have an "Energy Review Board" to look at the energy implications of projects. Each agency should be required to address such matters. Fourthly, an education program must be formulated to teach the public about the energy implications of present patterns of sprawl and transportation. Fifthly, plans must be implemented to allow the timely integration of alternate energy sources with future land use patterns. Sixthly, land must be evaluated for its resources. Those areas which seem promising from the standpoint of energy must be preserved much as national scenic wonders are now protected. Such action calls for "Resource Reserves," which are held for energy developments.

All these actions will require a greater degree of control over land use. Many people do not want such control regardless of the collective benefits. Greater control over land use does not mean full loss of freedom of action regarding land, but rather that there has not been enough energy-conscious planning in the past. It would mean increasing such control to a level where it could be effective in cutting energy consumption.

There are many possible and sensible ways in which the relation between land use and energy development can be addressed. It is surprising, therefore, that this relationship has received so little attention. Undoubtedly this will change in the future. As the public becomes more concerned with the relationship between land use and energy, relatively few general themes will emerge: urban forms and function, building designs, population densities, growth rates, means of transportation, facility siting, land commitments, migrations, and legal means to an end. How these themes are treated will depend on public priorities and individual decisions.

Notes

1. H. Caudill, *Night Comes to the Cumberlands* (Dubuque, Iowa: Atlantic-Little, Brown, 1962).
2. HRB-Singer, Inc. *Overview of Subsidence Potential in Pennsylvania Coal Fields* (Washington, D.C.: Appalachian Regional Commission, 1975).
3. J. Poland and G. H. Davis, "Land Subsidence Due to Withdrawal of Fluids," *Geological Society of America, Reviews in Engineering Geology* 2 (1969): 187–261.
4. National Academy of Sciences, *Rehabilitation Potential of Western Coal Lands* (Cambridge, Mass.: Ballinger, 1973).
5. M. J. Pasqualetti and S. Bender-Lamb, "Energy Related Forced Migration," paper delivered at the Annual Meeting of the Arizona/Nevada Academy of Science, Tempe, 1979.
6. M. J. Pasqualetti, "Geothermal Energy in Imperial County, California: Environmental, Socio-Economic, Demographic, and Public Opinion Research Conclusions and Policy Recommendations," *Energy: The International Journal* 4 (1979): 67–80.
7. W. Zelinsky, "Population Patterns and Energy: Some Unanswered Questions," *Earth and Mineral Sciences* 49 (1979): 1, 6–7.
8. Real Estate Research Corporation, *The Costs of Sprawl*. Prepared for the Department of Housing and Urban Development, 1974.
9. O. Carroll and R. Nathans, "Land Use Configurations and the Utilization of Distributed Energy Technology," in *Distributed Energy Systems in California's Future*. Interim Report vol. 2 (Washington, D.C.: U.S. Department of Energy, 1978).
10. M. Fels and M. Munsun, "Energy Thrift in Urban Transportation: Options for the Future," in *The Energy Conservation Papers*, ed. R. H. Williams, (Cambridge, Mass.: Ballinger, 1975).

11. L. F. Wheat, *Regional Growth and Industrial Location* (Lexington, Mass.: D. C. Heath and Co., 1973).

12. As cited in Little et al., "Energy and Land Use: A Study of Interrelationships." Prepared by the Congressional Research Service, Library of Congress, Washington, D.C., 1976.

13. M. J. Pasqualetti and B. Miller, "Solar Energy and Coal: A Comparison of Land Use Requirements." Paper delivered at the Southwestern and Rocky Mountain Division American Association for the Advancement of Science, 56th Annual Meeting, April 9–12, 1980.

14. U.S. Department of Energy, *Geothermal Direct Heat Use, Market Potential/Penetration Analysis for Federal Region IX,* October 1979.

15. C. J. Weinberg, "Environmental Aspects of Geysers Geothermal Operations." Paper delivered at Environmental Aspects of Non-Conventional Energy Resource II—American Nuclear Society Topical Meeting, Denver, Sept. 26–29, 1978.

16. M. J. Pasqualetti and B. Miller, "Solar Energy and Coal: A Comparison of Land Use Requirements." Paper delivered at the Annual Meeting of the Arizona-Nevada Academy of Science, Las Vegas, April, 1980.

17. T. O. Carroll, R. Nathans, P. F. Palmedo, and R. Stern, *The Planner's Energy Workbook* (Brookhaven, New York: State University of New York, Brookhaven National Laboratory, 1977).

18. Little, "Energy and Land Use: A Study of Interrelationships."

19. Carroll and Nathans, "Land Use Configurations and the Utilization of Distributed Energy Technology."

20. C. Backus, Professor of Engineering, Arizona State University, Tempe, personal communication.

21. P. Pollock, *The Implementation of State Solar Incentives, Land-Use Planning to Ensure Solar Access* (Golden, Colorado: Solar Energy Research Institute, 1979).

22. State of California, "Residential Energy Conservation Manual New Residential Buildings" (Sacramento, Calif.: Energy Resources Conservation and Development Commission, 1977).

23. Living Systems, Inc., "Indio, California Energy Conservation Project" (Washington, D.C.: U.S. Department of Housing and Urban Development, 1977).

Chapter 11

Management and Regulation of Areas Subject to Natural Hazards

Earl J. Baker
Florida State University

Introduction

Not all geographical locations are equally prone to vagaries of nature such as earthquakes, hurricanes, floods, and landslides. Some regions of a country are more hazardous than others, and some locations within a community are more hazardous than others. This spatial variation in risk from a given natural hazard leads to the obvious notion that more hazard-prone sites are less suitable for some types of development than are safer sites.

Obvious or not, individual decision makers characteristically underestimate the costs of occupying sites subject to natural hazards. In some cases the underestimation stems from total ignorance that a hazard exists, and in others complex psychological processes result in a denial of the hazard or a miscalculation of its likelihood or consequences. Other individuals willingly accept the risks with full and accurate information; still others accept housing in hazardous areas because it may be the only housing they can afford.

When a hazardous event occurs and damage ensues, part of the losses are almost invariably shifted to the public sector through disaster relief programs. For this reason, as well to protect people from themselves, the concepts of hazard-zone management and regulation have found their way into public policy. The increased reliance on these techniques came about, however, only after a recognition that traditional dependence upon large-scale structural adjustments to hazards (e.g., dams, seawalls, levees, jetties) was failing to reduce the trend in losses and in some cases might actually have increased certain types of losses.

Development in hazardous areas continues at a frightening pace. A recent study done for the United States Department of Housing and Urban Development estimated that without regulation of urban floodplains in the United States, average *annual* flood losses in those areas would increase by more than $500 million by the year 1990, raising the average annual loss figure to more than $2 billion.[1] Perhaps the most dramatic cases of development in hazard-prone areas occur in coastal zones. A summary of coastal development between 1960 and 1970 is depicted in figures 11.1 and 11.2. Growth within one to five miles of the coastline was almost four times the national average, and growth seaward of the twenty-foot contour was probably considerably greater.[2]

Delineation of Hazard Zones

The degree to which an area can be managed or regulated to reduce risk from a given hazard depends upon the accuracy with which risk from the hazard can be differentiated spatially. Some hazards are of such a nature, and enough is known about them, that some parts of a neighborhood

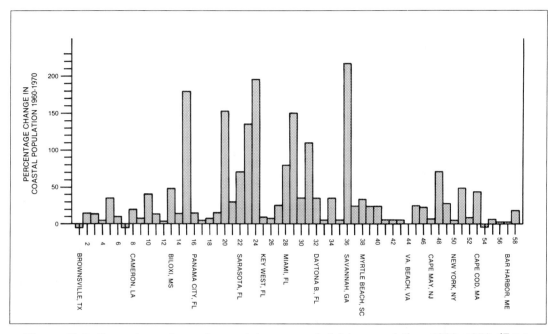

Figure 11.1. Percentage change in coastal census subdivision population, 1960–1970. (From Baker, 1979; reproduced from *Coastal Zone Management Journal* 5(4) by permission of Crane, Russak, and Co., Inc.)

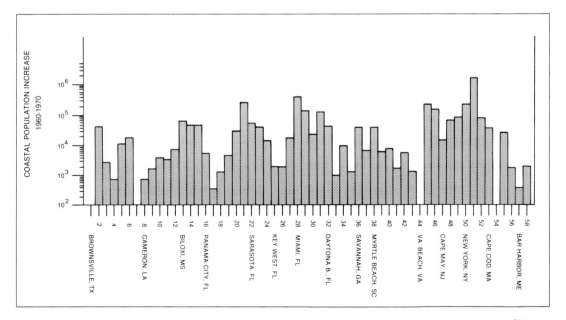

Figure 11.2. Changes in number of inhabitants in coastal census subdivisions, 1960–1970. (From Baker, 1979; reproduced from *Coastal Zone Management Journal* 5(4) by permission of Crane, Russak, and Co., Inc.)

can be identified as being more hazardous than others. It is sometimes possible to state exactly how much more hazardous one site is than another in probabilistic terms. Other hazards may be so geographically pervasive without clear patterns of concentration within small areas that the only reliable distinctions regarding the distribution of risk can be made for large areas such as states or even the entire country. Flooding is an example of the former case and lightning the latter.

Map Scale

One of the key elements of maps attempting to delineate hazardous areas is map scale. Maps may be categorized as (1) national scale maps (approximately 1:5,000,000), (2) state scale maps (approximately 1:500,000) and (3) local scale maps (approximately 1:25,000). For most purposes the larger the map scale, the more useful the map, especially if stringent regulations are being applied to areas identified as most hazardous. The larger scale allows one to differentiate among levels of risk even within small geographical areas such as city blocks.

For some hazards, it is currently impossible to make reliable distinctions regarding risk within small areas. In some cases the reason might be a lack of data indicating risk levels, but the more common reason is that the risk simply appears to be relatively uniform over very large geographical areas. For hazards of this type the only useful maps are of national or state scales. Local scale maps are used when risk distinctions can be made over small areas.

Table 11.1 summarizes the scales at which various hazards can be mapped reliably. Hurricane winds vary little locally, but zonations can be noted at the state scale. Storm surge hazard can be mapped locally because risk is a function of land elevation, and the same is true of riverine flooding. Tornado risk is so spatially pervasive that the most reliable distinctions must be made at the national scale, although some variation in risk can be identified within a number of states. Hailstorms and lightning are similar to tornadoes in their mapping potential. Frost is generally mapped at the state scale, but low-lying areas and land bordering on bodies of water (which retain heat better overnight) can be identified locally in the case of radiated frost. A large scale can be used for certain types of coastal erosion maps, most notably those differentiating zones that face increasing risk over time (i.e., the projected ten-year erosion line or the projected twenty-five-year line). Maps that indicate reaches of coastline eroding most rapidly must usually employ a state scale. Drought is one of the most difficult hazards to differentiate spatially. Most maps are of national scale and do not usually attempt to indicate that some areas are more risky than others. Rather, one usually finds drought areas around the country differentiated on the basis of the nature of drought conditions when they occur (e.g., long, moderate, or short duration).

Earthquake risk mapping is relatively recent and is severely constrained in some areas by the paucity of data—both regarding geologic substructure and seismic history. In certain well-studied areas such as California, however, state and even local-scale distinctions can be made regarding earthquake risk. Additional distinctions can be made at the local scale depending upon soil type, as some soils transmit energy to the structures they support more efficiently than others. For purposes of indicating likelihood of tsunamis striking a coastline, only state-scale distinctions are feasible, but within a local area, given a certain magnitude of wave height, risk can be differentiated on the basis of elevation.

Landslide-prone slopes can be identified locally in many situations, as can avalanche areas. In volcanic areas, likely paths of lava and mudflows can also be identified locally. Windstorm

Table 11.1. Delineation of Hazardous Areas

Hazard	Mapping Potential		Scale**
	Risk Propensity*		
Hurricane			
Wind	Probabilities		State
Storm Surge	Probabilities		Local
Riverine Flood	Probabilities		Local
Tornado	Ordinal Zones		National
Hailstorm	Ordinal Zones		National
Lightning	Ordinal Zones		National
Frost	Probabilities		State
Coastal Erosion	Ordinal Zones		Local
Drought	Ordinal Zones		National
Earthquake	Ordinal Zones		Local
	Probabilities		National
Tsunami	Ordinal Zones		State
Landslide	Ordinal Zones		Local
Snow and Ice	Ordinal Zones		National
Volcanoes	Ordinal Zones		Local
Avalanche	Ordinal Zones		Local
Wind	Ordinal Zones		Local

* "Probabilities" implies that the absolute (and thus relative) likelihood of a hazardous event of a given magnitude can be estimated for a given location. "Ordinal zones" indicates that a location can only be assigned to some category of relative risk such as low, moderate, and high.

** National scale refers to a scale of approximately 1:5,000,000
State scale refers to a scale of approximately 1:500,000
Local scale refers to a scale of approximately 1:25,000

areas can usually be differentiated only at state and national scales, but certain types such as the downslope winds of the Rockies can be mapped at large scales. Snow and ice storm zones are reliably mapped at the national scale and within some states. Local variations can sometimes be identified from the presence of water bodies and other influences.

Risk Information

The other key feature of maps showing hazardous areas is the sort of risk information depicted. The above discussion dealt with the task of delineating some areas as being more hazardous than others. The distinction among areas might be probabilistic or simply ordinal. Probablistic information can depict the actual likelihood (usually in annual probabilities) of a given area experiencing a hazardous event of a certain magnitude. This is the most useful sort of risk information. One can ascertain the absolute level of risk for various sites; average annual losses can be projected (given additional information); and precise determinations regarding the relative risk among sites made. Alternatively, probabilistic information may be used to show the spatial distinctions in magnitude of events, given a certain likelihood (or "return interval," which does *not* imply cyclical nature). For example, figure 11.3 depicts the magnitude of horizontal ground acceleration for different seismic risk areas of the country. The magnitudes have a 90 percent chance of not being exceeded in a fifty-year period.

Other risk information is less precise than probabilistic information. A map might simply show the historical pattern of occurrences of hazardous events without estimating probabilities, or a map might indicate one area as being of high risk, a second of moderate risk, and so on. These distinctions are ordinal, however, rather than interval or ratio.

Hazards mapped probabilistically are hurricane winds and storm surges, riverine flooding, frosts, and occasionally snow and ice storms and earthquakes. The potential exists for mapping hail, lightning, coastal erosion, and windstorms probabilistically. Data deficiencies or lack of understanding of the processes involved in generating the hazardous events necessitate mapping of the remaining hazards listed in table 11.1 only by risk zones or by historical example or summary.

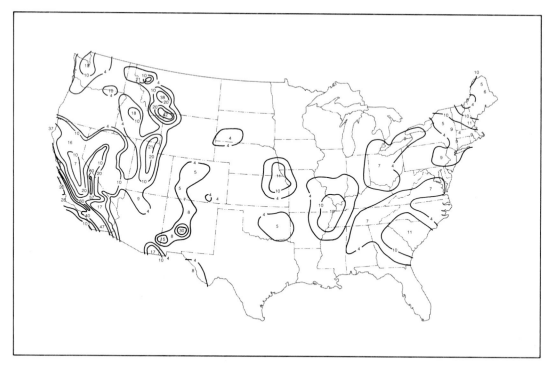

Figure 11.3. Horizontal rock acceleration, as a percent of gravity, having a 90% chance of not being exceeded in a 50-year period. (From Algermissen and Perkins, USGS, 1976.)

Local Hazard Zone Management Tools

State governments have typically delegated their authority to regulate land use to local government. Since the enabling acts were adopted permitting local units to regulate land use, almost all land use regulation has occurred at the local level. The justification for such delegation has been that local officials best know local problems and how to solve them.

Zoning

Zoning simply divides the governmental entity into units of land, or zones, which are uniform with respect to risk from the hazard. Zoning is the traditionally preferred tool for regulating land use in areas where a definite hazard zone can be delineated, because the hazard zone can be specified and restrictions imposed consistent with the hazard. Zoning can specify permitted uses and where various activities may be conducted. It can also establish standards, such as minimum elevations or structural prerequisites, to be applied in a specified area. For example a multihazard ordinance was adopted for Little Cottonwood Canyon Utah (Alta-Snowbird Ski Resort) which prohibits construction of permanent structures in areas subject to hazards such as floods, landslides, and avalanches.

A second approach to hazard regulation specifies graduated use zones. Use restrictions are more severe the more hazardous the area. For example, Warrick, Rhode Island, permits only noncommercial boat docks, beach cabanas, and open space uses in "areas of extreme hurricane danger," whereas a wide range of structures with first floor minimum elevation requirements are permitted in the more general "areas of hurricane danger." The United States Water Resources Council has drafted a model zoning ordinance for use by coastal communities that also employs a graduated use zone approach. In the "high hazard district" only open space activities are permitted (agriculture, golf courses, parking areas), but special exception uses may be granted (circuses, drive-in theaters, marinas). In the "general hazard district" first floor elevation and construction guidelines are established, and flood-proofed structures may be granted special exceptions.

A special category of zoning-type laws requires "setback lines." A high hazard area is identified, and construction is required to be located behind the border of the zone, except by special permit. Glynn and Chatham Counties in Georgia have coastal setbacks and Portola Valley, California requires setbacks of up to 175 feet from the San Andreas fault line (fig. 11.4).

Subdivision Regulations

Subdivision regulations establish guidelines for the division of large parcels of land into smaller lots which will subsequently be sold or commercially developed. In most cases subdivision regulations deal with large residential developments.

The subdivider is required to prepare a plat of the area to be sold or developed. The plat is a detailed map showing individual parcels, streets, and other proposed aspects of the development. The subdivider is not ordinarily required to indicate hazardous zones on the plat. The regulatory board then reviews the plat and can modify it to make activities in the area more compatible with

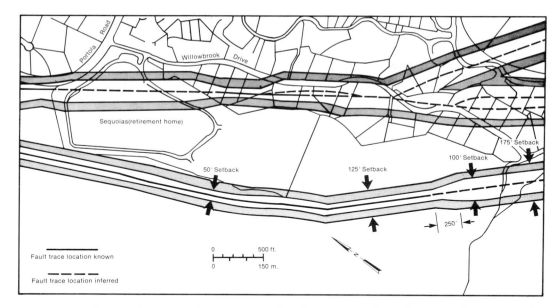

Figure 11.4. Construction setback zones along the San Andreas Fault, Portola Valley, California. (From Nichols and Buchanan-Banks, USGS, 1974.)

the comprehensive plan, or it can reject the development altogether. If subdivision regulations require explicit consideration of natural hazards, flooding and geologic hazards are most commonly included. An example of an ordinance that requires consideration of natural hazards is the Portsmouth, Virginia subdivision regulation. That ordinance prohibits the subdivision of land if it is subject to flooding or other hazards, unless such hazards can be overcome by filling or special construction techniques.

Building Codes

Building codes are regulatory measures that set minimum standards for new structures. Building codes usually apply throughout a community, unlike structural provisions incorporated into zoning ordinances. For some hazards this broad application makes zoning preferable to codes, but for other hazards, such as earthquakes or hurricane winds, codes may be preferable because the entire community may be susceptible.

Building codes are designed to help assure that structures in a hazardous area can withstand a hazard of a prescribed magnitude. The details of the code can establish minimum floor elevations, prohibit or restrict the use of inferior building materials, and require proper anchorage or foundation stabilization. Several counties in South Florida have adopted a building code specifying wind load provisions and construction techniques and materials eclipsing the wind provisions of the Southern Standard Building Code.

Miscellaneous Ordinances

Sanitary and well codes were conceived for the purpose of protecting the quality of water supply and establishing minimum standards for waste disposal. In areas where these goals might be affected by natural hazards, particular safeguards can be required to assure that water and waste facilities are located and constructed to achieve greater compatibility with the hazard.

Grading regulations exist in some communities to govern the process of smoothing or leveling a slope to the desired gradient. Zoning boards can refuse to permit the grading of areas regarded as unstable or otherwise hazardous. The most common application of grading regulations is in areas of landslide, slippage, or settling potential, but they are also applied to prevent the lowering of elevation of sites or removal of protective sand dunes. Palm Beach, Florida is one of many communities that protects its dunes, which serve as a natural barrier against storm surge.

Evacuation from some coastal areas is becoming a critical problem due to high population densities and inadequate transportation routes. Sanibel, Florida, an island community connected to the mainland by a single, two-lane causeway, adopted a residential density ceiling in an attempt to prevent impossible evacuation difficulties from developing.

Mobile homes present special problems. Because of their light weight, mobile homes are very susceptible to wind damage. Such units have overturned in winds less than 65 mph. However, securely anchored homes have withstood winds of over 100 mph.

There are presently very few communities with tie-down regulations, but an exception is Boulder County, Colorado. Boulder County has been divided into four graduated zones. The zones specify the wind pressures that mobile homes must be able to withstand (fig. 11.5).

Laws have also been enacted to prevent encroachment of development in floodways. In addition to amelioration of direct loss potential, prohibiting channel encroachment decreases secondary effects if floodwaters are obstructed or if debris is in the path of floodwaters. Drainage codes are also sometimes imposed in flood-prone areas to reduce the likelihood of accumulation of storm waters.

The Planned Unit Development (PUD)—based on a combination of high density structures and open spaces—is a fairly recent development in land use planning. It provides satisfactory ways to reduce propensity of loss in hazardous areas. Most PUD ordinances are passed to encourage developers to construct apartment buildings or office parks in certain areas, and to surround them with open spaces, but a PUD can be easily used to develop a unit of land with a known natural hazard in it. The hazardous area is simply left as open space. Encouragement of high-density structures in combination with open space may be desirable in some situations. Miami, Florida has developed plans to use high rise buildings as temporary evacuation shelters during hurricanes.

Public Acquisition

Public acquisition of land in hazardous areas, particularly in urban communities, is becoming common. Several goals may be accomplished simultaneously through public acquisition of hazardous areas. First, it places management of the hazardous areas in the hands of public officials. Second, the land itself may be managed on a multiple use basis, providing greenbelts, parkland and recreation opportunities near centers of population. Third, such acquisition can be used as a

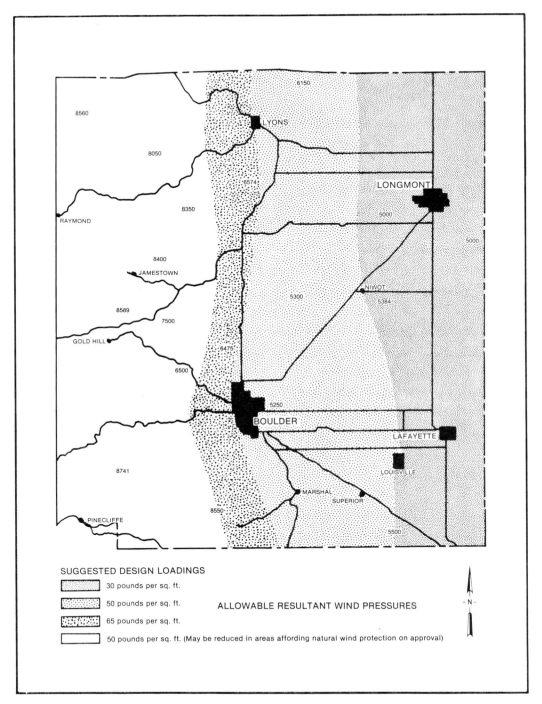

Figure 11.5. Wind hazard zones governing mobile home tie-downs in Boulder County, Colorado. (From Baker and McPhee, 1975; reproduced from *Land Use Management and Regulation in Hazardous Areas* by permission of the University of Colorado.)

tool in carrying out the goals of the community's comprehensive plan, particularly in controlling and guiding growth in the local area.

Public acquisition of land, especially in urban areas, is expensive. There are several possibilities for funding which will be enumerated in a later section. Rapid City, South Dakota was given Federal Urban Renewal Funds to acquire real estate destroyed by the June 1972 flood. Over fourteen hundred parcels of floodplain land were acquired, and the residents and businesses were relocated on higher ground. This land is now used for greenbelt, bridle paths, bicycling and hiking trails, golf courses, and tennis courts. Although isolated, sporadic cases of flood plain acquisition have occurred since 1972, none have been on such a grand scale. The public generally reacts favorably to equitable relocation and to imposition of controls after a disaster.

State Hazard Zone Management Tools

Though state governments can take any of the regulatory actions outlined for local governments, state officials have been reluctant to interfere with local land use efforts in the past. The belief that local decision makers should regulate land use is now giving way to the realization that few land use problems are truly local in nature. Many policies and actions affect an area larger than the local community. The states' increasing willingness to assert their authority to regulate land use is well documented.[3]

State Comprehensive Land Use Laws

A few states have passed land use bills that apply to the entire state or to generically defined areas. Hazard considerations are usually a minor part of the measures; instead emphasis is given to environmental quality.

Comprehensive state land use legislation is two-pronged. It provides for a state land use planning program and establishes various guidelines to regulate land use and development. Planning legislation is more common than strict controls and usually precedes regulations by several years. One example of land use planning legislation that includes consideration of hazards is the Oregon law creating the State Land Conservation and Development Commission. The commission is charged with developing land use goals and guidelines for flood plains and areas of geologic hazards. California uses an integrated state planning approach in dealing with hazards. The California Division of Mines and Geology, in formulating the Urban Geology Master Plan for California, divided the state into cells of 7.5 minute parcels and studied the role of ten hazards in planning for each cell.

In establishing regulations for guiding land use, states generally deal with two categories of problems—areas of critical state concern and developments having regional impact. Both elements may involve hazardous areas. Areas of critical concern may include fast growing urban communities, historical and archaeological sites, or (more commonly) critical environmental areas. A bill considered by Washington State specified controls for "Areas of Statewide Significance," and includes "areas of high potential for natural disaster." The Florida law, on the other hand, does not explicitly include hazardous areas under its "Areas of Critical State Concern."

Developments having a regional impact include large residential subdivisions. Such subdivisions can have repercussions on places outside their immediate area. The regional impact clause is supposed to prevent development that creates a negative impact. Such developments coming under state review are characteristically evaluated with respect to their effects on flood and drainage problems internally and on neighboring sites.

Some states require that localities consider hazards in their zoning ordinances. California goes about this in an indirect manner. In addition to providing for coastal zone management, the state's government code requires that cities and counties adopt a "general plan," which must include a seismic safety element in which seismic hazards are identified and appraised. The state also requires that local zoning ordinances be in conformity with the general plans. Wisconsin's statute is more direct. It explicitly requires local flood plain zoning and provides for state-imposed zoning should local entities fail to enact their own.

A more recent approach is the statewide "zoning" prescribed in major land use legislation by Hawaii and Maine. The Hawaii Land Use Commission Act classifies all land of the state as urban, rural, agricultural, or conservation, and specifies permitted uses for land in each zone. Similarly, the Maine Land Use Regulation Commission is charged with classifying about half the state's land (mostly in remote areas) into protection (including flood plains and precipitous slopes), management, holding and development districts. Each category has guidelines for permissible uses. Most major state land use legislation requires that a regional or state appeal board rule on applications for permits to deviate from legislative land use guidelines.

In 1974 the Colorado State Legislature passed a bill requiring all communities to review their zoning maps and comprehensive plans and to identify specified natural hazards of statewide concern. After identifying these hazards, the communities are required to enact appropriate ordinances to prohibit encroachment into these areas.

Coastal Legislation

As a result of the Federal Coastal Zone Management Act of 1972, several coastal states have developed comprehensive coastal legislation, often dealing quite explicitly with natural hazards. North Carolina's Coastal Area Management Act, for example, provides for state-local joint permitting in Areas of Environmental Concern. One type of "Critical Area" is recognized as a natural hazard area, "where uncontrolled or incompatible development could unreasonably endanger life or property."

More common are wetlands protection laws. These acts are designed to prevent ecologically detrimental development of inland and coastal wetlands marshes, tidelands and estuaries. These areas are subject to hazards such as floods, hurricanes, tsunami, and coastal erosion. Laws controlling wetland development protect people from these natural hazards. In recognition of this, some wetlands acts deal explicitly with natural hazards. A Massachusetts law provides for state review of any proposed development that will alter land subject to tidal action, coastal storm flowage, or flooding.

Another class of coastal regulations protects dunes, beaches, and other natural protective barriers. These natural barriers protect people from hurricane storm surge, tsunami, and erosion. Delaware regulates the removal of sand and gravel from coastal areas. North Carolina protects against sand dune destruction, and Florida has a beach setback requirement to protect dunes, beaches, and property.

Subdivision Regulations

State level subdivision controls vary greatly. More permissive legislation simply requires registration by subdividers. Several states require "full disclosure" reports prior to sale of property to protect buyers from misinformation. Others, such as Michigan, make it mandatory for hazardous conditions (flood hazards) extant on the land to be specified in the reports. A few states, notably Michigan and Wisconsin, require state agency review of subdivision plats before they can be approved. Most states, though, simply authorize local governments to review subdivision proposals. Colorado, on the other hand, requires local entities to develop their own subdivision regulations. Failure to do so results in the state establishing the subdivision regulations for the local unit. By issuing guidelines for local governments, Colorado assures that new developments do not unknowingly produce risks for property owners or the state. The emphasis is upon providing counsel to local government by state agencies. In cases where states prescribe guidelines for local subdivision regulations, flooding, drainage and grading are often given attention.

Floodway Encroachment and Obstruction

The most common hazard regulated at the state level is the periodic flooding of rivers. At least thirty eight states have some form of regulation pertaining to licensing, inspecting, or the construction of dams, levees, or other obstructions to the floodway. An important type of regulation is the "encroachment line." These are controls that prohibit new construction from obstructing the flow of floodwaters or adding debris to the flood flow. Such regulations are intended to keep development from compounding the danger of floods.

Hazard Control Legislative Packages

At least eight separate laws dealing with seismic hazards have been enacted in California. Several deal with land use regulation either directly or indirectly. The Seismic Safety Element law requires that city and county general plans contain a seismic safety element. Another law requires that public school buildings not be located over active fault traces and that special construction practices be employed to reduce risk to seismic activity. Similar construction practices are required of hospitals. The Alquist Priolo Geologic Hazards Act is designed to limit construction above active fault traces. The state geologist prepares maps of "Special Studies Zones," which are usually no more than a quarter of a mile wide. All proposed development in those zones must be approved by municipal governments according to state guidelines. Development can be prohibited if undue hazards are created. Taken together, the California legislation provides a good example of multipronged efforts to reduce losses from a natural hazard via land use management.

Federal Hazard Zone Management Tools

National Flood Insurance Act

Although the federal government lacks the constitutional authority to regulate land use per se, there are nevertheless numerous federal incentives for state and local governments to act. The premiere federal legislation is the National Flood Insurance Act of 1968 as amended. Over twenty thousand communities (cities, towns, and unincorporated areas of counties) have been identified by the Federal Insurance Administration (FIA–FEMA) as being flood prone. FIA will make flood insurance available in those communities if the respective governments agree to impose federal guidelines regulating development in areas subject to flooding. The operation is referred to as the National Flood Insurance Program (NFIP).

Initially a community enters the "emergency" phase of the program before actuarial maps have been drawn. During this period the community must enact fairly minimal controls over new building in flood hazard areas. When a Flood Insurance Rate Map (FIRM) has been adapted, the community must implement more restrictive controls—basically requiring structures to be elevated or flood proofed to the level of the 100-year flood. Additional regulations deal with encroachment in the floodway, "filling" of the floodway fringe, and destruction of natural buffers in coastal areas. Other aspects of the legislation, such as the provision of funds for purchase of damaged property after a flood, are only recently receiving attention.

Property already built in floodplains can be insured at federally subsidized rates, but new construction (after the FIRM has been adopted) must pay actuarial rates, as must "substantial" improvements and repairs of older buildings. Thus, over the long run the program is intended to shift flood losses from relief programs onto floodplain occupants (through their premiums), while at the same time reducing losses by requiring better building practices.

The program is not mandatory, and before 1973 few communities were participating. Subsequent amendments penalized non-participating communities, and now over sixteen thousand communities participate, with over twenty-three hundred in the regular (post-FIRM) program.

Criticisms of the program fall into two categories. The first alleges that the regulations are too restrictive (infringing on property rights, increasing housing costs, and eroding tax bases by depressing land values).[4] A court challenge to the constitutionality of the NFIP by a group calling itself the Flood Insurance Litigation Coalition recently failed. The other criticisms allege that the program is too weak (sometimes suggesting that the program actually induces loss-prone development).[5] A report cited earlier projected that even with compliance with minimum FIA land use regulations, annual flood losses in urban areas would increase by $125 million by 1990.[6]

Coastal Zone Management Act

The other principal federal law affecting land use in hazardous areas is the Coastal Zone Management Act of 1972. The Office of Coastal Zone Management (OCZM), a part of the National Oceanic and Atmospheric Administration, funds 80 percent of a state's expenses in developing and implementing a coastal zone management plan and regulations if the state does so in accordance with federal guidelines. The guidelines include identification of "Areas of Particular Concern," which may be generically defined or may be geographically specific. One criterion to be used in identifying such areas is hazardousness, including susceptibility to hurricanes. Some states have had their regulatory schemes approved by OCZM, while others are still developing their plans. The federal initiative has been extremely successful in inducing several states to take steps in this area which they would not have taken without the federal carrot. It is expected that OCZM will scrutinize more closely the hazard aspects of plans submitted in the future than the first plans it approved.

Other Federal Activities

Several other federal laws affect the use of coastal hazardous areas but will be mentioned only briefly. Two primarily environmental measures, the National Environmental Policy Act (NEPA) and Section 404(b) of the Federal Water Pollution Control Act Amendments of 1972, have aspects which directly or indirectly mitigate disasters. The Water Resources Development Act of 1974 requires that nonstructural alternatives be considered when federal agencies (primarily the United States Army Corps of Engineers in coastal areas) design water-related projects. The Land and Water Conservation Act of 1965, the State and Local Fiscal Assistance Act of 1972 (Revenue Sharing), and the Housing and Community Development Act of 1974 (Community Block Grants) provide major sources of funds for land acquisition in hazardous areas to preclude highly loss-prone development. The Interstate Land Sales Full Disclosure Act of 1968 provides consumer protection by requiring that hazard propensity be included in property reports. The National Seashore Program involves direct federal purchase and management of oceanfront property, and the recent Executive Order 11988 sets forth guidelines for evaluating flood risk when planning construction of facilities funded by federal monies. The Mobile Home Construction and Safety Standards Act of 1974 prescribes structural performance criteria that must be met for mobile homes to be designated "hurricane resistive." The Occupational Safety and Health Administration could become active in restricting manufacturing and commercial employers from endangering employees by siting their facilities in hazardous areas. Finally the Disaster Relief Act Amendments of 1974 provided up to $250,000 to each state for preparation of disaster preparedness plans, which were to include a hazard mitigation element generally interpreted to mean land use planning and building codes.

Environmental Benefits

One of the strongest selling points for certain types of land use controls in hazardous areas is that in addition to reducing risk from the hazard a number of environmental quality goals can be achieved simultaneously. Policies preserving natural features which afford protection from the hazard, which are open space in nature, and so forth fall into this category. On the other hand building codes per se have no inherent environmental quality assets. A policy requiring filling of low-lying, flood-prone areas before construction is permitted would clearly be a liability to many natural processes.

A common integration of the two goals is reflected in public acquisition of shorelines and floodplains for recreation areas or natural area preserves. Littleton, Colorado decided that rather than receive protection from floods by a channel improvement on the South Platte River it would prefer to acquire the land and use it for open space purposes. Under the Water Resources Development Act of 1974 it was authorized to supply funds which would have been spent on engineering works for land purchase. The remaining cost was covered by municipal bonds of more than $500,000.

The example of Rapid City, South Dakota was mentioned earlier. Federal funds allowed the city to purchase fourteen hundred parcels of land on which structures had been destroyed or damaged in its 1972 flood. The acquired land is now used for hiking and biking trails, activity fields for soccer, baseball and the like, wilderness parks, and a golf course. A similar transition, though not on the same scale, followed the Big Thompson flood of 1976 in Colorado. These transitions will probably become increasingly common after disasters, given current inclinations of federal agencies. It appears that for the first time the principle of postdisaster land acquisition for the public domain will be applied in a coastal area in the wake of Hurricane Frederick in 1979. There have been over forty floodplain acquisition projects thus far undertaken with federal assistance.

Coastal areas probably provide the best example of the compatibility of hazard loss reduction goals and environmental quality goals. Three sets of considerations are convenient for organizing the discussion: problems unique to beaches and wetlands and general density criteria.[7]

Beaches and Beach Processes

Sand beaches, both on barrier islands and on the open coast, are highly dynamic, geologically unstable systems. Both the natural chronic erosion of shorelines and severe coastal storms make beach areas hazardous for human habitation, but development that minimizes the destruction of the natural features and processes of the beach environment faces the least risk.

The beach itself provides a measure of protection from the sea by helping to regulate the rate of erosion caused by storms. If sand is removed from the beach artificially, if the beach is narrowed by artificial action, or if structures are built that interfere with the sediment transport exchange system, the protection afforded by the beach against storm and seasonal erosion will be diminished.

Dunes are perhaps the most salient topographic feature of beach environments, especially the primary or frontal dunes. During major storms part or perhaps all of the dune is eroded, with some of the eroded sand eventually being redeposited on the beach. Thus the dunes serve as reservoirs of sand for the beach system. Furthermore, in absorbing the wave energy from the storms, they dissipate the force gradually, not causing further destruction of the beach. The other important function served by the dune system is similar to that of a dike or levee. In small and moderate strength storms—even hurricanes—the dunes can prevent the storm surge from inundating the areas behind them, obviously producing a major benefit to property sited there.

In efforts to build ever-nearer the water's edge, dunes are leveled to facilitate construction, thereby subjecting the property to almost certain undermining during storms and diminishing the dune's ability to protect against flooding. Cutting roadways through dunes to improve beach access also reduces the dike-effect of dunes and increases erosion. Vegetation such as sea oats tends to hold the dunes in place.

Wetlands, Marshes and Swamps

In low-energy coastal areas and on the "back" or lagoonal side of barrier islands, one finds low-lying land with salt-water tolerant vegetation. Nearest the ocean, lagoon, or bay are salt marshes and mangrove swamps. They are inundated by normal high tides and sometimes referred to as vegetated tidelands. These environments are important producers and storers of food and nutrients for marine life and as purifiers of polluted runoff from upland areas.

More directly related to hazards from coastal storms and erosion, vegetation can help mitigate risk. Root systems help stabilize the shoreline, thus slowing erosion, and the bodies of vegetation absorb energy from waves and surges, slowing the waves and reducing the distance inland they will travel. Mangroves can be particularly effective in this regard and even create land areas by trapping sediment and detritus in their root structures.

Construction, notably dredge and fill activity, in wetlands, marshes and swamps inhibits all of the functions listed above. Drainage disruption, increased siltation, and heightened contamination of runoff impair the hydrologic and biotic activities. Buildings in these areas are going to be subject to high risk from flooding due to the extremely low elevations. The areas are inundated daily or yearly under normal circumstances. That problem is the principal motivation for filling planned building sites with earthen material (thereby raising its elevation). The most convenient source of fill is spoil from dredging adjacent to the site. The ecological problems with dredge and fill operations have already been noted, and the degree of safety from storms afforded by such filling is minimal. In most Atlantic and Gulf coastal areas the height of the storm surge produced by a 100-year storm is between 10 to 12 feet. This is about the same height as the 25-year surge plus a 3-foot wave.[8] Filling to that height is prohibitive—both economically, ecologically and practically. Elevation on pilings is feasible, but even then filling in these areas becomes necessary to provide access to homesites and other infrastructures, as well as for many commercial activities. The type of residential structures is constrained if they must be raised on pilings rather than on fill. For these reasons developers whose projects involve large areas of wetlands have vocally opposed the application of conventional floodplain management regulations to their areas; that is, they recognize that safe development of those environments is prohibitively expensive.

General Density Constraints

High population densities create problems in low-lying coastal areas because of environmental damages, health risks, and evacuation difficulties. Massive withdrawals of underground water have resulted in saltwater intrusion in some areas and subsidence, which exacerbates flood potential, in others. Due to soil and water table conditions, particularly in floodprone areas, many coastal environments can tolerate only low densities of septic tanks, thereby imposing limits on housing units, unless more centralized sewage treatment facilities are available. High population densities lead to critical evacuation problems as well. Nine of ten deaths from hurricanes result from drowning, thus necessitating evacuation of areas which will be inundated by the storms—up to the 20-foot contour in major storms. Many coastal areas, especially barrier islands, are poorly served by transportation routes to high ground. In some areas it is estimated that evacuation must begin twenty hours in advance of landfall in order to safely relocate the entire population at risk. Based on past experience it is unlikely that adequate numbers of coastal residents will begin leaving that early, giving rise to concerns that a disaster involving a thousand deaths is possible.

Economic Effects

There is no shortage of papers proposing rigorous procedures for evaluating the advisability of hazard zone management policies.[9] Methods from traditional benefit-cost analysis to geologic suitability matricies to recursive non-linear programming have been suggested, but few are ever used. Part of the reason that so little use is made of formal procedures appears to be that the time and expertise to do such sophisticated, explicit analysis is seldom available at the state and local levels where many such decisions are made. The principal reason, however, is probably a preference for a decision-making process that is more accommodating to political considerations.

Evaluating Land Use Policies

Even in the least formal methods, most of the same considerations appear which one finds in the more rigorous models.[10] Figures 11.6 illustrates the primary steps in the process.

Loss management goals might not be so obvious as they seem. The traditional criterion is average annual losses (in dollars, lives, or whatever), which can be viewed historically or can be projected, based on probabilities of various magnitudes of hazardous events and their consequences. Over 50 percent of total flood losses, however, are attributable to events more rare than the 100-year flood.[11] It has been shown that the length of time a community requires to recover from a disaster increases not linearly but exponentially as a function of the proportion of the population lost in the disaster.[12] This gives rise to the concept of catastrophe potential—the case of extreme losses concentrated spatially and temporally. Thus, two policies might result in the same level of average annual losses, but one might produce relatively frequent losses of small to moderate magnitude while the other might result in very few loss occasions but huge losses when they do occur. A third criterion for loss management might be thought of as a distributional consideration. For example, the very young and very old are more vulnerable to disasters than are others; therefore a policy might seek to redistribute risk more uniformly by concentrating on reducing the hazard faced by the young and the old. Another distributional example has to do with the degree of reliance which a community places on various activities. It might be advisable to be careful, for example, about the siting of hospitals and "lifeline" activities.

Land use management strategies affect hazard losses in most cases by altering the rate of growth of loss-prone uses in hazardous areas. This might be done by reducing the total amount of lives and property in hazardous areas or by increasing the resistance of structures and activities to loss. In a few cases such as watershed management, the natural event system itself is modified.

The most obvious set of beneficial effects is the aversion of losses from the hazard. There can be other benefits of the policy, however, most notably the enhancement of environmental quality discussed at length earlier. The worth of these and other secondary benefits is determined by the goals of the community.

There are, of course, costs to land use regulations and other strategies as well as benefits. If public acquisition is being employed, then capital outlay becomes significant. Most regulatory schemes involve considerable administrative expense, and certain land use policies—requiring filling of low-lying areas, for example—can damage the natural environment. The most important cost from an economic efficiency standpoint is often the loss of land use benefits that would have accrued to society from the hazardous area's unregulated use.

In calculating the cost of land use benefits, most approaches seem to neglect the fact that regulation can also enhance the utility of land bordering the restricted (hazardous) area. Therefore, to recognize that possibility, the best measure of this "opportunity cost" of nondevelopment for a given parcel of land appears to be the price of the preferred site within the hazard zone *without* regulation, minus the price of the best alternative site outside the hazard zone *with* regulation of the zone. Land values do, however, have a drawback as indicators of the actual stream of rents,

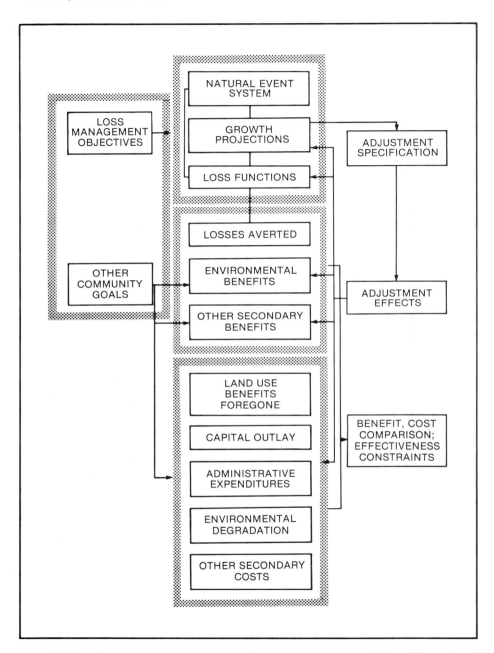

Figure 11.6. Steps involved in evaluating hazard zone management policies. (Reproduced by permission from PROCEEDINGS of the Association of American Geographers, Volume 7, 1975, p. 34, fig. 1, E. J. Baker.)

especially in hazardous areas, because managers characteristically underestimate the losses their use of the parcel will incur, thereby overestimating the rent from the land. The error lies in what is usually called "hazard perception." The psychological process often results in an underestimation of hazard losses, and therefore an overestimation of net benefits.[13]

Like it or not, when choosing among alternative land use policies, it is rare to find one that is superior with respect to each and every criterion being used for evaluation. Thus, tradeoffs must be performed which unfortunately are usually never articulated and made explicit. Benefit-cost analysis, in which all effects are converted to monetary units, is the most explicit technique, but it requires significant resources in order to be applied properly, and many regard expression of such things as human life in pecuniary terms as distasteful. Goals-achievement matrix-type schemes give an illusion of quantitative rigor while hardly ever, if ever, demonstrating any valid claim for reflecting true social preferences for the various effects of the policy. Thus, the final "integration" of the various effects—partly because of limitations on expertise and resources, partly because of an unwillingness to be explicit about the decision-making specifics—is finally performed informally usually by elected officials or by administrators.

Examples of Economic Effects

Thorough, beginning-to-end, comprehensive evaluations of the economic merit of land use policies are rare, despite the fact that federal agencies are not required to consider nonstructural alternatives in flood planning (the nonstructural alternative is usually floodproofing), but certain economic effects have been calculated for a variety of hazards.

On the most general level, the effects of land use management on both catastrophe-potential and average annual losses from flooding have been compared to the effects of other adjustments to flooding (fig. 11.7). Of the six loss abatement strategies considered, only land use management has been found to result in substantial positive net benefits on an average annual basis while simultaneously reducing catastrophe potential. Other figures cited earlier indicate that continuation of the current NFIP land use regulations will result in slowing the rate of increase in urban flood losses in the United States by more than $500 million per year by 1990.[14]

A study of landslides in Los Angeles, California is also encouraging. Before 1952 there were no grading codes, soils engineering, or engineering geology studies required before construction on slopes. Between 1952 and 1962 there was a semiadequate grading code in effect, soils engineering was required, but very little engineering geology was performed. Since 1963 (actually between 1963 and 1969 as far as the ensuing data are concerned) grading codes have been imposed, and soils engineering and engineering geology studies have been required. After torrential winter rains in Los Angeles in 1969, an assessment of damages to structures built under each of the three sets of regulations was performed. The average damages in 1969 per site constructed before 1952 (not per pre–1952 sites damaged) was $330. The 1952–1962 losses were $100 per site constructed, and the post–1962 figures were only $7. Put another way, 10.4 percent of the pre–1952 sites suffered damage compared to 1.3 percent of the 1952–1962 sites and .15 percent of the post–1962 sites.[15]

In hurricane areas similar computations have been performed. Following Hurricane Eloise in 1975 the cost-effectiveness of Florida's Coastal Construction Setback Line was found to have been very successful in reducing losses to structures built in compliance with it. Its overall benefits

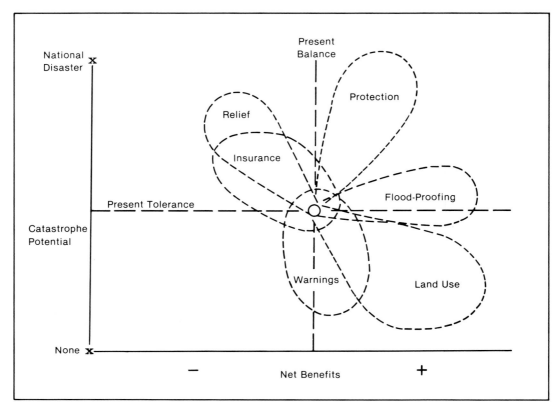

Figure 11.7. Simultaneous effects on net average annual benefits and on catastrophe potential from alternative adjustments to floods. (From White, 1975; reproduced from *Flood Hazard in the United States* by permission of the University of Colorado.)

were found to exceed its costs.[16] Calculations have shown that modifications formulated in Texas to the Southern Standard Building Code to make structures more resistant to hurricanes (primarily winds) would increase overall finished development costs between 1 and 3 percent (depending on type of structure). Wind damages would be only 10 percent as high with the modified code.[17]

Legal Issues

The legal issues of land use regulation are dealt with at length in a previous chapter. Most of those generalizations, including much of the fundamental case law, apply to controls in hazardous areas. Only a few particulars pertaining to hazard zone regulations will be pursued here.

Almost all case law involving application of the police power to hazardous areas has dealt with floodplain zoning. A 1959 article by Dunham was the first exposition on the legality of floodplain regulations. The arguments posed are still often applied in defending such laws. Dunham suggested that floodplain controls could (1) protect unwary investors, (2) prevent "safely" sited owners from suffering increased damages due to flood level increase stemming from floodplain encroachment, and (3) protect the public from costs associated with emergency "floodfighting" and rescue and relief to flood victims.[18]

The courts have widely upheld floodplain regulation in principle. The only decisions against specific regulations have been in cases in which the law appeared to constitute a "taking" by preserving an individual's land for a public-benefit function and when the regulation precluded any economically profitable use of the property at all. Even in these decisions laws were found invalid only in the particular cases brought before the courts; that is, the ordinances themselves were not wholly invalidated. A concern often expressed by local officials—that the regulation might be found arbitrary or unfairly discriminatory due to charges of imprecision in the delineation process—has not been a problem. Related case law suggests that it will not be, so long as the delineation procedure is grounded in rational scientific principles reflecting the state-of-the-art, even if it is not uniformly accepted as being the penultimate.[19]

While government officials are usually concerned about legal repercussions if their ordinances go too far, questions have been raised recently concerning a government's legal liabilities for not going far enough. A study conducted by the Association of Bay Area Governments in Berkeley, California asked whether local governments could be held liable for earthquakes. It was concluded that governments could be held liable for some damages and injuries occurring during an earthquake. The two most likely cases are injuries or damages which (1) were made more likely by conditions of the jurisdiction's own property (e.g., county hospitals) and (2) occur on public property made hazardous by private property (e.g., a parapet from a private building falling on a sidewalk).[20]

Summary

As the "new land ethic" widely cited in the literature of land use management continues to pervade policy, the application of ideas consistent with that notion to hazardous areas increases. Large-scale engineering solutions are no longer seen as an exclusive panacea for the problems the nation faces from natural hazards. Such efforts alone have proved inadequate, and policy makers have turned to the ideas of land husbandry to mitigate losses from hazards while providing environmental benefits as well. It is hoped the decade ahead will see more innovative applications of these principles and that they will be used to cope with a greater variety of hazards.

Notes

1. Sheaffer and Roland, Inc., "Evaluation of the Economic, Social and Environmental Effects of Floodplain Regulations" (Washington, D.C.: Department of Housing and Urban Development—Office of Policy Development and Research, 1979).
2. F. J. Baker, "Geographical Variations in Hurricane Risk and Legislative Response," *Coastal Zone Management Journal* 5 (1979): 263–283.
3. E. J. Baker and J. G. McPhee, *Land Use Management and Regulation in Hazardous Areas,* Program on Technology, Environment, and Man Monograph NSF–RA–E–75–008 (Boulder, Col.: University of Colorado, Institute of Behavioral Science, 1975).
4. T. Keeling, "The National Flood Insurance Program: A Local Perspective." Paper presented at the National Conference on Hurricanes and Coastal Storms, Orlando, Florida, May 29–31, 1979.

5. H. C. Miller, "Coastal Flood Plain Management and the National Flood Insurance Program: A Case Study of Three Rhode Island Communities," *Environmental Comment* (1975): 2–14.
6. Sheaffer and Roland, Inc., "Evaluation of the Economic, Social, and Environmental Effects of Floodplain Regulations."
7. E. J. Baker, "Coastal Ecology and Hazard Mitigation," *Bulletin of the Coastal Society* 3 (1979): 6–8.
8. D. G. Friedman, "The Storm Surge Hazard along the Gulf and South Atlantic Coastlines" (Hartford: The Travelers Insurance Company, 1971).
9. E. J. Baker, "Some Problems in Evaluating Land Use Policy Alternatives," *Proceedings of the Association of American Geographers* 7 (1975): 32–36.
10. Ibid.
11. R. C. Holems, "Composition and Size of Flood Losses," in *Papers on Flood Problems,* ed. G. F. White (Chicago: University of Chicago, Department of Geography, 1961).
12. R. W. Kates and D. Pijamka, "From Rubble to Monument: The Pace of Reconstruction," in *Reconstruction Following Disaster,* eds. J. E. Haas, R. W. Kates, and M. J. Bowden (Cambridge: M.I.T. Press, 1977).
13. I. Burton and R. W. Kates, "The Perception of Natural Hazards in Resource Management," *Natural Resource Journal* 3 (1964): 412–441.
14. Sheaffer and Roland, Inc., "Evaluation of the Economic, Social and Environmental Effects of Floodplain Regulations."
15. J. Slosson, "The Role of Engineering Geology in Urban Planning," in *The Governor's Conference on Environmental Geology* (Sacramento: State of California, 1969).
16. W. E. Shows et al., *The Economic Impact of Florida's Coastal Setback Line: A Study of Bay County, Florida* (Tampa: University of South Florida, Department of Economics, 1976).
17. W. G. Lesso, "The Effect on Building Costs Due to Improved Wind Resistant Standards." Paper presented at the National Conference on Hurricanes and Coastal Storms, Orlando, Florida, May 29–31, 1979.
18. A. Dunham, "Flood Control via the Police Power," *University of Pennsylvania Law Review* 107 (1959): 1098–1132.
19. R. H. Platt, "The National Flood Insurance Program: Some Midstream Perspectives," *Journal of the American Institute of Planners* 42 (1976): 303–313.
20. Association of Bay Area Governments, "Fact Sheet on ABAG Earthquake Liability Study" (Berkeley: ABAG, 1979).

Selected References

Algermissen, S. T., and Perkins, D. M. "A Probabilistic Estimate of Maximum Acceleration in Rock in the Contiguous United States." Open-File Report 76–416. Washington, D.C.: U.S. Geological Survey, 1974.
Nichols, D. R., and Buchanan-Banks, J. M. *Seismic Hazards and Land Use Planning,* Circular 690. Washington, D.C.: U.S. Geological Survey, 1974.
White, G. F. *Flood Hazard in the United States: A Research Assessment,* Program on Technology, Environment, and New Monograph # NSF–RA–E–75–006. Boulder, Col.: University of Colorado, Institute of Behavioral Science, 1975.

Chapter 12

Hazardous Waste Management and Land Use

Roy C. Herndon
Florida State University
Tallahassee, Florida

Overview of Hazardous Waste Problem

The production of hazardous wastes is not a new phenomenon. In fact, it would be difficult to find a period in human history when potentially hazardous wastes were not produced. What is relatively new is the awareness that the mismanagement of such wastes can cause major environmental and human health problems. This chapter will discuss the nature of hazardous waste and some of its impacts on land use.

Before proceeding "hazardous waste" needs to be defined. Although much has been written about the subject, the concept remains somewhat diffuse. There are numerous definitions, but many are too all-inclusive to be useful as a tool for discrimination. A point to keep in mind when formulating a definition is that toxic is not a synonym for hazardous, and these terms should not be used interchangeably. Toxic refers to intrinsic characteristics of a substance; hazardous refers to its extrinsic properties. As pointed out by the National Academy of Sciences, toxicity is the capacity of a substance to produce injury including effects such as teratogenicity, mutagenicity, and carcinogenicity, whereas hazard is the probability that injury will result from use of (or contact with) a substance in a given quantity or manner.[1]

With these caveats in mind, the following working definition of a hazardous waste is adopted: " . . . any waste which requires special management provisions in waste handling (process, storage, collection, hauling and disposal) because of its acute and/or chronic effects on the public health and welfare, the individuals who handle it, or on the environment."[2] In the context of this definition waste will be interpreted as a material that is rejected from a process and then either disposed of on site, shipped off the premises for disposal, or used as a feedstock by another firm. If the rejected material is recovered and made into some other product in-plant, then it is not considered a waste, but a byproduct. For the purposes of this chapter it is not necessary to formulate a more technical definition. However, it should be emphasized that in order to establish rules and regulations governing the disposal of hazardous waste, it is necessary to deal with specific criteria such as concentration, tolerances and cutoff levels. Also, the possible cumulative effect of certain chemicals in the body must be considered.

Hazardous Waste and Land Use

As a consequence of the increasing industrialization of society, the quantity of wastes generated has grown to staggering proportions in the last few decades. The United States generates billions of tons of solid waste each year, the major sources being mining, agricultural, industrial, municipal and sewage waste. Most of this waste is managed using land disposal techniques.

Although the volume of mining waste is far greater than that generated by other sources, this waste is largely made up of overburden which does not usually present as great an environmental and human health threat as does industrial waste. Similarly, agricultural waste is largely crop and feedlot materials, which are potentially less hazardous than industrial wastes and can be handled more easily.

Of these billions of tons of solid waste generated annually in the United States, approximately 350 million (wet) metric tons are produced by the industrial sector of the economy. It is estimated that 10 to 15 percent (or over 50 million metric tons) of this industrial waste, which comes from manufacturing and pollution control equipment, is potentially hazardous.[3] (Radioactive hazardous waste will be discussed separately although many of the management procedures are similar to those used for nonradioactive hazardous waste.)

In the past industrial wastes have generally been deposited in or on the land, at times with severe negative human impact. Recent examples in Kentucky, Louisiana, New Jersey, and New York (described later in this chapter) as well as other places clearly point to a need for proper land use techniques if potentially hazardous wastes are to be safely managed over both the short and long term. A report prepared for the United States Environmental Protection Agency estimated that there may be over 30,000 sites in the United States containing hazardous waste.[4] A nationwide survey of open dumps is scheduled to be completed in the early 1980s and should provide a much better estimate of the number of hazardous waste sites.

Since land disposal will probably remain a primary means of hazardous waste disposal for some time, it is useful to obtain an order of magnitude estimate for the land area that might be needed for hazardous waste disposal in the United States. Using the estimated figure of 50 million metric tons of hazardous waste produced annually in the United States, and assuming an average waste density of three times that of water, approximately 10 square kilometers per year are rendered unavailable for other uses if the average depth of land disposal is one meter. This calculation is based on the use of secure landfills. These secure sites could be located on land of very low permeability to protect against ground water contamination. Other desirable geological and hydrological characteristics should also be considered in the selection of landfill sites. As an alternative, artificial means such as specially constructed plastic liners could be employed on sites that would otherwise be unsuitable. In unsecured landfills, the secondary pollution area may be one hundred times the primary area due to flooding and leaching effects. These effects could increase the land made unavailable for other uses to 1,000 square kilometers per year. If the lifetime of the hazardous waste is arbitrarily assumed to be twenty years (for some wastes, this is a very conservative estimate), then the land made unavailable for other uses over the next twenty years would be about 20,000 square kilometers or 0.2 percent of the total land area of the United States.

There are important land use considerations with regard to hazardous waste management other than just providing a safe disposal site. Proper land management requires an analysis of the impacts that may occur on land contiguous to such a disposal site. For example, even if individuals who live near the disposal area do not object to the site in principle, they still might object to the truck traffic and possible increased litter. Also, there may be individuals or groups who view this type of land use as an esthetic threat to nearby recreational areas and residential neighborhoods. These perceptions may prove to be as crucial in the site selection process as technical considerations. Land use managers must realize therefore that the selection of a suitable hazardous waste disposal site is a psychological as well as a technical challenge.

It is not only the quantity of hazardous waste that is important, but the type or quality of the waste is of equal concern. Extremely low concentrations of certain chemicals can be hazardous to people, although the total mass of such chemicals produced may appear small. This high (i.e., negative) quality hazardous waste is largely a result of our "chemical society" in which science and technology have evolved an everincreasing number of man-made compounds for specific purposes. When not used for defense or military purposes, the intent of these chemicals is usually to improve the quality of life, e.g., by developing new pesticides to combat agricultural pests. However, more and more attention is being given to the negative aspects of relying on the "chemical cure". The possibility of environmentally caused illnesses such as cancer, respiratory disease and nervous disorders from even small concentrations of certain chemicals has caused a reevaluation of the net benefits of these chemicals.

Hazardous Waste Management/Disposal Alternatives

A major problem has occurred in the management of hazardous waste because many states have not provided the rules, regulations, and enforcement procedures that are necessary to avoid improper land disposal of hazardous wastes. Public Law 94–580, the Resource Conservation and Recovery Act (RCRA) of 1976, was the first attempt by Congress to provide comprehensive federal legislation to insure that hazardous wastes are managed safely and uniformly. Individual states still have the option of implementing their own hazardous waste management programs provided that they are "equivalent and consistent" with the federal requirements.

In the past the land use practices in hazardous waste management have been quite variable. There are examples in California, Texas and Alabama of landfills that accept hazardous waste and appear to be safely designed and operated. On the other hand there are numerous examples of carelessly and irresponsibly run sites which have the potential for causing serious human and environmental problems. The land disposal of hazardous waste must be accomplished using facilities that are specifically located, designed, operated and monitored—even after the facilities are no longer active—in a manner that protects life and the environment.

There are a number of disposal alternatives for hazardous wastes. Although at present surface land disposal is the most widely used method, it is by no means the only possibility. Other alternatives that need to be considered in providing for the adequate and safe disposal of hazardous wastes are subsurface land disposal (well injection), disposal in water or air, recycling (waste exchanges), incineration and pyrolysis, above or below ground short-term storage, above ground long-term storage, waste decontamination at the source, and waste decontamination after collection but prior to disposal.

The use of some or all of these alternatives could provide safe and effective means of handling the hazardous wastes generated in the United States. California has, for example, specifically addressed the land disposal practices for hazardous wastes although the state's report emphasizes that "it is not the intention [of this report] to universally endorse the disposal of hazardous waste to land; when possible, hazardous wastes should be neutralized prior to disposal."[5]

Deep-well injection as a land disposal option requires extensive and detailed studies. Puri and Winston state that in order to accomplish safe disposal by deep-well injection, " . . . it is important to understand the hydrologic and geologic factors which control horizontal and vertical fluid movements in the aquifer in order to be able to predict the ultimate direction of migration and rate of flow of the liquid wastes which may be injected into the system."[6] This implies that land use managers must either have the scientific data in hand or have the data collected to evaluate a potential site for hazardous waste disposal. Typically this means that other experts must be included in the decision-making process in order for land use managers to arrive at sound decisions with regard to land use as a safe disposal option (see chapter 4 for a model of the land use decision-making process).

Direct disposal of hazardous waste into the air or water on the rationale that the ocean or atmosphere seems big enough to adjust to endless environmental insult appears unwise. For example, it is indeed tempting when stored nerve gas containers begin leaking to look for the final solution in "deep water dumping." However, the adage "out of sight, out of mind" may be inappropriate for hazardous waste disposal. The oceans and atmosphere are still not well enough understood to assume they can inevitably recover from abuse.

Another possibility for reducing the quantity of hazardous waste is to use the waste products from certain industries as the raw materials or feedstock for another industry. This alternative utilizes known recovery techniques and holds promise of becoming economically attractive as stricter laws and regulations are brought to bear on the problem of safe hazardous waste disposal.

One particular aspect of recycling that has application for the management of hazardous waste is the establishment of a "waste exchange." The most common type of waste exchange acts as a clearinghouse for information about types of quantities of industrial waste materials. It gathers and distributes information about industrial wastes available, and forwards inquires to appropriate firms. Usually, an effort is made to protect the identity of participating firms from regulatory agencies as well as industrial competitors. Although the role of the waste exchange in a management program is limited, the Director of the United States Environmental Protection Agency's Hazardous Waste Management Division pointed out that "waste exchanges . . . can make a very valuable contribution to the overall waste-management program."[7] Certainly the concept deserves consideration although a regional waste exchange concept may make more sense than a single-state approach.[8]

Incineration and pyrolysis as alternatives for managing selected chemical wastes have not been used to their full potential, because technical development is in progress and high capital investment is required. For example, a facility such as a fluidized bed incinerator to incinerate 24 million liters per year of aqueous phenol waste requires a capital investment of $6 million, not including land costs, and an operating cost of $124 per metric ton.[9] These figures are high when compared to typical land filling costs. However, as development proceeds and costs decline, certain classes of particularly hazardous wastes may best be handled using this type of facility even if costs remain relatively high.

A variation of this technique is to incinerate certain hazardous waste far out at sea using specially equipped ships. It might be possible to burn wastes for as little as $80 per ton since the dilution and isolation factors eliminate the need for many of the expensive pollution control devices, such as scrubbers, which are used to clean flue gases before venting to the atmosphere. There are presently two such ships in operation.[10]

The storage of hazardous waste, either above or below ground, may be a suitable temporary solution to a vexing problem; that is, what to do with certain classes of wastes that have no satisfactory permanent solution that is immediately available (see section on radioactive wastes). The operation of such a facility requires the close attention of state and federal regulatory agencies in order to ensure its secure and safe operation.

One method for ameliorating the hazardous waste management problem is to decontaminate the waste immediately after generation by converting it to a nonhazardous form and then using the more conventional and less costly disposal methods available. Under the present system, however, economic incentives are insufficient to make this a popular alternative even in areas where the technology exists. Of particular interest also is the introduction of production methods in industry to produce less hazardous waste initially. This requires, in many cases, the introduction of new technologies or the development of existing ones, often necessitating a sizeable economic investment. However, as disposal costs rise over the next few years as a result of the public demand for safe and secure disposal methods, these technologies may become economically feasible. From the point of view of land use managers these methods are appealing because they decrease the amount of hazardous waste that might otherwise be deposited in the land. Reducing the amount of hazardous waste going to the land decreases the risk of potential environmental and ecological damage.

The disposal alternatives discussed above offer land use managers a variety of options to manage hazardous waste other than land disposal. It is only by evaluating a specific set of conditions, including such factors as the nature and quantity of the waste for disposal, that land use managers can determine if a particular site should be considered for hazardous waste disposal.

A Special Problem Area: Radioactive Wastes

Radioactive wastes, produced by the nuclear industry, present special problems although the procedures for their proper management are essentially the same as those for other types of hazardous waste. For the purposes of discussion, radioactive wastes may be classified as high level wastes, low level wastes, and uranium mine and mill tailings. High level wastes are strongly radioactive and include either intact reactor fuel assemblies discarded after use or the portion of wastes generated in the reprocessing of spent fuel. Reprocessing simply means that the spent reactor fuel is sent to a plant where the usable fissionable material is extracted and subsequently used to fabricate more reactor fuel. These wastes as well as high level wastes generated from the development of nuclear weapons and other defense purposes are being considered for disposal in geologic repositories or by other options designed to provide long-term isolation of the wastes from the biosphere. Low level wastes require little or no shielding, and have low but potentially hazardous quantities of radionuclides. Low level wastes are generated in almost all activities involving radioactive materials, such as medical laboratories, universities, and hospitals, and are typically disposed of by shallow land burial. Uranium mining and milling operations produce tailings that contain low concentrations of naturally occurring radioactive materials. The tailings are generated in very large volumes and are stored on-site.

In Grand Junction, Colorado tailings have been used as construction fill dirt for over fifteen years. Public buildings, including schools, shopping centers and homes have been built using these low level radioactive wastes. In Florida the phosphate mining industry produces vast quantities of mining wastes that are slightly radioactive. Residential subdivisions have been built using this reclaimed land. Not all experts agree about the potential danger presented by such low level wastes, but it is probably better to err on the part of caution when dealing with such potentially hazardous wastes. The proper management of these wastes presents a challenge to land use managers since the only practical solution is land disposal.

The final or interim deposition of radioactive wastes, in particular the high level wastes, is a subject of much controversy. Radioactive wastes are typically regulated by both federal and state agencies, the primary general objective being that "existing and future nuclear waste from military and civilian activities (including discarded spent fuel from the once through nuclear power cycle) should be isolated from the biosphere and pose no significant threat to public health and safety."[11] To accomplish this end the chosen technology must meet all the relevant radiological protection criteria as well as any other regulatory requirements. Four possible technologies, including both land and non-land disposal alternatives, for the final disposal of high level wastes are: placement in mined repositories or very deep drill holes, placement in deep ocean sediments, transmutation of the heavy radionuclides, and ejection into space.

Of these options, mined respositories, i.e., geologic formations, probably will be technically feasible before any of the others. Nevertheless, the interim surface storage of spent fuel on land near reactors or at away-from-reactor storage facilities is an important component of the United States' overall waste management program until such underground repositories are available. Surface storage should not be viewed, however, as an alternative to ultimate disposal.[12]

An interesting aspect of nuclear wastes, in particular high level wastes, is that the total land area needed to dispose of such wastes is relatively small: " . . . the mass and volume of the waste generated by nuclear power activities are very small—all such waste that will be produced by the operation of all nuclear electric power plants between now and the end of the century will have a volume of less than 500,000 ft.³—the volume of a one-story warehouse 200 feet on a side."[13] The preceding statement is somewhat oversimplified in that only high level wastes are included. However, lower level reactor wastes, although ten to twenty times the volume of the high level wastes, are much easier to handle since their heat and penetrating radiations are considerably less. In addition, volume reduction techniques could reduce these lower level reactor wastes to about the same volume as that of the high level wastes.

Only commerical reactor wastes were considered in this example, and the volume was calculated on the basis of reprocessed fuel with residual waste solidification. It is important to keep in mind that the policy of the United States, out of concern for nuclear proliferation and possible diversion of fissile material, is to prohibit the commercial reprocessing of reactor fuel. This policy means that in the United States spent reactor fuel is itself high level waste and so will occupy a greater volume than that estimated in the example cited above. However, even a volume increase of ten or a hundred does not require an inordinate land area. There are, of course, radioactive wastes from defense installations, which increase the total volume of wastes but these wastes can be reprocessed.

The point to be made is that although the total land area needed for disposal of all radioactive wastes may be relatively small, the potential for large-scale environmental contamination may be quite large. The time scales required for containment of these high level wastes until they decay to safe levels range from a few hundred to many thousands of years. Leakage of these wastes into the biosphere could render vast land areas (and water supplies) unsafe for many years. It should be emphasized that some nonradioactive hazardous wastes also persist for very long or indefinite periods of time. Therefore, the necessity for long-term containment and monitoring applies, in general, to both radioactive and nonradioactive hazardous wastes.

Selected Case Studies

In order to gain an appreciation of the kinds of problems that arise from the lack of proper land use planning in the management of hazardous wastes, it is worthwhile to look at a number of specific case studies. No conclusions are stated at the end of these case studies. This is not an oversight. The incidents speak for themselves without need for subjective evaluation. What is clear from studying these examples is that many, if not all of them, could have been avoided if proper land use planning and management techniques had been implemented initially.

Case Study: New York[14]

In the late 1800s a 20-yard wide navigation channel, designed to carry water from above the falls at Niagara, New York back to the river below the falls, was planned and partially constructed. Named the Love Canal after its designer, William Love, the canal was only one mile long when abandoned due to insufficient financial resources. For more than ten years prior to its closure in 1953, the unfinished canal served as a municipal and chemical waste dump for several area chemical firms. The most notable contributor to this disposal site deposited over 21,000 tons of potentially hazardous chemical wastes during this period.

Shortly after the dump site was closed and sold to the city of Niagara Falls in 1953 for one dollar, a public elementary school was built on the site and homes were constructed immediately adjacent to the dump. As early as 1959 chemical waste began to ooze up out of the ground and seep into the basements of these homes, but it was 1978 before large numbers of homes were affected and an investigation launched. This investigation ultimately resulted in the evacuation of families from hundreds of residences.

Over a hundred different chemicals have been identified in the Love Canal including dioxin, lindane, carbon tetrachloride, benzene, and trichloroethylene. Some of these, such as dioxin, are acutely toxic. Many others are known to cause cancer and birth defects. Other chemicals remain unidentified, and the quantity of some of the identified substances remains unknown. The amount of dioxin, for example, is estimated by chemical company officials as "very, very small" although records indicate that enough trichlorophenol was deposited in the canal to generate over 125 pounds of dioxin.

The problem was deemed serious enough by the state that over 230 families living adjacent to the site were ordered evacuated. New York has spent over 22 million dollars buying these homes and cleaning up the area. In addition the federal government has given millions of dollars in assistance, and lawsuits have been filed against private companies totaling billions of dollars.

As a result of the investigations into the Love Canal site, the city of Niagara Falls has found additional buried chemical wastes, much of them deposited by the same chemical company in three abandoned landfills. In a dump directly across a road from the Love Canal is buried more than 23,000 tons of hazardous waste, including toxic chemicals such as chlorobenzene, lindane, and mirex. Several miles from these dumps, on a creek named "Bloody Run," is a large 16-acre site containing another 80,000 tons of stored chemical waste. This creek runs from the dump site underneath a steel products plant and through a neighborhood of about twenty residences. Here, as at the Love Canal, there is suspicion that some of the health problems suffered by residents may be related to the effects of these wastes.

Case Study: Louisiana[15]

Economically, Louisiana is heavily dependent on the oil, gas, and chemical industries. These industries provide jobs and revenues for the state, but they also produce considerable quantities of hazardous waste.

The Louisiana Department of Natural Resources recently surveyed dump sites in the state and identified four that pose a "serious" problem. The four sites, which the governor said "the public should stay away from," are Devils Swamp, East Baton Rouge Parrish; Bayou Sorrell, Iberville Parrish; Tate Cove, Evangeline Parrish; and Sorrento, Ascension Parrish.

Additional sites may also present serious problems, for example, a disposal site near Taft, Louisiana, but these were not included in the study because the governor felt not enough testing had been done. However, three confidential reports indicate that for fourteen years toxic wastes were disposed of on the Taft site in an entirely unregulated fashion. The reports document broken dikes, pits for toxic wastes excavated out of porous soils, and contamination of surface waters by toxic materials from rainwater runoff. In addition, tests of monitoring wells have shown contaminated subsurface water. Some of the materials disposed of on-site were asbestos, capacitors containing polychlorinated biphenyls (PCBs), and lead, all of which are either toxic or suspected of causing cancer. The company operated this site without getting a permit for hazardous waste disposal.

Another company, a small waste disposal firm, was permitted to locate adjacent to a large cattle farm, which had operated for over thirty years, in the bayou country of Louisiana. The company used open pits to dispose of waste from oil and chemical companies. Within months of beginning operations, the chemical waste site overflowed, flooding more than 500 acres of farm land with thousands of gallons of hazardous waste containing carbon tetrachloride, hexachloro-butadiene, and other petrochemical wastes. These chemicals, considered lethal to animals, plants and people, killed 149 cattle.

One incident in Louisiana that received national attention occurred in Bayou Sorrell, a small fishing village. Hazardous wastes from at least thirty-nine different companies were brought to the area for deep-well injection disposal, a procedure in which the waste is pumped deep into the ground. Instead of being disposed of as permitted by the state of Louisiana, it appears that much of this waste was simply dumped into open pits. In July 1978 a driver backed his tank truck up to this waste site and pumped chemical waste into one of the open pits. A chemical reaction occurred, and the coroner's report showed that the driver died of asphyxiation due to hydrogen sulfide gas.

Case Study: Kentucky[16]

In 1978 the state of Kentucky issued a hazardous waste survey report, which stated that over 1.3 million tons of hazardous waste are generated each year in Kentucky. Although most of these wastes are recycled by various processes, over 180,000 tons of this waste are disposed of each year by methods that have the potential for causing environmental damage if improperly managed.

About the time this report was released, a major problem resulting from improper hazardous waste disposal practices was discovered in a valley about 20 miles south of Louisville. In this valley, known as the Valley of the Drums, over 17,000 steel drums were found, many rusting and filled with potentially hazardous waste. These visible drums, plus an unknown quantity still buried, had been left by a company hired by several Kentucky firms to dispose of their hazardous wastes. Over $325,000 has been spent for cataloging, organizing, and sampling the drums, and early plans called for the location of an incinerator at the site to faciliate clean-up. However, local opposition thwarted a necessary zoning change, and it appears that the clean-up process will take a long time.

In another incident the president of a liquid recycling firm was convicted of discharging pollutants into a federal waterway in connection with the dumping of chlorinated hydrocarbons in Louisville's sewer system. This surreptitious dumping forced the shutdown of Louisville's sewage treatment plant for three months. Due to this forced closure, 100 million gallons of raw sewage were dumped into the Ohio River every day during this period.

About 20 miles south of Louisville, on flooded property owned by relatives of the president of the same liquid recycling firm, over 600 steel drums, some leaking, were discovered. Rusty drums were also found floating nearby in Stump Gap Creek, where flood waters from the Ohio River had carried them. The United States Environmental Protection Agency tested the contents of twenty seven drums and found thirteen toxic chemicals, two of which—xylene and toluene— are suspected of causing cancer. Personnel from the Environmental Protection Agency and the state of Kentucky, soldiers from Ft. Knox, and workers from a chemical spill cleanup company met at the site to retrieve the drums. Once the operation began, it became clear that the problem was more extensive than authorities had first thought. After 520 drums had been collected, over 200 were still visible. In addition, military personnel equipped with metal detectors found thirty sites on the property where metal appeared to be buried. When the soldiers dug at the first site they found a cache of drums with unknown contents. The Environmental Protection Agency, under emergency authority of the 1977 Federal Water Pollution Act, alloted $100,000 to be used to prevent any further chemical spills into the Ohio River watershed as a result of these drums.

Case Study: New Jersey[17]

New Jersey produces an estimated five million wet tons of hazardous waste annually, or about 10 percent of the fifty million tons produced yearly in the United States. Of these five million tons, three million are presently being dumped in the ocean. In addition to wastes generated in-state, unknown amounts of hazardous wastes are being transported into the state and being disposed of illegally.

As a result of this high volume of hazardous waste production and importation, New Jersey has many chemical waste dump sites. Some of these pose serious problems. For example, a 40-acre section of the New Jersey Meadowlands surrounding a now-razed mercury processing plant, which abandoned 286 tons of mercury on the site, has been found to contain the highest level of mercury contamination in the world. Tests conducted by the New Jersey Department of Environmental Protection have found soil concentrations of mercury to be as high as 123,000 parts per million in some spots. The United States Environmental Protection Agency restricts mercury concentrations in drinking water at 2 parts per billion and considers 160 parts per million as lethal. Investigations show this mercury contamination to be spreading, and it has been detected in Berry Creek, which connects with the Hackensack River.

Another striking example of improper and potentially dangerous disposal practices is located along the Elizabeth River in Elizabeth, New Jersey. Here a chemical company was discovered storing approximately 35,000–40,000 drums of various explosive and toxic chemical wastes such as nitrogylcerine, picric acid, nitrocellulose, nitric acid, and perichlorates. Originally issued a temporarily permit in 1974, the facility was ordered closed by the state of New Jersey in January 1979, at which time an estimated 20 percent of these drums were found to be deteriorating and leaking. Some of the companies from which the chemicals were originally collected for disposal have been asked to reclaim the drums. However, many of the drums are unlabelled. Costs of identifying and disposing of the chemicals have been placed at greater than $10 million. With Manhattan Island across the river, costs of a disaster such as occurred on April 21, 1980, could have been substantially higher. On this date a fire erupted at the firm's warehouse site, which led to fishing being suspended in the Hudson River and the temporary closing of some schools. Eight firefighters were treated for injuries during the eight-hour fire, which sent many barrels hundreds of feet into the air.

Conclusions

The marriage of hazardous waste disposal to land use requires particular care on the part of land use planners and managers. A wrong decision in land use planning with regard to hazardous waste can lead to both short and long-term problems that may affect not only the future aesthetic and market value of the land, but also the health and safety of communities. Land use managers play a particularly important role since they may be in a position early in the decision-making process to make influential recommendations and decisions with regard to land use for waste disposal.

Land use managers must recognize that they will need information and data from experts other than planners if they are to commit land resources for the proper management of hazardous waste. Indeed, four basic elements must be considered by land use managers in their decision-making process. They include, in addition to current land use practices, hydrologic, biological, ecological and socioeconomic considerations, all of which may require help from experts in disciplines other than land use management. The hydrologic, biological and ecological considerations provide the physical description of the environment that will be affected by committing a given tract of land to the disposal of potentially hazardous waste. Land use practices and socioeconomic conditions are somewhat more flexible in that they can be changed by legislation, regulations or changes in lifestyle.

Certainly land use managers can play an important and decisive role in helping society use its land resources wisely with regard to hazardous waste disposal. It is a challenge which land use planners and managers must meet in concert with experts in other disciplines. Land, like all resources, typically has competing interests involved for its use, especially with regard to such uses as the disposal of hazardous waste. Land use managers stand in a unique position to help resolve these competing interests in a way consistent with the present and future needs of society.

Notes

1. *Report of the Food Protection Committee* (Washington, D.C.: National Academy of Sciences, 1970).
2. *A Report on Industrial and Hazardous Wastes* (Olympia: State of Washington Department of Ecology, 1973), p. 3.
3. *Solid Waste Facts: A Statistical Handbook* (Washington, D.C.: U.S. Environmental Protection Agency, 1978).
4. *Preliminary Assessment of Clean-up Costs for National Hazardous Waste Problems* (New York: Fred C. Hart Associates, Inc., 1979).
5. *Guidelines for Hazardous Waste Land Disposal Facilities* (Sacramento: State of California Department of Health, 1973), p. 1.
6. H. S. Puri and G. O. Winston, *Geological Framework of the High Transmitting Zones in South Florida.* Special Publication No. 20 (Tallahassee: State of Florida Bureau of Geology, 1974), p. 1.
7. L. J. Ricci, "Chemical Waste Swapping: Promising But No Panacea," *Chemical Engineering* 83 (14) (1976): 44–48.
8. *Hazardous Waste Survey for the State of Florida* (Tallahassee: State of Florida Department of Environmental Regulation, 1977), p. 202.
9. U.S. Department of Commerce, *Destroying Chemical Wastes in Commerical Scale Incinerators* (Washington, D.C.: U.S. Environmental Protection Agency, 1977).
10. T. H. Maugh, II, "Incineration, Deep Wells Gain New Importance," *Science* 204 (1979): 1188–1295.
11. *Report to the President by the Interagency Review Group on Nuclear Waste Management* (Washington, D.C.: Interagency Review Group on Nuclear Waste Management, 1979), p. 15.
12. Ibid., p. 35.
13. F. K. Pittman, "Management of Radioactive Wastes," *Water, Air and Soil Pollution* 4 (1975): 215–219.
14. M. H. Brown, "Love Canal and the Poisoning of America," *Atlantic* 244 (December 1979): 33–47; "An Environmental Time Bomb Gone Off," *Science* 24 (June 1979): 820; "Hazardous Waste Control Efforts: A Frightful Mess," *Conservation Foundation Letter* (April 1980); C. Holden, "Love Canal Residents Under Stress," *Science* 208 (June 1980): 1242–1244; N. P. Cheremisinoff, P. N. Cheremisinoff, F. Ellerbush, A. J. Perva, "Addendum to Chapter 13—The Love Canal Incident", *Industrial and Hazardous Wastes Impoundment* (Ann Arbor: Science Publishers, Inc., 1979): 316–318; Statement by Michael C. O'Laughlin, Mayor of Niagara Falls, New York before the Subcommittee on Environmental Pollution of the U.S. Senate Committee on Public Works, July 19, 1979; G. McGarry, "Love Canal: What Happened?" *Palladium-Times,* Oswego, New York (April 16, 1979).
15. J. Wardlow, "4 Toxic Waste Sites in La. called 'Serious Problems,' " *New Orleans States—Item* (April 19, 1979); L. Michaud, "Waste Reports Show Hooper Plant Problem" *Morning Advocate,* Baton Rouge (May 4, 1979): 1; M. Desmond, "Chemical Waste Haunts Louisiana Swamp," *Buffalo Courier Express* (1978): 23; *Revised Status Report—Hazardous Waste Sites* (Washington, D.C.: U.S. Environmental Protection Agency, 1979); P. Davis, "A Death in Louisiana," *EPA Journal* 5(2) (1979): 14–15.
16. State of Kentucky, *Hazardous Waste Survey of Kentucky* (Frankfurt, 1978); Courier-Journal, Louisville, Kentucky, Special Report, "Warning: Toxic Waste" (1979).
17. "Explosion of a Toxic Time Bomb," *Time* 115 (May 5, 1980): 67; "Cleanup Goes Slowly in Chemical Warehouse," *Chemical and Engineering News* 57 (May 21, 1979): 5; "Justice, EPA Sue Under RCRA," *Chemical Week* 124 (February 14, 1979): 13; Joanne Omang, "A $6 Million Hassle Over Spilled Poison," *Washington Post* (November 26, 1978): C1; "Chemical Control Explosion Threatens Wide Area," *Hazardous Waste Report* 1(20): 17–18; R. Jeffrey Smith, "EPA Announces Toxic Waste Controls," *Science* 208 (May 9, 1980): 581; Testimony of Senator Bill Bradley before the Joint Hearing of the U.S. Senate Subcommittee on Environmental Pollution and Resource Protection (June 21, 1979).

Section D

Implications for the Future

Chapter 13

The Future and the Need for Rational Land Use Decisions

Edward A. Fernald
Florida State University
John F. Lounsbury
Arizona State University
Lawrence M. Sommers
Michigan State University

Introduction

Land Use planning and analysis are complex processes. The chapters in this book have covered critical points that concern land use specialists. However, the responsibilities of land use specialists do not end with the present. Decision makers must anticipate future land use prospects and problems to the best of their abilities to ensure rational land use in the future. This final chapter will suggest a procedure for guiding decisions about land use changes and suggest a few areas of needed research in the spatial analysis of land use.

Land Use Problems of the Future

Prediction of the future in a dynamic society in which social and economic factors as well as values and attitudes are rapidly changing is difficult. Unstable conditions have occurred in the United States during the last few decades as adjustments have been made by society to unprecedented developments in technology. However, the current land use problems, issues, and conflicts discussed in previous chapters are likely to become more acute in the 1980s. Some of these problems will have national impacts because they either affect the country as a whole or are so common to many localities as to cause national awareness and concern. The most serious and demanding problems perhaps will be the preservation of prime agricultural land in face of increasing urban populations, conflicts between future residential land and development of energy resources, degradation of the environment, and conflicts concerning the control of the land.

Preservation of Farmland

The conversion of farmland to other land uses is not a threat to the production of sufficient foods and fibers for the American people, at least not in the foreseeable future; rather, the problem lies in the changing role of agricultural commodities in foreign trade. Agricultural exports have increased to the point where they offset, to a significant degree, the fiscal drain of acquiring energy and manufactured goods from abroad. They have become major economic and political weapons in international affairs, making the loss of almost 3 million acres of cropland annually (over one-third of which is prime land) to permanent non-farm uses alarming. The demand to retain the best agricultural land for farming will grow stronger year by year.

Development of Energy Resources

The "American Dream," to own a single-family home situated on a separate plot of ground in an aesthetically pleasing setting, is being threatened. It is becoming increasingly difficult to leave the relatively crowded city and move into open space surrounding urban centers. Until recently, cheap fossil fuels encouraged this trend by allowing people a great degree of flexibility in choosing a place to live. They did not need to rely on public transportation to get to work or to procure the necessities and amenities of life. This type of settlement pattern is now being severely challenged as the price of energy continues to rise. The shortage and cost of energy will no doubt act as a deterrent and containment to urban sprawl. The density of new and existing developed areas will have to be increased to foster energy conserving measures such as district heating, public transportation, and recycling of urban wastes for energy. A major problem confronting governments, individuals, groups and private enterprises is to find ways to change the attitudes and perceptions of people toward finite resources and rational land use policies. People, accustomed to the advantages provided by the cheap energy era, appear to be unwilling or slow to accept the fact that current wasteful and inefficient uses of the land and resources must change. Further, changes in the source and type of energy will have a major impact on the future character of land use, both rural and urban. More land areas will be devoted to the production of nonconventional energy supplies—solar power, biomass, wind, and small-scale hydroelectric—which will drastically influence the patterns of settlements.

Degradation of the Environment

The list of real and imagined land uses that degrade the environment is long and diverse. The more visible examples include air and water pollution, accelerated soil erosion, draining of wetlands, coastline erosion, forest depletion, and destruction of wildlife habitats. Many of these conditions result in irreversible changes in the environment and many concern the interrelation of the atmosphere, hydrosphere and biosphere. Changes in one aspect of the environment trigger changes in other features of the landscape. In a dynamic society, changes in land use are inevitable and will alter the natural setting. The land use problems of the future lie not with the changes per se, but with the resulting differences of opinion as to whether changes are damaging or otherwise undesirable.

Degradation of the environment is in the eyes of the beholder, and is dependent upon the values of a given society at a given location and time. As economic growth continues and populations increase, trade-offs are essential and the conflicts and debates, often emotional, regarding these trade-offs will be characteristic of the 1980s. Land use changes with subsequent alterations of the environment will proceed at faster rates in the coming decade as the pattern of energy sources change and new technology develops.

Land Use Controls

At this time, there are no standardized land use controls and no national guidelines in the United States. As discussed in previous chapters, the states have traditionally delegated land use controls to local governments via planning and zoning acts. There is great diversity regarding land use controls and land use planning from one local jurisdiction to another. The states are now beginning to assume a more direct role in land use planning, not only for public lands, but also in the control of developments on nonstate-owned lands. It may be anticipated that major conflicts over land use will continue in the 1980s among local groups, or between local and regional or state interests, or between state and national groups over mineral rights, power plant and mining sites, conversion of agricultural land to other uses, water rights and controls, development of energy resources, and so on. It is conceivable that these conflicts could become so acute and long lasting as to pose serious threats to local, regional or national economic growth.

The Need for Rational Land Use Planning

Contemporary and future land use problems and issues can only be resolved if sufficient research is devoted to their solution. Unfortunately, many land use decisions and plans today are based on insufficient or inaccurate information. It is essential that accurate and up-to-date inventories be made at the scale pertinent to particular land use problems. The acquisition of the necessary land use data may be costly in terms of both time and money, but it is the basis of all planning, modeling, and future activities. Land use plans or decisions can be no more accurate or meaningful than the data upon which they are based.

Further, if the United States is to make optimum use of the land resource, it is imperative that rational land use controls and land use decisions be developed at various scales or levels of resolution. National land use regulations are needed to protect or develop regional resources that cross state boundaries. New land use policies need to be developed for state and local governmental units, and these local controls must be coordinated. The development of such regulations at various levels, all highly compatible with one another, is a goal for the future. It cannot be accomplished quickly. In the meantime, land use changes will occur, and it is important to the local area, region, state and country as a whole that impacts of proposed land use changes be understood as fully as possible.

Guiding Land Use Change

In all land use changes there are trade-offs. It is incumbent upon land use analysts to have a clear understanding of those compromises. As stated in earlier chapters, this is done by setting of objectives, collecting and analyzing data, understanding laws, policies and regulations available to planners, and developing new tools to help achieve objectives. After the analysts or decision makers have gained an understanding of the land as it exists in its unchanged state and an understanding of what they want to do, it is important for them to be aware of land use change methods that will help institute the change with minimum negative impacts on urban as well as rural environments.

To aid decision makers in their efforts to guide national land use change, methodologies need to be developed and evaluated to serve everyone, from individuals who are thinking about optimizing a short-term profit on small parcels of land to regional decision makers who wish to develop a series of institutional changes with a metropolitan area or river basin wide impact. Economic models[1] may be used to explain land use patterns, but much work is needed before analysts can use these models as a practical tool in making decisions. McHarg's (1969) computerized overlay system[2] is a step in the right direction and can be modified for small areas at a large scale by utilizing hand drawn maps and overlays. A practical land use change methodology is described below. Such a procedure should be a part of any land use plan or strategy.

A common problem in the past has been the unsuccessful use of the "master" or the "comprehensive" land use plan. The idea of developing such a plan is good, but too often plans have been developed with less than the necessary understanding of the physical and cultural characteristics of the study area. Another problem has been that solutions are often provided by the plans before necessary studies have been undertaken. Land use analysis and planning must be an objective exercise, undertaken to meet the needs of society rather than those of special interests. One rational procedure to provide direction to a land use change is a simple input/intervening variable/output process (fig. 13.1). By using such an outline, the decision maker is able to consider criteria and parameters that may otherwise be overlooked. When applied to a specific site, the input includes the identification of the objectives of land use change, a history of the land use of the site, and an analysis and mapping of the site's physical, biological, and cultural characteristics.

The intervening variable step requires planners to superimpose a project's specifications on maps. Through a series of overlays not only can the specific site changes be shown, but the internal physical and cultural relationships can be identified to allow a measure of the impacts of the change. Research is needed on ways to develop an acceptable quantification of land use change impacts. Nevertheless, a simple measurement scale can guide the practitioner. A measure of the impacts allows evaluation of the project for optimum and acceptable land use. Optimum and acceptable are defined as the maximum economic, social, political, aesthetic and other benefits projected by the land use change that are acceptable to society at large. For example, a shopping center development of a forested site might be economically desirable to individuals but unacceptable to society because of loss of wildlife habitat, decrease in water quality, and loss of an aesthetically pleasing landscape.

The output of this procedure, depending on how it is organized, provides either an optimum land use or identifies several alternatives and their impacts. These data can then be used to guide the decisions of elected officials. The output of such a model or outline provides an optimum land use map. The accompanying text explains land use changes, their liabilities and their benefits. This output can be used as input to recycle the process for any subsequent land use change.

In guiding land use changes, it is ultimately important for people to adopt a very conservative policy. Unless the land use changes are understood fully and agreed on by the vast majority of those affected by them, the change should not be implemented. At any later date the proposed change can be made. For example, a forest can be cut, a dune can be destroyed, a marsh can be filled, or a mineral can be mined. In nearly every case, after a lapse of several years, the marsh, the forest, the dune or the mineral will be worth more in terms of dollars than at the time the modification was rejected. On the other hand, once a marsh, sand dune, or forest has been modified, it is impossible to recreate the original landscape. In every case, it is the long-term profit, not only in terms of money but in terms of environmental benefits and societal amenities, that should be considered before land use change is permitted. The applicability of this generalization increases as one moves from individual land parcels to regions. A primary reason for following such a land use change procedure, as suggested in figure 13.1, is that negative or irreversible land uses may be identified when the changes are in the map stage and not made on the landscape.

Implementing land use decisions, whether in single purpose projects or in overall comprehensive or master plans, is the final activity in the land use planning procedure. It should not, however, be a stopping point in the planning and analysis process. A rational land use plan should present and explain the best societal use for land at a specific time for a designated space. These plans should not be considered final blueprints for environmental protection or for development. Implementation should begin only when and where the needs of society are met and should call for preservation when the data substantiate such action. The major objective should be to suggest best land uses and identify development limits based on the support capabilities of the physical and cultural systems.

Well-organized, objectively developed land use plans are no more than statements of the best thinking of the moment in terms of citizens' attitudes and available fiscal, natural, social and technological resources. Plans should be used not only for present analysis, information and education, and decision making, but for input into a continuing recycling of the land analysis and planning process.

As recognized earlier, the master or comprehensive plan has often been misused and it has rightfully drawn criticism by citizens. Nevertheless, the comprehensive land use plan is the best instrument to use if it is objectively developed on the basis of accurate and complete data. Like any other tool, it still must be used with caution. It is an error to accept a plan with a completion date that does not allow time for modifications. A weakness of some plans is that they are too complicated for local people to implement. In other cases, they require a much higher level of funding or technology than the local area can afford. Still another problem with a comprehensive land use plan approach is the possibility of creating a situation where the planning agency is without the power to execute the plan. In this case, the development of a planning program is an

Input:
1. Alternative Objectives
2. Historical Land Use
3. Physical and Biological Analysis
4. Cultural Analysis

Intervening Variables
1. Superimposed Project / Specifications on Map
2. Evaluate Physical / Cultural Impacts
3. Evaluate Project for "Optimum and Acceptable" (O/A) Land Use

Output:
1. Choose O/A Use
2. Identify Alternatives and Their Impacts
3. Present O/A Use in Map and Text Form for Implementation, Communication, and Input to Recycle of Model

Figure 13.1. Simplified land use change process.

exercise in futility. Finally, the land use plan should have self-correcting steps or it can become a self-fulfilling prophecy.

The development of a land use plan is not a linear exercise. Any change in availability of money, in the cultural or physical resources (including technology) or in the objectives of the populace should be considered new information. Dynamic plans of this kind will always allow for modification based on the careful analysis of legitimate input. This point, however, does not invite the modification of a land use plan in the same sense as issuing a variance to a zoning ordinance. All changes should occur because of the recycling of the entire procedure and not because of pressures applied by individuals outside of the planning context.

Land use planning and analysis are basically activities of government, feared by many Americans because of the power governments have over their lives. The solution to this dilemma is not simple, but it is well to remember certain facts. One is that as more people are added to any given space, more rules must be adopted to regulate their activities. Experience has shown that written rules and governmental administration are necessary in modern society.

Assuming agreement with this position, it should be kept in mind that government is of and for "the people." Rules and administrative apparatus of government are tools that are used for good or evil. In the area of land use, citizens must become involved in the development and administration of acceptable land use rules and regulations. Land use analysts are technical experts and assistants in that process. Citizens must participate in land use planning or the infamous "they" (the decision makers) will do it for them.

Conclusions

In order to help citizens and governments do a better job of land use analysis and planning, the data must continue to be developed, evaluated and used to create long-term higher levels, and, in many areas, higher densities of land use.

New technical methods for analyzing land must be developed and research expanded in areas such as, but not limited to, planned unit developments, moratoria, phased development ordinances, preferential tax assessments, purchase of development rights, preemptive purchase, purchase and lease-back, sell-back, land banking, impact taxes, transfers of development rights, windfalls for wipeouts, carrying capacity studies, growth management strategies and the impact of technology change on land use and its analysis. In every case both the rights of the individual and those of the majority must be considered. Land use analysis is complex but offers a challenging and demanding career. Other land use problems of political, social and economic significance such as the "taking issue" are being studied at this time by many groups and have not been included in this book.

Land use analysts must understand that some questions can evoke very emotional responses. For example, the role of land costs in the present housing dilemma may lead to questioning the practice of land speculation. Rising land costs are a significant portion of the increase in housing costs. Historically, land costs have increased because of the investment of excess dollars in potential residential land by speculators who did not buy land for a production (housing) purpose. In the past, this practice has not had as large an impact as it has today because of the great supply of land. Today the practice encourages inflation by changing the use of potential residential land as it becomes utilized as a vehicle in the speculative process. In the broader areas of land use, studies show that agriculture, open space, recreation, and low income housing are the most needed societal land uses. As any parcel goes through the speculation process, the first four land uses that are lost are agriculture, open space, recreation, and low income housing. Should people with excess money be able to have an inflationary impact on housing costs and other low density uses? If not, how can this be discouraged within the law and without branding land speculators as "evil" people?

As we move into the 1980s it appears that the early 1970s trend for land use legislation is near a standstill. Energy, unemployment, inflation, and other problems are not only taking our minds off land use legislation but, as in the case of economic development, are working against such programs. In many cases, land use analysts see land use programs as major parts of an answer to such closely related problems as energy and land use developments. In most cases, states will react to individual land use problems rather than considering and enacting rational holistic programs. This is an unfortunate but probably true prediction. The land use program developed by each state or locality will consist of combined legislation and programs such as those for energy, pollution, coastal zone utilization, and economic development. If the above prediction takes place, it will impose more responsibility on local governments and individual citizens. First, they must decide what kind of land uses they want in their communities and be responsible for implementing them. Secondly, they must anticipate the effects that state and federal legislation and policies will have on their land use plans and support or oppose legislation and policies based on the best information available. In summary, it is vital that planners, politicians, business people, scientists and private citizens think through the various aspects of the land use decision-making process. This approach applies to urban, rural, or any kind of land use. In every case, the decision maker needs to understand and appreciate the value of scientific data; the scientist needs to develop a better means of communicating with the land use decision maker; and citizens need to participate meaningfully in the process. The solutions to these problems, which are multidisciplinary in scope, are dependent upon the talents and best thinking that scientists, decision makers, and citizens have to contribute.

Land use problems will inevitably become more complex with the pressure of increasing population on resources and earth space. Thus, it seems likely that the spatial approach will be of growing significance in achieving understanding of and finding solutions to future land use issues. The insights, methods, techniques, and approaches of this volume are fundamental to future decisions about the best use of land in the United States.

Notes

1. B. J. L. Berry, E. C. Conklin, and D. M. Ray, *The Geography of Economic Systems* (Englewood Cliffs, N.J.: Prentice Hall, Inc., 1976).
2. I. L.McHarg, *Design with Nature* (New York: The American Museum of Natural History, 1969).

Selected References

Abler, R. *Human Geography in a Shrinking World.* Belmont, Calif.: Duxbury, 1975.

Berry, B. J. L.; Conklin, E. C.; and Ray, D. M. *The Geography of Economic Systems.* Englewood Cliffs, N.J.: Prentice Hall, Inc., 1976.

Council on Environmental Quality. *Environmental Quality.* 8th and 9th annual reports. Washington, D.C.: U.S. Government Printing Office, 1977, 1978.

David, B., and Belden, J. *A Survey of State Programs to Preserve Farmland.* Washington D.C.: Council on Environmental Quality, Executive Office of the President, 1979.

Ford Foundation. *A Time to Choose: America's Energy Future.* Cambridge, Mass.: Ballinger, 1974.

Frazier, J., and Esptein, B. *Applied Geography Conference.* vols. 1 and 2. Binghamton, N.Y.: SUNY Binghamton, 1978, 1979.

Healy, R. G., and Rosenburg, J. S. *Land Use and the States.* 2d ed. 1979. Resources for the Future, Baltimore: Johns Hopkins University Press, 1979.

Moss, E. ed. *Land Use Controls in the United States.* New York: Dial, 1977.

Schumacher, E. F. *Small is Beautiful.* New York: Harper and Row, 1973.

Schwartz, B. *The Changing Face of the Suburbs.* Chicago: University of Chicago Press, 1976.

Zeimetz, K. A.; Dillion, E.; Hardy, E. E.; and Otte, R. C. *Dynamics of Land Use in Fast Growth Areas.* Economic Research Service, Agricultural Economic Report No. 325, Washington, D.C.: U.S. Department of Agriculture, 1976.